THE CELEBRITY MOGUL

The Celebrity Mogul

BILL VINCENT

Contents

Introduction: The Making of a Celebrity Mogul 1

Chapter 1: The Trump Legacy 5
Chapter 2: The Young Mogul 23
Chapter 3: Glitz, Glamour, and the Art of the Deal 41
Chapter 4: The Media Magnet 61
Chapter 5: The Apprentice—A Star is Born 81
Chapter 6: Crafting the Celebrity Persona 99
Chapter 7: The Brand Beyond Business 117
Chapter 8: Navigating Public Controversies 135
Chapter 9: Politics and Power 153
Chapter 10: The 2011 Turning Point—Obama and the B 171
Chapter 11: Transition to Politics—A New Arena 187
Chapter 12: The Celebrity Candidate 205
Chapter 13: Building a Populist Brand 223
Chapter 14: Leveraging Celebrity in the White Hous 241
Chapter 15: The Power of the Trump Brand Post-Pres 263
Chapter 16: The Legacy of a Celebrity Mogul 283

Epilogue: Reflections on Fame and Influence 304

Copyright © 2024 by Bill Vincent
All rights reserved. No part of this book may be reproduced in any manner whatsoever without written permission except in the case of brief quotations embodied in critical articles and reviews.
First Printing, 2024

Introduction: The Making of a Celebrity Mogul

Donald J. Trump is a name that has become synonymous with wealth, power, and fame. His journey from a successful real estate mogul to a household name and ultimately a political figure is a story of reinvention, media mastery, and relentless brand-building. In a world where celebrity often paves the way for influence, Trump stands as a striking example of how fame, carefully cultivated and strategically leveraged, can open doors not only in business but in the highest echelons of political power.

This book, *The Celebrity Mogul: Donald J. Trump's Rise to Fame and Influence*, explores how Trump transformed himself from a brash New York City real estate developer into a pop culture icon and a global figure. His larger-than-life personality and his deep understanding of the power of media allowed him to construct a brand that transcended the industries he worked in. Trump didn't just build skyscrapers—he built an image of success that resonated with millions.

In the 1980s, Trump's ambition and flamboyance turned him into a fixture of the Manhattan social scene. His properties—opulent, gilded, and larger-than-life—became symbols of his growing empire. But Trump's real genius was his ability to attract media attention. He understood that in the modern world, publicity could be as valuable as profit, if not more so. Whether it was a high-profile divorce, a public spat, or a new business venture, Trump found a way to keep his name in the headlines. By the 1990s, he had solidified his place as one of America's most recognizable businessmen.

Yet, the turning point in Trump's career came not from his real estate ventures but from television. When *The Apprentice* premiered in 2004, Trump became more than just a wealthy businessman—he became a television star. The show, with its iconic catchphrase "You're fired," propelled Trump into the homes of millions of Americans each week. He was no longer just building hotels and casinos; he was building a persona. Through the carefully crafted character of the shrewd, tough, and seemingly omnipotent CEO, Trump became a symbol of success to many viewers. *The Apprentice* wasn't just entertainment—it was a masterclass in personal branding.

Over the years, Trump's celebrity only grew, and he expanded his influence far beyond business and entertainment. His brand—centered around the idea of winning, power, and wealth—was magnetic to a segment of the American public. By the time Trump announced his candidacy for president in 2015, he had spent decades cultivating an image of authority and success. His run for office was unconventional, but it was the culmination of everything he had been building for years. Trump wasn't just a businessman running for office; he was a brand that millions of Americans already recognized and, in many cases, admired.

This book will explore Trump's rise through the lens of celebrity, media manipulation, and branding. It will look at how he built his real estate empire, became a television icon, and ultimately used his fame to reshape American politics. Trump's story is one of ambition, spectacle, and self-promotion, and it offers a glimpse into the intersection of fame and power in the 21st century.

From the luxurious heights of Trump Tower to the Oval Office, Donald J. Trump's journey is one that defies conventional expectations. He blurred the lines between business, entertainment, and politics in ways no one had done before. As we delve into his rise, we will explore the forces that made his celebrity possible and examine how he turned that celebrity into influence, reshaping not just his own career, but the political landscape of the United States.

In *The Celebrity Mogul*, we will follow the evolution of Donald Trump's persona, from the ambitious son of a real estate developer to a global figure whose name became synonymous with wealth, fame, and power. More than just a businessman, Trump became a brand, and this brand paved the way for one of the most remarkable and unprecedented political ascents in American history.

This is the story of Donald Trump—the Celebrity Mogul.

Chapter 1

Chapter 1: The Trump Legacy

The Origins of the Trump Family

The story of the Trump family's rise to prominence in American business begins, like many American success stories, with an immigrant seeking better opportunities. Friedrich Trump, Donald Trump's grandfather, was born in 1869 in the small village of Kallstadt, Germany. At the age of 16, Friedrich made the bold decision to leave behind the poverty of his homeland and set sail for America in 1885. His story of humble beginnings would mark the starting point of a family legacy that, within two generations, would see the Trump name become synonymous with wealth, luxury, and influence.

Friedrich arrived in New York City as a young man with little formal education and no connections. Like many immigrants of his time, he sought to make a new life for himself through hard work and perseverance. His first years in America were spent as a barber, plying his trade in the bustling city. However, Friedrich was ambitious, and he soon grew restless with the limited opportunities that this profession afforded him. In 1891, Friedrich decided to leave New York and head west, chasing the American dream in one of the most exciting and perilous arenas of the time: the Gold Rush.

While Friedrich Trump never struck gold in the traditional sense, his venture into the goldfields of the Pacific Northwest laid the foundation for his fortune. He opened a series of hotels and restaurants in the boomtowns that sprang up around mining camps, catering to the waves of fortune-seekers who flocked to these areas. His establishments offered not only food and lodging but also entertainment for the miners, providing services that ranged from gambling to prostitution. Though this period of Friedrich's life was marked by controversy, it also demonstrated his entrepreneurial spirit and his willingness to seize opportunities in challenging environments. Friedrich's ventures were highly profitable, and by the time he returned to New York in 1901, he had accumulated enough wealth to start a new chapter for the Trump family.

Upon his return to New York, Friedrich married and settled in the Bronx, where he began investing in real estate. His initial investments were modest, but they provided the Trump family with financial stability and a foothold in the competitive world of New York property. Friedrich's time in the West had taught him valuable lessons about risk-taking and capitalizing on growing markets—principles that would later shape the business strategies of his descendants. Unfortunately, Friedrich's promising real estate career was cut short when he died of pneumonia in 1918 at the age of 49, leaving behind a young family and a modest estate.

Friedrich's son, Fred Trump, was only 13 when his father passed away, but it was Fred who would carry the family's real estate ambitions to new heights. Despite Friedrich's relatively brief involvement in New York real estate, the foundation he laid—both financially and in terms of entrepreneurial spirit—would prove pivotal. The Trump family was no longer scraping by in the way many immigrants had to; they were beginning to establish themselves as serious players in the world of property development.

Fred Trump inherited his father's work ethic and ambition, and it was he who truly transformed the Trump family from modest real estate investors into one of the most successful property developers in New York. Under Fred's leadership, the Trump name would become known throughout the outer boroughs of the city, particularly in Queens and Brooklyn, where he built thousands of affordable housing units for middle-class families. These developments marked the beginning of the Trump real estate empire, a legacy that Fred would pass on to his son, Donald, who would take the family name to unprecedented levels of fame and wealth.

The origins of the Trump legacy are rooted in the classic immigrant story: hard work, ambition, and a willingness to seize opportunities in the face of adversity. Friedrich Trump's journey from a small German village to the goldfields of the Pacific Northwest, and eventually to New York's real estate market, set the stage for the Trump family's future success. Though Friedrich's role in the family history was brief, his entrepreneurial spirit and the wealth he accumulated provided the foundation on which his son, Fred, and later his grandson, Donald, would build their empires.

The Trump legacy did not begin with skyscrapers, casinos, or television shows—it began with a young immigrant's desire to make a better life for himself, a desire that would echo through generations of the Trump family and ultimately lead to a name that would become known across the world.

Fred Trump's Influence on Donald's Business Education

Fred Trump, Donald Trump's father, was the architect of the Trump family's rise to prominence in the New York real estate market. While Donald would go on to expand the Trump brand into Manhattan, television, and even politics, it was Fred who laid the foundation for Donald's success, both in terms of wealth and business acumen. Fred Trump was a shrewd, disciplined, and methodical businessman, and from an early age, he imparted these values to his son, helping to shape Donald's approach to business.

Born in 1905 in the Bronx, Fred grew up in a household still recovering from the sudden loss of his father, Friedrich Trump. With Friedrich's death in 1918, Fred, barely a teenager, became the man of the house. While his mother, Elizabeth, took control of the family's modest real estate holdings, Fred was learning the ropes by her side. Elizabeth Trump may have been the family's formal business leader at the time, but it was Fred's drive and instinct for property development that began to set the Trump family apart from other small-time landlords in Queens and Brooklyn.

Fred's business career took off in the 1930s when he began building homes in Queens during the Great Depression. Where others saw economic despair, Fred saw opportunity. He capitalized on federal loan programs that incentivized housing construction, quickly gaining a reputation as a reliable and efficient builder. His developments focused on affordable housing for middle-class families, and by the 1940s and 1950s, Fred Trump was one of the most prolific home builders in the outer boroughs of New York City. It was in this environment—amid construction sites, negotiations, and rental properties—that young Donald first began learning the ropes of the real estate business.

Fred believed in involving his children in the family business early on, and Donald was no exception. By the time he was a teenager, Donald was shadowing his father, visiting construction sites, meeting with contractors, and observing how Fred dealt with architects, tenants, and city officials. Fred's approach to business was methodical and grounded in practical realities. He believed in managing costs meticulously, taking a hands-on approach to every aspect of his projects, and, above all, avoiding unnecessary risks. These lessons were drilled into Donald from a young age. In fact, Fred's frugality was legendary—he was known to re-use nails at construction sites to cut costs, and he expected his children to inherit that same attention to detail.

Yet, while Fred emphasized conservative, long-term thinking, Donald began to develop a taste for the grander, more high-profile aspects of business. He admired his father's success, but even as a teenager, he yearned for something more. Fred operated in the outer boroughs, building practical homes for working-class families. Donald, on the other hand, had his sights set on Manhattan, where he dreamed of developing towering skyscrapers and luxury buildings that would become landmarks in the city's skyline.

Though their business styles would later diverge, Fred's influence on Donald during these formative years cannot be overstated. It was Fred who taught Donald the importance of hard work, the value of a strong work ethic, and the necessity of being hands-on with every aspect of a business. Fred also instilled in his son a deep understanding of the financial side of real estate, from securing loans and managing debt to navigating the complex world of New York's regulatory environment. These lessons would serve Donald well as he began to carve out his own career in the real estate world.

Fred Trump was also a master of navigating the political and bureaucratic systems of New York City. In an era when political connections could make or break a developer, Fred knew how to leverage his relationships with local politicians and city officials to secure lucrative contracts and favorable zoning decisions. He understood that success in real estate wasn't just about building—it was about managing the many external forces that could affect a project's profitability. Donald learned this lesson early, watching his father expertly handle the intricate web of city politics, a skill that would become crucial to Donald's later business ventures and his eventual political career.

While Donald Trump would later become famous for his brash style, his bold moves, and his embrace of high-risk, high-reward ventures, Fred's steady hand and conservative approach to business laid the groundwork. Donald may have had bigger ambitions, but his foundation in real estate—built under his father's watchful eye—gave him the tools to pursue those ambitions. The lessons Fred imparted to Donald were not just practical; they were ideological. Fred believed in building things that lasted, in creating value through hard work, and in keeping a tight grip on the financial aspects of any deal.

Fred Trump's influence on Donald was also deeply personal. Fred was a figure of immense authority in Donald's life, and much of Donald's drive to succeed came from a desire to impress his father and earn his respect. Fred was tough, demanding, and often critical—traits that Donald would later embody in his own business dealings. This father-son relationship was complex and competitive, but it was also foundational. Fred set the bar high, and Donald spent much of his early career striving to exceed it.

In the end, while Donald would later become a public figure in ways his father never could have imagined, Fred Trump's legacy as a businessman is evident in the way Donald approached the world of real estate and beyond. The discipline, financial acumen, and work ethic that Fred instilled in Donald were critical elements of his success. Fred may have built homes in the outer boroughs, but he built a son who would take the Trump name to the pinnacle of wealth, fame, and influence.

Growing Up in Queens—Donald Trump's Early Ambitions

Donald Trump's childhood in Queens, New York, was marked by privilege and expectation. He was born into a family that was already well on its way to establishing a formidable real estate empire, but for Donald, growing up under the shadow of his father, Fred Trump, was both a blessing and a challenge. The wealth and status his father had built in the outer boroughs of New York provided Donald with a comfortable upbringing, but it also sparked within him an intense drive to achieve even greater success, a desire to step out from his father's shadow and make a name for himself on a much larger stage.

Donald was born on June 14, 1946, in Jamaica Estates, a wealthy enclave in Queens. The Trump family home, a sprawling red-brick mansion, stood as a symbol of Fred Trump's success, a testament to his achievements in the construction business. Growing up in such an environment, Donald was surrounded by the trappings of wealth from an early age. His father's business was thriving, with Fred developing thousands of affordable housing units for middle-class families in Queens and Brooklyn. Donald was not just a child of privilege—he was also a child of ambition, one who had a front-row seat to his father's business empire and the opportunities it created.

But life in the Trump household was not one of complacency. Fred Trump was a strict, demanding figure, both as a father and as a businessman. He instilled in his children the importance of hard work and discipline. For Donald, the expectations were especially high. He was Fred's second son, but from a young age, it was clear that Donald was different—more aggressive, more confident, and more eager to prove himself. His father saw this and pushed him hard, molding him into a mini version of himself, but with even greater ambitions.

Donald's early education took place in the private Kew-Forest School, where he quickly gained a reputation for being energetic, outspoken, and, at times, rebellious. His tendency to challenge authority figures and his natural assertiveness often got him into trouble, traits that would later define his public persona. By the time he was 13, Donald's behavior had become so disruptive that his parents decided to send him to the New York Military Academy, hoping that the discipline and structure of a military school would help channel his energy more productively.

Attending the New York Military Academy proved to be a pivotal experience for Donald. It was there that he began to develop the leadership skills and sense of discipline that would carry him through his future business ventures. The academy offered a regimented environment that fostered competitiveness, and Donald thrived in it. He quickly rose through the ranks, becoming a student leader and excelling in both academics and sports. This experience was formative for Donald; it reinforced his natural instincts to lead, to win, and to dominate. It also gave him a taste of the power and prestige that come with being in command, lessons he would carry into his business career and, eventually, his political life.

Donald's time at the military academy also deepened his relationship with his father. Fred was a frequent visitor to the academy, and the two bonded over Donald's growing sense of discipline and achievement. Fred admired his son's leadership abilities and his competitive spirit, seeing in Donald the potential to take the Trump family name to new heights. By the time Donald graduated from the academy in 1964, it was clear that he had internalized many of his father's values—hard work, discipline, and an unwavering commitment to success.

Yet, despite his father's guidance and the success Fred had achieved in the outer boroughs, Donald's ambitions were much larger. While Fred was content building middle-class housing in Queens and Brooklyn, Donald had his sights set on Manhattan. To him, Queens, where his father had built his empire, was too small, too limiting. Manhattan represented everything Donald craved—wealth, power, glamour, and, most importantly, recognition. For Donald, Manhattan was not just a place to do business; it was the ultimate stage, where the most influential people in the world played, and he was determined to be one of them.

This ambition became clear as Donald began planning his future. After graduating from the military academy, Donald enrolled at Fordham University but quickly transferred to the Wharton School of Finance at the University of Pennsylvania, one of the most prestigious business schools in the country. Donald frequently emphasized his time at Wharton as proof of his intelligence and business acumen, but even during his college years, his focus was less on academic achievements and more on the future. He spent summers working for his father's business, learning the ins and outs of the real estate trade, but always with an eye toward something bigger.

By the time Donald graduated from Wharton in 1968, his ambitions were fully formed. He had learned the basics of real estate development from his father, but he was not content with following in Fred's footsteps. Donald wanted to expand the Trump brand beyond the outer boroughs, beyond affordable housing, and into the world of luxury, skyscrapers, and high-profile deals. He wanted to build something grander, something that would carry his name not just across New York City but around the world.

Donald's childhood and early adulthood were shaped by his father's influence, but they were also marked by a growing desire to forge his own path. The discipline he learned at the military academy and the lessons he absorbed from his father's business shaped him into a young man with a clear sense of purpose. Donald Trump wasn't just another child of privilege—he was a young man determined to transform the Trump name into a symbol of success, power, and prestige. Queens had been Fred Trump's domain, but Donald was already looking across the East River, to the towering skyscrapers of Manhattan, where his future lay.

Entering the Business World—Donald's First Ventures

By the time Donald Trump graduated from the Wharton School of Finance at the University of Pennsylvania in 1968, he had already spent years learning the real estate trade under the watchful eye of his father, Fred Trump. Armed with a prestigious education and a lifetime of firsthand business experience, Donald was ready to enter the world of real estate with ambitions that far surpassed the foundations laid by his father. However, despite his clear desire to break into the glitzy world of Manhattan real estate, Donald's early ventures began in the same terrain his father had mastered—the outer boroughs of New York City, specifically Queens and Brooklyn.

Fred Trump was a firm believer in hands-on training. He had no intention of handing Donald a golden ticket into Manhattan's elite circles right away. Instead, Fred wanted Donald to prove his worth by working on the same kinds of projects that had made the Trump family successful: middle-income housing developments. In Fred's view, these projects were the backbone of the family's business, profitable, stable, and relatively low-risk. Donald, eager to prove himself, took on this challenge, working with his father to manage and develop properties in Queens and Brooklyn throughout the late 1960s and early 1970s.

One of Donald's earliest experiences in the business was his involvement in the construction and management of apartment complexes that were part of the Trump family's existing portfolio. Fred had built thousands of units across New York's outer boroughs, focusing on affordable housing for middle-class families, often with the help of government incentives and subsidies. These projects weren't glamorous, but they were profitable, and they provided Donald with a crash course in the day-to-day management of large-scale real estate holdings. He was responsible for overseeing construction crews, negotiating with contractors, and dealing with tenants—a gritty introduction to the realities of real estate development.

Donald's first significant independent project came in 1971 when he was put in charge of managing a troubled development called Swifton Village in Cincinnati, Ohio. Fred Trump had purchased the 1,200-unit apartment complex for a bargain price in the early 1960s, but by the time Donald took the reins, the property had fallen into disrepair and was losing money. This was Donald's opportunity to show his father that he could handle a complex and challenging project on his own, and he approached the situation with a sense of determination and confidence that would later define his career.

At Swifton Village, Donald implemented a series of aggressive cost-cutting measures and initiated an extensive renovation of the complex. He also focused on improving tenant relations and increasing occupancy rates by marketing the apartments to a broader demographic. Within two years, the property's fortunes had turned around, and the Trumps were able to sell Swifton Village for a substantial profit. This success marked an early victory for Donald, proving to his father—and to himself—that he had the skills to manage large-scale projects and make them profitable.

However, while Donald's early ventures with his father were successful, they were not enough to satisfy his growing ambitions. He had spent years learning the ropes in Queens and Brooklyn, but he had his sights set on something much bigger: Manhattan. For Donald, the outer boroughs represented the past—a world of modest developments, affordable housing, and quiet success. Manhattan, on the other hand, was where the titans of real estate operated, where skyscrapers reached into the sky and where the wealthy and powerful lived, worked, and played. To Donald, breaking into Manhattan was the ultimate test of his abilities, and it was there that he believed he could truly make his mark.

Throughout the early 1970s, Donald continued to work alongside his father, but he also began plotting his move into Manhattan. He saw opportunity in the city's declining real estate market. The New York City of the early 1970s was a far cry from the glittering metropolis it would later become. The city was grappling with financial turmoil, crime rates were soaring, and many once-grand properties in Manhattan were falling into disrepair. For Donald, this represented an opportunity. He believed that he could revitalize the city's decaying properties, turning them into profitable, high-profile developments that would not only generate wealth but also establish his reputation as a major player in the real estate world.

The first step in Donald's journey into Manhattan came in 1973, when he began scouting for potential development sites in the city. He knew that if he wanted to succeed, he would need to find the right deal—one that would allow him to make a splash in the city's competitive real estate market. That opportunity came in the form of a decaying, near-bankrupt property: the Commodore Hotel.

The Commodore, once a symbol of luxury and elegance in midtown Manhattan, had fallen on hard times by the 1970s. Located adjacent to Grand Central Terminal, the hotel had become a symbol of the city's broader decline, with occupancy rates plummeting and the building falling into disrepair. Donald saw an opportunity to transform the dilapidated property into a high-end luxury hotel, one that would signal not only the resurgence of the hotel itself but of Manhattan real estate as a whole.

To pull off the deal, Donald needed to navigate a complex web of financial and political challenges. He approached the Hyatt Corporation, convincing them to partner with him on the redevelopment of the hotel. Then, with the help of his father's political connections, Donald secured a generous tax abatement from the city, which was desperate for any form of economic revitalization. The deal was risky, but it was exactly the kind of high-stakes, high-reward project that Donald craved.

This venture into Manhattan would be the first of many bold moves that would define Donald Trump's career. With the Commodore Hotel deal in motion, Donald was finally on his way to realizing his dream of becoming a major force in Manhattan real estate. For Donald, this wasn't just about making money—it was about making a name for himself, establishing his brand, and proving to the world that he was not just Fred Trump's son, but a visionary businessman in his own right.

Breaking Into Manhattan—The Commodore Hotel Deal

Donald Trump's ambition to break into the Manhattan real estate market culminated in one of the most pivotal moments of his early career: the acquisition and redevelopment of the

Commodore Hotel. This deal would become a defining project for Trump, marking his transformation from a promising young real estate developer into a major player in one of the most competitive and prestigious real estate markets in the world. The Commodore Hotel deal wasn't just a financial transaction—it was a symbol of Trump's larger-than-life ambitions and his ability to maneuver through complex challenges to achieve success.

The Commodore Hotel, originally built in the 1920s, was located on 42nd Street, right next to the iconic Grand Central Terminal. Once a glamorous destination for travelers in midtown Manhattan, the hotel had fallen into disrepair by the 1970s. New York City, in general, was facing economic decline during this time, with rising crime rates, high unemployment, and crumbling infrastructure. The hotel, like much of the city, was struggling to stay afloat, and its owners were desperate to sell. While many saw the Commodore as a liability, Trump saw it as an opportunity. He believed that with the right vision and investment, the hotel could be restored to its former glory and become a key player in the revitalization of Manhattan.

In 1974, Trump set his sights on acquiring the Commodore. He had already been laying the groundwork for his entry into Manhattan's real estate scene, and this project seemed like the perfect launching pad. However, securing the deal would require a combination of bold negotiations, financial acumen, and political savvy. Trump knew that the hotel's purchase and redevelopment would be a massive undertaking, requiring both significant capital and strategic partnerships. As a newcomer to Manhattan's high-stakes real estate world, Trump would need to convince a number of powerful stakeholders that he could pull it off.

The first major hurdle Trump faced was financing. While Fred Trump had built a considerable fortune in Queens and Brooklyn, the scale of the Commodore project was beyond what the family business had previously taken on. To finance the redevelopment, Donald approached the Hyatt Corporation, a company looking to expand its presence in the New York hotel market. Trump's pitch to Hyatt was simple but compelling: with a prime location next to Grand Central Terminal and his plan for a modern luxury hotel, the Commodore had the potential to become a premier destination for travelers and a symbol of Manhattan's resurgence.

Hyatt agreed to partner with Trump, but even with their support, the deal was far from guaranteed. The real challenge lay in the financial condition of New York City itself. The city was teetering on the edge of bankruptcy, and high taxes, along with a poor business environment, made large-scale real estate developments nearly impossible. Trump, however, saw this as an opportunity. He believed that if he could secure tax incentives from the city, he could make the deal financially viable.

This is where Trump's political skills came into play. With the help of his father's connections, Donald arranged a meeting with key city officials, including then-Mayor Abraham Beame. Trump argued that the Commodore Hotel's redevelopment could serve as a catalyst for revitalizing the entire area around Grand Central Terminal. He positioned the project as a win-win for both the city and his company—by granting a tax abatement, the city would not only avoid the hotel falling further into decline but would also see increased tourism and tax revenue in the long run.

After months of negotiation, Trump succeeded in securing an unprecedented 40-year tax abatement from the city, a major coup that made the Commodore deal financially feasible. The agreement meant that the Trump Organization and Hyatt would pay significantly reduced property taxes for decades, making the investment in the hotel far more attractive. This tax deal, a hallmark of Trump's early career, showcased his ability to leverage government incentives to create value in his business ventures. It was also a testament to his growing reputation as a dealmaker—a developer who could navigate the complex intersection of business, politics, and finance.

With financing in place and the tax abatement secured, Trump moved forward with the redevelopment of the Commodore. His vision was clear: he wanted to transform the aging hotel into a modern, luxurious property that would stand as a symbol of Manhattan's rebirth. To achieve this, Trump hired Der Scutt, an acclaimed architect known for his work on other high-profile Manhattan projects. Together, they designed a sleek glass façade that would replace the hotel's old brick exterior, giving it a fresh, contemporary look. The design was bold and modern, reflecting Trump's desire to stand out in Manhattan's crowded real estate market.

The renovation was completed in 1980, and the newly christened Grand Hyatt Hotel opened to great fanfare. It was an immediate success, both financially and symbolically. The hotel's transformation from a crumbling relic into a gleaming symbol of modern luxury was seen as a triumph, not just for Trump, but for New York City itself. The Grand Hyatt became a popular destination for tourists and business travelers alike, and its success helped spur the redevelopment of the surrounding area. For Donald Trump, the project was a validation of his vision and his ability to execute on a grand scale.

The Commodore Hotel deal solidified Trump's position as a major force in Manhattan real estate. It was the first of many high-profile projects that would define his career and establish the Trump brand as synonymous with luxury, power, and ambition. But beyond the financial success of the deal, the project was also a personal milestone for Trump. It marked his official entry into Manhattan, the place he had long dreamed of conquering. No longer was he simply Fred Trump's son, operating in the shadow of his father's outer-borough empire. He was now Donald Trump—the man who had taken on Manhattan and won.

This deal laid the groundwork for Trump's future projects, which would follow a similar formula: identify undervalued properties, secure favorable terms through negotiation, and transform them into high-profile successes. The Grand Hyatt was just the beginning. With the Commodore under his belt, Trump now had the confidence and the reputation to pursue even larger and more ambitious developments. He had arrived in Manhattan, and there was no turning back.

Chapter 2

Chapter 2: The Young Mogul

The Shift to Manhattan—Donald's Vision for High-Stakes Development

By the mid-1970s, Donald Trump had proven his abilities as a real estate developer working alongside his father in the outer boroughs of New York. But Donald's ambition went beyond the family business of building middle-income housing in Queens and Brooklyn. He saw something grander on the horizon—something that would take him from the relative anonymity of his father's empire into the spotlight of Manhattan's elite real estate market. For Donald, Manhattan wasn't just another borough; it was the ultimate stage where only the boldest, most daring developers could truly make their mark. This vision, more than anything else, would shape the trajectory of his early career.

Manhattan in the 1970s was a city in turmoil. New York was on the brink of bankruptcy, crime was rampant, and entire neighborhoods were in decline. To many developers, the city's real estate market seemed like a risk not worth taking. However, Donald saw it differently. Where others saw decay and danger, Trump saw opportunity. He believed that the city's downturn presented the perfect time to invest, when prices were low and risks were high, because the rewards for success would be even higher. He was determined to make his move into the heart of the city, regardless of the obstacles in his path.

For Donald, breaking into Manhattan represented much more than financial opportunity—it was personal. He had grown up admiring the power and glamour of Manhattan from a distance, but his father, Fred Trump, had stayed away from it, choosing to focus on the more stable and profitable outer boroughs. While Fred was content to build middle-class housing, Donald had a different vision. He didn't just want to be rich; he wanted to be recognized as a major player in New York's most prestigious real estate market. To him, Manhattan was the place where reputations were made, and he believed that only by conquering it could he truly differentiate himself from his father and create his own legacy.

Trump knew that his first step into Manhattan real estate would have to be a bold one. He couldn't afford to take small, cautious steps. In a city filled with skyscrapers and iconic landmarks, subtlety wouldn't get him noticed. To make his presence felt, he would need to embark on a project so ambitious, so grand in scale, that it would announce his arrival in a way that no one could ignore. Trump's early experiences in Brooklyn and Queens had taught him how to navigate the complexities of real estate development, but Manhattan was different. It wasn't just about the business—it was about status, influence, and public perception.

The challenges that came with entering Manhattan's high-stakes market were numerous. For one, the established developers in the city viewed outsiders with skepticism. The world of Manhattan real estate was insular, dominated by old money and long-standing relationships. Donald, young and brash, would need to prove himself in an environment where newcomers were often met with disdain. Moreover, Manhattan real estate deals required vast sums of capital, far more than anything Donald had worked with in the outer boroughs. This meant securing partnerships, financing, and often navigating complex political landscapes to get deals done.

But Trump had a natural talent for deal-making, and he understood that in Manhattan, success was often about more than just money—it was about relationships, leverage, and timing. He began building relationships with powerful figures in the city's political and financial circles, positioning himself as someone who could get things done. He made it clear that he wasn't just another developer looking to build a few apartment complexes; he had a grand vision for what New York could become, and he wanted to be the man to lead its transformation.

Trump's decision to target Manhattan during this period reflected his deep understanding of timing and risk. He knew that the city's financial troubles would eventually pass, and when they did, those who had invested early would reap the rewards. More importantly, Trump understood the power of branding and perception. He knew that if he could establish himself in Manhattan, even just by landing a single major project, it would elevate his status far beyond that of a typical real estate developer. It wasn't enough for him to be wealthy—he wanted to be seen as one of the most influential and successful figures in the city.

Trump's move to Manhattan also marked a key moment in the evolution of his personal brand. He was no longer just the son of a successful builder; he was becoming Donald Trump, a name that would eventually be synonymous with luxury, ambition, and larger-than-life projects. Manhattan wasn't just a business venture for him—it was the stage on which he would perform for the world, where every deal and every building would be a reflection of his ambition and vision.

In the years to come, Donald Trump would indeed leave an indelible mark on Manhattan's skyline. But it was this initial shift—this bold decision to leave behind the safety of his father's success and strike out on his own—that laid the foundation for everything that followed. Trump's entry into Manhattan real estate was more than just a career move; it was the beginning of his transformation into the public figure and brand that would eventually capture the attention of the entire world.

The Trump Tower—A Monument to Luxury and Power

Donald Trump's ambitions to conquer Manhattan found their ultimate expression in a single, audacious project: Trump Tower. This glittering skyscraper, which would rise on Fifth Avenue in the heart of New York City, became more than just another real estate development—it was the embodiment of Trump's larger-than-life persona and his vision for luxury and power. In many ways, Trump Tower symbolized the very essence of Donald Trump himself: bold, opulent, and impossible to ignore.

By the late 1970s, after his successful redevelopment of the Commodore Hotel (which became the Grand Hyatt), Trump had established himself as a force to be reckoned with in Manhattan real estate. But he wasn't content with merely being a player in the game—he wanted to stand above the competition. His next project would have to be something monumental, something that would put his name front and center in the city's most prestigious neighborhood.

Trump's opportunity came in 1978 when he acquired the Bonwit Teller building, a historic art deco department store located at 725 Fifth Avenue, one of the most coveted addresses in Manhattan. Fifth Avenue was home to some of the most famous luxury retailers and landmarks in the world, and owning a piece of this prime real estate was a dream for any developer. Trump envisioned replacing the aging department store with a state-of-the-art skyscraper that would not only serve as a luxury residential and commercial space but also as a lasting monument to the Trump name.

The idea behind Trump Tower was simple yet revolutionary: it would combine ultra-luxury residential apartments with high-end retail space, catering to the world's wealthiest individuals and businesses. Trump wanted to create a building that exuded prestige and sophistication at every level. From the gleaming glass exterior to the lavish marble-filled interiors, Trump Tower would be designed to attract the rich, the famous, and the powerful.

But acquiring the land and securing the necessary approvals for the project was no easy task. Trump faced significant opposition, particularly from preservationists who were concerned about the demolition of the historic Bonwit Teller building. The building's art deco sculptures were especially prized, and Trump initially promised to preserve them for donation to the Metropolitan Museum of Art. However, as demolition began, the sculptures were destroyed, a decision that ignited public outrage. For Trump, though, the controversy was secondary to the larger goal—his focus was on building the tower and completing the project on his terms.

Trump's boldness didn't stop with the demolition. He understood that for Trump Tower to succeed, it couldn't just be another high-rise—it had to be extraordinary. To design the building, Trump hired Der Scutt, an acclaimed architect, and together they developed plans for a sleek, reflective glass tower that would rise 58 stories above Fifth Avenue. The tower's striking black glass façade was unlike anything else on the street, setting it apart from the more traditional stone buildings that surrounded it. The design was cutting-edge for its time, making Trump Tower a standout among the city's luxury buildings.

Inside, Trump spared no expense in creating an opulent atmosphere. The building's lobby, which would eventually become a tourist attraction in its own right, was lined with pink marble and adorned with a waterfall cascading down its interior walls. Trump insisted on using only the highest-quality materials, such as Italian marble and brass, to ensure that every detail reflected the sense of luxury and power that he wanted the building to convey. For Trump, the building wasn't just a place to live or work—it was an experience.

Trump Tower opened in 1983, and it quickly became a symbol of 1980s extravagance. The residential units were sold to some of the wealthiest individuals in the world, including celebrities, foreign dignitaries, and business moguls. Trump himself moved into the penthouse, which he decorated with gold and crystal, further cementing his image as the ultimate purveyor of luxury. The building's commercial spaces were leased to high-end retailers, including Tiffany & Co., whose flagship store was right next door. Trump Tower wasn't just a building—it was a lifestyle, and living or working there became a status symbol.

The marketing of Trump Tower was as much about selling the Trump brand as it was about selling real estate. Trump's name was emblazoned across the building's entrance in bold gold letters, and from the beginning, Trump understood the power of association. By making his name synonymous with luxury, he was able to elevate both the value of the building and his personal brand. Trump Tower wasn't just a successful real estate development—it was a brand-building exercise that positioned Donald Trump as the face of New York luxury.

While Trump Tower was undoubtedly a financial success, its greatest impact may have been in how it solidified Donald Trump's identity in the public eye. The tower became the physical representation of the Trump brand, a place where wealth, luxury, and power converged in one glittering skyscraper. The building's prominence, combined with Trump's ability to generate media attention, ensured that Trump Tower would become a cultural icon as much as a real estate success.

The media couldn't get enough of Trump Tower. It was covered in magazines, featured in television programs, and even became a popular tourist destination. Celebrities and dignitaries were frequently spotted in the lobby, and Trump made sure to cultivate an image of exclusivity and glamour around the building. By the mid-1980s, Trump Tower wasn't just another development—it had become a symbol of success in its own right, and it helped catapult Donald Trump from being a local real estate developer to a national celebrity.

In many ways, Trump Tower was the culmination of Donald Trump's early vision: to not just succeed in Manhattan but to dominate it. It was a physical manifestation of his belief in the power of perception, luxury, and branding. For Trump, this wasn't just about building a profitable development—it was about creating a monument to his ambition and securing his place in the pantheon of New York's elite developers. More than just a building, Trump Tower marked the point where Trump's name became synonymous with the bold, brash, and unapologetically lavish persona that would define him for decades to come.

The Branding of Trump—Establishing a Personal Brand

As Donald Trump's real estate empire grew, so did something even more valuable: his personal brand. From the early stages of his career, Trump understood that in the world of high-profile real estate, image and reputation were just as important as bricks and mortar. His name was more than a signature—it was a symbol of luxury, ambition, and success. Trump wasn't just building skyscrapers; he was building a public persona that would carry him far beyond the confines of New York real estate and into the national and global spotlight.

In the late 1970s and early 1980s, as his projects in Manhattan began to take shape, Trump realized that his greatest asset wasn't just his ability to secure financing or close deals—it was his ability to sell a vision, and that vision was intimately tied to his own image. He understood that if people associated his name with success and luxury, it would elevate not only his projects but his entire business. The Trump brand was born out of this realization, and Trump himself became its most powerful ambassador.

Trump's approach to branding was unique, particularly for someone in the real estate business. While many developers chose to remain behind the scenes, letting their buildings and projects speak for themselves, Trump made sure that his name—and face—were front and center in everything he did. He appeared on magazine covers, in television interviews, and at high-profile social events, always presenting himself as the face of success. For Trump, publicity was not a byproduct of his work; it was an essential component of his business strategy. He knew that media exposure could be leveraged to enhance the value of his developments and attract attention to his growing empire.

One of Trump's early strategies was to associate his name with high-end luxury and exclusivity. His projects, like the Grand Hyatt and Trump Tower, were marketed as the epitome of sophistication and class. By branding his buildings with the Trump name, he created an immediate sense of prestige and desirability. The name itself became shorthand for high-end living, attracting a clientele that wanted to be associated with the Trump lifestyle. But more than just targeting wealthy buyers and tenants, Trump aimed to capture the imagination of the public. He wanted his name to evoke a sense of aspiration, so that even those who couldn't afford to live in a Trump property would associate his name with the idea of success.

The branding of Trump went beyond real estate. As Trump became more famous, his persona began to shape public perceptions of wealth, ambition, and power. He cultivated an image of the ultimate dealmaker—a man who always won, no matter how high the stakes. In interviews, Trump spoke about his projects with an air of absolute confidence, often exaggerating the scale of his successes to reinforce the idea that everything he touched turned to gold. This larger-than-life image became central to the Trump brand. By presenting himself as a winner, Trump convinced others that his projects, too, were destined for success. His confidence became contagious, attracting investors, partners, and buyers who wanted to be part of his winning streak.

Trump's ability to manipulate the media played a crucial role in building his brand. He had an instinctive understanding of how to generate publicity and keep his name in the headlines. Whether it was through strategic leaks about new projects, high-profile social appearances, or even personal controversies, Trump made sure that the public was always talking about him. He cultivated relationships with journalists and columnists, often feeding them stories that painted him in a favorable light. In return, the media gave him exactly what he wanted—constant exposure that helped solidify his image as a successful, high-profile businessman.

A key element of Trump's branding success was his willingness to blur the lines between truth and perception. While many of his real estate ventures were successful, Trump was equally skilled at using media to exaggerate his achievements and downplay his failures. He created a narrative of unstoppable success, even when the reality was more complex. For instance, during times when his businesses faced financial challenges, Trump never allowed the public to see him sweat. He maintained his persona as the ultimate dealmaker, carefully controlling the image he presented to the world. In Trump's world, perception was often more important than reality.

The Trump brand also extended to his personal life. Trump's marriages, children, and lifestyle were all carefully curated elements of his public image. His relationships with high-profile celebrities and socialites added to his mystique, while his extravagant lifestyle—private jets, luxury homes, and designer clothes—reinforced the idea that he was living the American dream. Trump understood that people were fascinated by wealth and power, and he played into that fascination by constantly showcasing his success. Whether it was a photoshoot of his gilded apartment or interviews about his personal philosophy on winning, Trump ensured that the public saw him as someone who had mastered the game of life.

By the mid-1980s, Trump's brand had transcended real estate. He was no longer just a developer; he was a cultural icon. His name was synonymous with success, luxury, and ambition, and he was constantly in the public eye. People weren't just buying Trump properties—they were buying into the Trump vision of success. The Trump brand had become one of the most recognizable in the world, and it was built on the foundation of Trump's ability to sell not just buildings, but himself.

In the years to come, Trump would continue to leverage his personal brand to expand into new industries, from entertainment to sports and beyond. But it all began with his understanding that in the world of real estate, and in business in general, success was not just about the deals you made—it was about the image you projected. For Donald Trump, branding wasn't just a marketing strategy—it was the key to his rise to fame and influence. His name, emblazoned in gold on the front of buildings, became his most powerful asset, propelling him from a real estate mogul to a global icon.

The Rise of a Media Personality—Trump in the Spotlight

By the 1980s, Donald Trump was no longer just a real estate mogul—he had become a media sensation. As his projects became more ambitious and his brand grew stronger, Trump understood that his public image could be just as valuable as the buildings he constructed. He wasn't content to stay in the background like many of his peers in the real estate world. Instead, Trump sought out the spotlight, leveraging the media to amplify his persona and extend his influence far beyond the borders of New York City. His ability to navigate and manipulate the media would soon become one of his most powerful tools, turning him into a cultural phenomenon.

Trump's rise as a media personality can be traced back to his understanding of the media's hunger for larger-than-life characters, particularly during the excess and glamor of the 1980s. This was a decade when Wall Street was booming, wealth was worshipped, and America was fascinated with the so-called "masters of the universe"—the men who seemed to control the flow of money and power. Trump fit perfectly into this narrative, and he was more than willing to play the part. He crafted an image of himself as the ultimate dealmaker, a man who could turn every venture into gold, and he knew how to ensure that image was reflected in the headlines.

It wasn't just the real estate press that took notice of Trump; mainstream media quickly latched onto his story. He became a fixture in magazines and newspapers, not only for his business deals but for his high-profile lifestyle. Trump's name appeared in articles that mixed business reporting with society gossip, blurring the lines between business news and celebrity culture. In this way, Trump elevated himself beyond the world of real estate, becoming a symbol of success that resonated with a much broader audience. His ability to connect with the public was unmatched—people were fascinated by his confidence, his extravagance, and his boldness.

One of the key moments that cemented Trump's media stardom came in 1983 when he graced the cover of *Time* magazine. The cover photo showed Trump standing confidently against the backdrop of the New York skyline, with the headline: "This Man May Be the Best Businessman in America." For Trump, appearing on the cover of *Time* wasn't just a personal triumph—it was a declaration that he had officially arrived on the national stage. In the years that followed, he would appear on countless magazine covers and television shows, each time reinforcing the carefully cultivated image of himself as a man who was always winning, always in control.

Television became another powerful platform for Trump to expand his public persona. He was a frequent guest on popular talk shows like *The Tonight Show*, *Late Night with David Letterman*, and *Larry King Live*. These appearances allowed Trump to showcase his personality, which was as much a part of his brand as his business acumen. He exuded confidence, often using his appearances to boast about his latest deals, offer his opinions on the economy, or share his thoughts on what it took to succeed in business. His sound bites—often blunt, always attention-grabbing—were perfectly suited for television, and they made him a favorite guest of talk show hosts looking to entertain their audiences with a dose of Trump's brash, unapologetic style.

In addition to his television appearances, Trump also began cultivating relationships with New York City's most influential columnists and media personalities. He often fed them tips and stories about his latest business ventures or his personal life, ensuring that his name remained a constant presence in the city's tabloids and gossip pages. This symbiotic relationship with the media allowed Trump to control the narrative around his success. He knew that attention—positive or negative—was valuable, and he skillfully used the media to keep himself in the public eye. The more people talked about Trump, the more his brand grew, and with it, his power and influence.

Trump's flair for self-promotion reached new heights with the publication of his first book, *The Art of the Deal*, in 1987. Co-written with journalist Tony Schwartz, the book was part memoir, part business manual, and entirely a marketing tool for the Trump brand. In it, Trump detailed his rise in real estate, offering readers a behind-the-scenes look at how he made deals and built his empire. But more than that, *The Art of the Deal* served as a platform for Trump to solidify his image as the ultimate negotiator—a man who knew how to win no matter the odds. The book was a massive success, spending weeks on the *New York Times* bestseller list and further cementing Trump's status as a media-savvy mogul.

The Art of the Deal was more than just a business book; it was a manifesto for Trump's approach to life and business, and it resonated with a wide audience. In the pages of the book, Trump outlined his rules for success, which included a mixture of bravado, showmanship, and an unshakable belief in his own abilities. The book became a bible of sorts for aspiring entrepreneurs, many of whom admired Trump not only for his financial success but for his relentless pursuit of the limelight. Trump's willingness to put himself out there, to court both admiration and criticism, was part of what made him so compelling to the media and the public alike.

By the late 1980s, Trump had fully embraced his role as a media personality. His name was everywhere—on buildings, in newspapers, on television, and in bookstores. He had crossed over from being a wealthy businessman to being a full-fledged celebrity, and he knew how to capitalize on that. The media had made him larger than life, and Trump, ever the showman, used his platform to continue building his empire and expanding his influence.

What set Trump apart from other businessmen of the era was his understanding that fame and fortune could feed off each other. His media appearances weren't just vanity projects; they were strategic moves that enhanced his business prospects. The more famous he became, the more valuable his projects became, and the more he could command higher prices for his properties. His celebrity status allowed him to blur the lines between business and entertainment, and in doing so, he created a template for the modern celebrity entrepreneur.

In the end, Trump's rise as a media personality was about more than just vanity—it was a calculated move that would pay dividends for decades to come. By transforming himself into a cultural icon, Trump ensured that his name would always be synonymous with success, wealth, and power. He had entered the public consciousness not just as a businessman, but as a symbol of American ambition, a man who had mastered both the art of the deal and the art of media manipulation. It was this dual mastery that would carry him to even greater heights, as he leveraged his celebrity status to further expand his empire—and, eventually, his political ambitions.

Expanding the Empire—Trump's Diversification Beyond Real Estate

By the late 1980s, Donald Trump had established himself as one of the most recognizable names in real estate, but he wasn't content to remain within the confines of the property business. Trump had always envisioned himself as more than just a developer—he saw himself as an empire builder. To fulfill that vision, he began expanding into new ventures that would not only diversify his business interests but also amplify his brand. Trump understood that to maintain his image as a titan of industry, he needed to branch out, conquering different sectors and, in the process, making the Trump name synonymous with luxury and success across a variety of industries.

One of Trump's first major moves outside of real estate was his foray into the world of casinos. In the mid-1980s, Atlantic City was emerging as a hotspot for gambling, and Trump recognized an opportunity to capitalize on this burgeoning market. In 1984, Trump opened his first casino, the Trump Plaza Hotel and Casino, on the Atlantic City boardwalk. Like his real estate ventures, Trump Plaza was marketed as a high-end destination, a luxurious escape for gamblers seeking a taste of the good life. The casino quickly became a symbol of Atlantic City's new wave of growth, and Trump's name on the property lent it an air of prestige.

Not satisfied with one casino, Trump doubled down on Atlantic City, acquiring two more major properties: Trump Castle and, later, the massive Trump Taj Mahal. The Taj Mahal, which opened in 1990, was billed as the "eighth wonder of the world," a lavish, sprawling complex that cost nearly $1 billion to build. Trump spared no expense in creating a casino that was both opulent and larger-than-life. The Taj Mahal boasted over 2,000 rooms, the world's largest casino floor at the time, and ornate décor designed to impress visitors at every turn. Trump, ever the showman, ensured that the grand opening was a spectacle, complete with fireworks and a ribbon-cutting ceremony attended by high-profile celebrities.

With his casinos, Trump made a statement: he wasn't just a player in real estate, he was a mogul with the ability to dominate entire industries. His Atlantic City properties weren't just business ventures—they were expressions of Trump's desire to build an empire that spanned far beyond New York. And yet, while his casinos initially generated substantial revenue, the high costs of construction and stiff competition in the Atlantic City market put financial strain on Trump's growing portfolio. His aggressive expansion into the casino business, combined with the mounting debt associated with his new projects, would eventually lead to financial troubles that surfaced in the early 1990s. But at the height of his casino ventures, Trump was undeniably a major force in Atlantic City's transformation into a gambling destination.

Trump's diversification efforts weren't limited to casinos. He also ventured into the world of sports, purchasing the New Jersey Generals, a team in the short-lived United States Football League (USFL). Trump's acquisition of the Generals in 1983 was part of his broader ambition to expand into sports and entertainment. He saw the USFL as an up-and-coming league that could eventually rival the NFL, and he believed that owning a team would provide him with both financial returns and additional media exposure. However, Trump's involvement in the USFL was marked by controversy. He pushed for the league to move its schedule from the spring to the fall to compete directly with the NFL, a move that many believed contributed to the league's collapse. The USFL folded in 1986, and Trump's foray into professional football ended in disappointment.

Still, Trump's appetite for expanding his influence in the entertainment world didn't wane. He was drawn to ventures that would increase his visibility and cement his status as a public figure, which led him to dip into the world of beauty pageants. In 1996, Trump acquired the Miss Universe, Miss USA, and Miss Teen USA pageants. For Trump, the pageants were more than just business investments—they were platforms to further promote the Trump brand on a global stage. The glitz and glamour of the pageants fit neatly with Trump's personal image of wealth, beauty, and success. Under his ownership, the Miss Universe pageant, in particular, grew in popularity, becoming a highly televised global event. Trump's involvement in the pageants provided him with even more media exposure and reinforced his connection to the world of high-profile entertainment.

In addition to sports and entertainment, Trump also made a play for the airline industry with the launch of Trump Shuttle in 1989. The airline, which operated shuttle flights between New York, Washington, D.C., and Boston, was an attempt to create a luxury air travel experience, complete with plush leather seats and gold-colored fixtures. Trump Shuttle was meant to embody the same lavish lifestyle that Trump had cultivated in his real estate ventures. However, like many of Trump's non-real estate projects, Trump Shuttle struggled to turn a profit, and after two years of financial losses, Trump was forced to sell the airline in 1992. While Trump Shuttle may not have succeeded, the venture was another example of Trump's willingness to take risks in his pursuit of a diversified empire.

Even as Trump explored new industries, he never fully stepped away from real estate. In fact, the diversification of his business interests often served to bolster his real estate ventures. For example, Trump's ownership of the Plaza Hotel in New York, which he purchased in 1988, was a prime example of how he used his media and entertainment ties to enhance his real estate holdings. The Plaza was one of New York's most iconic hotels, and under Trump's ownership, it hosted a number of high-profile events, including movie premieres and celebrity galas. Trump's presence at these events only heightened his visibility, further intertwining his real estate business with his personal brand.

Trump's ventures into new industries weren't always financially successful, but they were effective in one crucial way: they kept the Trump name in the spotlight. Every new acquisition, every high-profile launch, and every controversial decision fed the media narrative that Donald Trump was a man who couldn't be confined to any one sector. He was a mogul in the truest sense of the word—someone whose influence extended across multiple industries and who was willing to take bold risks to grow his empire. Each new venture added another layer to the Trump brand, making it even more recognizable and omnipresent.

By the time the 1990s rolled around, Donald Trump had positioned himself not just as a real estate developer but as a multifaceted entrepreneur whose name was synonymous with ambition and luxury. He had created an empire that stretched far beyond Manhattan, encompassing casinos, sports, entertainment, and more. Though some of his ventures faltered financially, Trump's ability to diversify his interests allowed him to remain relevant, constantly reinventing himself in the public eye. This adaptability would become a hallmark of Trump's career, ensuring that even in times of difficulty, the Trump brand would endure—and eventually, it would propel him into an entirely new arena: politics.

Chapter 3

Chapter 3: Glitz, Glamour, and the Art of the Deal

The Trump Tower—A Monument to Luxury and Power

The story of Trump Tower is the story of Donald Trump's ascent from a successful New York real estate developer to a national figure whose name became synonymous with luxury, power, and ambition. By the early 1980s, Trump had already made a name for himself with projects like the Grand Hyatt, but it was the construction of Trump Tower that would transform him into a larger-than-life figure. Trump Tower wasn't just a real estate project; it was a monument to Trump's personal brand and vision—a gleaming skyscraper that captured the ethos of opulence, power, and celebrity.

Located on Fifth Avenue, one of the most prestigious streets in the world, the site for Trump Tower was previously home to the Bonwit Teller department store. Acquiring this prime piece of Manhattan real estate was the first coup in what would become one of Trump's most iconic projects. In true Trump fashion, the acquisition was not straightforward. Bonwit Teller was owned by the Genesco Corporation, which had initially refused to sell the property. Trump's persistence, however, eventually led to a deal. The negotiations revealed a key element of Trump's approach to business: he had a keen eye for undervalued or underused properties and was willing to push hard to acquire them, often offering terms that others would not dare. Trump recognized that the site's location, right at the heart of Manhattan's elite shopping and business district, was worth the high stakes.

From the outset, Trump had grand ambitions for the project. He envisioned not just a high-rise but a symbol of luxury living and cutting-edge design, something that would rival and surpass the most prestigious buildings in New York. Trump Tower would blend residential apartments, office spaces, and high-end retail under one roof—an innovative concept at the time. Trump's vision was clear: the building needed to stand out, not just for its height but for its elegance and luxury. The building's design, created by architect Der Scutt, would include a distinctive, sleek bronze-tinted glass façade that would immediately set it apart from the surrounding concrete and stone buildings that dominated Fifth Avenue.

Inside, Trump spared no expense. The tower's public atrium was clad in pink marble, adorned with cascading waterfalls, and lined with high-end stores like Gucci and Tiffany & Co. It was a deliberate play to attract the wealthy and the powerful, people who would be willing to pay premium prices to live or work in a building that exuded class and sophistication. For Trump, every detail mattered, from the gold-colored fixtures to the mirror-polished surfaces. His commitment to creating an environment of pure luxury reflected his own personality—bold, flashy, and unapologetically opulent.

Building Trump Tower, however, wasn't without its challenges. From securing financing to navigating the city's stringent zoning laws, Trump had to use his considerable skills as a dealmaker to bring the project to fruition. He convinced a group of banks to provide the $200 million in financing needed to complete the tower, at a time when lending to such a large, speculative project was not common. But Trump's charm and persuasive ability won them over. Moreover, he used his relationships with city officials to secure crucial zoning allowances, including the right to build higher than regulations would normally permit, in exchange for providing public access to the atrium. This negotiation allowed Trump to increase the number of floors in the tower, adding to its profitability.

The marketing of Trump Tower was as important as the construction itself. Trump was a master of promotion, and he spared no effort in making the building a symbol of wealth and prestige. He held an extravagant opening ceremony in 1983, attended by celebrities, business leaders, and New York's elite. The media attention surrounding the event was intense, and Trump ensured that the coverage focused not just on the tower's architecture but on its association with luxury and power. Trump Tower quickly became one of the most sought-after addresses in the city. Apartments sold for millions, and commercial tenants were willing to pay premium rents to be associated with the Trump brand.

What set Trump Tower apart from other buildings in New York wasn't just its design or its location—it was the way Trump infused the building with his own persona. The tower was a reflection of everything Trump wanted to project about himself: success, wealth, ambition, and a touch of glamour. For Trump, this was more than just another business deal; it was a symbol of his place in the world, a declaration that he had arrived at the pinnacle of power and prestige. Trump Tower became a landmark, not just because of its physical presence but because it embodied the image that Donald Trump had so carefully cultivated—a man of vision, larger than life, and at the center of New York's elite.

The success of Trump Tower was a turning point in Donald Trump's career. It marked the moment when he transitioned from being a successful developer to being a household name, someone whose projects weren't just real estate ventures but cultural events. The tower also laid the groundwork for Trump's future brand-building endeavors. After the success of Trump Tower, every project he touched would bear his name, as the Trump brand became as important as the buildings themselves. In many ways, Trump Tower was the ultimate reflection of Trump's genius for self-promotion and his understanding of how to sell not just a product, but a lifestyle and an image.

The construction and marketing of Trump Tower established Donald Trump as one of the most powerful figures in New York real estate, and more than that, it launched him into the realm of celebrity. For Trump, it wasn't enough to be successful in business; he wanted to be recognized, to be seen as someone who shaped the world around him. In Trump Tower, he found the perfect stage for this performance, a place where wealth, power, and ambition intersected with glamour and celebrity.

The Renovation of Wollman Rink—Trump as a Master of Public Relations

In 1986, Donald Trump took on a project that would further solidify his reputation as a businessman who could get things done when others couldn't. It was a project that seemed relatively simple at first glance but had become a symbol of government inefficiency and incompetence—the renovation of the Wollman Rink in Central Park. The saga of Wollman Rink's failed renovation had been an embarrassment for New York City for nearly six years. The city had spent millions of dollars and countless hours trying to refurbish the beloved ice-skating rink, yet the project remained incomplete, bogged down by bureaucratic mismanagement and cost overruns. When Trump stepped in and offered to complete the job, it wasn't just a business move—it was a brilliant act of public relations.

The Wollman Rink had been a Central Park landmark since 1950, attracting New Yorkers and tourists alike during the winter months. But by the late 1970s, the rink had fallen into disrepair, and the city decided it needed a full-scale renovation. What followed was a tale of delays, missteps, and escalating costs. Between 1980 and 1986, the city had already spent over $12 million on the project, yet the rink remained unfinished, its construction halted as city officials argued over plans and execution. The project had become a symbol of everything wrong with the city's governance at the time—inefficiency, waste, and failure to deliver.

Trump, always on the lookout for ways to insert himself into the public spotlight, saw an opportunity. The failed rink renovation was front-page news, and New Yorkers were frustrated. Trump's offer to take over the project was as much a stroke of genius as it was a calculated move. He promised to complete the renovation in less than six months and at a fraction of the city's cost, an offer that was hard for the city to refuse given its embarrassment over the situation. Trump wasn't just offering to renovate a skating rink; he was offering to save face for the city, positioning himself as the man who could cut through red tape and inefficiency.

What set Trump apart in this situation was his knack for self-promotion and public relations. He framed the Wollman Rink project not simply as a construction job but as a personal crusade to show the city how things should be done. Trump approached then-Mayor Ed Koch with his proposal, and the media quickly picked up on the story. Trump promised that if he was given control of the project, he would finish it in record time and wouldn't charge the city for his services. The only condition he set was that the city would give him control of the project and allow him to manage it his way—no city interference, no bureaucratic red tape.

Trump's confidence in his ability to manage the project efficiently resonated with a public increasingly frustrated by the city's inability to get things done. Trump knew that the media attention surrounding the Wollman Rink debacle gave him a golden opportunity to position himself as a savior—a businessman with the know-how and determination to succeed where government officials had failed. Trump's proposal wasn't just about finishing the rink; it was about proving a point. It was about showing that the private sector, represented by Trump, was better equipped to handle large-scale projects than the inefficient and bloated public sector.

As soon as Trump took control of the project, he moved quickly to demonstrate his commitment to finishing the rink on time and under budget. He brought in his own team of engineers and construction workers, bypassing the city's bureaucracy entirely. His management style was hands-on and direct—he personally visited the site frequently, ensuring that everything was progressing according to schedule. Trump also implemented a streamlined construction process, cutting out unnecessary steps and focusing on practical solutions to the problems that had plagued the project for years. Instead of using the city's complex plans for an elaborate refrigeration system, Trump opted for a simpler, more cost-effective solution that had been overlooked by the city's planners.

The result was nothing short of remarkable. In just four months, Trump completed the renovation of the Wollman Rink, well ahead of his promised six-month deadline. And, true to his word, the project was finished under budget—at a cost of around $2.25 million, a fraction of the $12 million the city had already squandered. The rink reopened in November 1986, just in time for the winter skating season, and it quickly became a source of pride for New Yorkers who had watched the city fail to complete the job for years.

The reopening of Wollman Rink was a triumph for Trump, but perhaps more importantly, it was a public relations masterstroke. The media coverage was overwhelmingly positive, portraying Trump as the hero who had swooped in to save the day. Trump made sure to capitalize on the moment, appearing in photo ops at the rink and giving interviews where he emphasized his role in cutting through the city's incompetence to deliver results. He was the man who got things done—a narrative that would stick with him throughout his career.

For Trump, the Wollman Rink project was more than just a success story in terms of construction; it was a branding opportunity. It showcased his ability to take on a high-profile, failing project and turn it into a success, all while capturing the media's attention and winning public admiration. It also fit perfectly into the image Trump was cultivating at the time: a larger-than-life businessman who could achieve the impossible, a dealmaker who knew how to navigate complex projects with ease, and a man who, above all, could turn a profit while making himself indispensable to the city. In the aftermath of Wollman Rink's reopening, Trump's star rose even higher, and his name became even more firmly entrenched in the minds of New Yorkers as synonymous with success and action.

The Wollman Rink renovation was, in many ways, a precursor to Trump's later moves in both business and politics. It demonstrated his ability to manipulate public perception, to position himself as a problem solver in the public eye, and to use his private business acumen to fill the gaps left by government. The project was an early example of Trump's unique talent for leveraging media attention to bolster his personal brand, a skill he would go on to perfect in the years ahead.

The Art of the Deal—Trump's Blueprint for Success

By the mid-1980s, Donald Trump had already solidified his reputation as one of the most dynamic and visible real estate moguls in New York City. His name was synonymous with luxury, power, and success, largely thanks to high-profile developments like Trump Tower and the renovation of the Wollman Rink. However, it wasn't just the properties that made Trump famous—it was the way he built a persona around himself as the ultimate dealmaker, a master of negotiation who always came out on top. This image would reach new heights in 1987, when Trump decided to share his business philosophy with the world through his bestselling book, *The Art of the Deal*.

The Art of the Deal wasn't just a business book; it was a manifesto for success as seen through Trump's eyes. Part autobiography, part guide to negotiation, the book captured the essence of Trump's rise to fame and explained the strategies he used to build his empire. For Trump, the book was more than a recounting of his business ventures—it was an opportunity to brand himself as the quintessential American businessman, someone who embodied the entrepreneurial spirit and could transform ambition into wealth.

The idea for *The Art of the Deal* came to Trump after realizing that people were fascinated not just by what he built, but by how he did it. Trump was a natural storyteller, and the public was eager to hear how he managed to negotiate high-stakes deals, navigate complex financial landscapes, and come out ahead every time. Trump approached the writing of the book with the same flair and self-promotion that had come to define his career. He enlisted journalist Tony Schwartz to help write the book, with Trump dictating stories and offering insights into his day-to-day life. Schwartz would later reveal that he spent hours shadowing Trump, capturing his voice, style, and larger-than-life persona.

The book itself was structured to highlight Trump's day-to-day approach to business while offering readers an inside look at his most significant deals. One of the key elements of *The Art of the Deal* was its pragmatic tone—Trump emphasized that success in business wasn't just about having vision or taking risks, but about mastering the art of negotiation, building relationships, and never backing down from a challenge. Trump explained that the essence of deal-making was being bold and persistent while also understanding when to walk away. His stories were filled with colorful anecdotes about his biggest real estate projects, from negotiating with the city over zoning laws to convincing banks to finance his massive developments.

A central theme of *The Art of the Deal* was Trump's ability to recognize and seize opportunities that others might miss. He outlined his philosophy of going big, taking calculated risks, and always aiming for projects that would make a statement. For Trump, deals weren't just business transactions—they were battles of strategy and wits. He described his approach to negotiations as a mixture of aggression, charm, and flexibility, stressing that one had to know when to push hard and when to make concessions. His negotiation tactics—such as offering seemingly outrageous terms as a starting point or knowing how to leverage media attention to gain an upper hand—became a blueprint for aspiring dealmakers.

Another key aspect of the book was Trump's insistence on the importance of self-promotion. In *The Art of the Deal*, Trump laid out his strategy for using the media to his advantage, understanding that the press could be a powerful tool in shaping public perception and driving interest in his projects. He was unashamed about courting the media and even using controversy to stay in the public eye. For Trump, there was no such thing as bad press, as long as it kept people talking about him. This was a tactic he would continue to use throughout his career, from his business ventures to his later political aspirations.

The timing of *The Art of the Deal*'s release couldn't have been more perfect. America in the 1980s was in the middle of a boom era—consumerism was at an all-time high, Wall Street was thriving, and the public was fascinated with the idea of wealth and power. Trump, with his flashy lifestyle and success, represented everything that many Americans aspired to be. The book, published in November 1987, quickly became a bestseller, with millions of copies sold. It struck a chord with readers who saw Trump as the embodiment of the American Dream—a self-made billionaire who had climbed to the top through grit, determination, and a relentless pursuit of success.

For Trump, the book wasn't just about telling his story—it was a strategic move to elevate his personal brand on a national, even global, scale. *The Art of the Deal* gave Trump a platform beyond real estate; it allowed him to position himself as a thought leader in business, someone whose advice and insights could be applied across industries. Trump began appearing on talk shows and giving interviews not just as a real estate developer, but as a guru on success. His persona as a business icon grew, and with it, his influence expanded beyond New York's real estate circles into broader pop culture.

The book also played a key role in creating the mythology around Trump that would follow him into his later career in television and, ultimately, politics. The narrative that Trump was a brilliant dealmaker who could turn anything he touched into gold became central to his identity. Even as critics pointed out that some of his claims were exaggerated, the perception of

Trump as a genius businessman stuck with the public. *The Art of the Deal* didn't just reflect Trump's business ventures; it shaped the way people saw him, creating a lasting legacy that would serve him in future endeavors.

In many ways, *The Art of the Deal* was the perfect vehicle for Trump to communicate his values: boldness, persistence, and an unshakeable belief in his ability to succeed. It was both a reflection of Trump's personality and a tool for his brand-building, allowing him to reach millions of readers and expand his influence far beyond New York. The book would go on to be considered one of the most famous business books of all time, but for Trump, it was much more than that—it was the beginning of his transformation into a celebrity mogul, a man whose name was as valuable as the deals he made.

With *The Art of the Deal*, Donald Trump had cemented his place not only as a top real estate developer but as a cultural figure, someone whose larger-than-life persona captivated the public. The book marked the peak of Trump's rise in the 1980s, turning him into a national celebrity and setting the stage for his future ventures into television and, eventually, politics. For Trump, the lessons of the book—about deal-making, branding, and the power of perception—would remain guiding principles throughout his life.

Atlantic City and the Casino Empire—A Gamble on a Grand Scale

As Donald Trump's reputation as a real estate mogul continued to grow in the 1980s, he set his sights on a new frontier: the world of casinos. Trump's move into Atlantic City was a bold expansion that reflected both his ambition and his desire to dominate yet another industry. He viewed casinos not just as lucrative business opportunities but as a way to expand the

Trump brand beyond New York. It was a high-stakes gamble, one that would lead to incredible highs and devastating lows, but for a time, Trump's casinos would make him the king of Atlantic City.

Trump's interest in Atlantic City began in the early 1980s when the city was attempting to reinvent itself as the East Coast's answer to Las Vegas. With legalized gambling in place, Atlantic City offered the potential for massive profits, and developers from across the country were rushing to build casinos along the boardwalk. Trump saw this as an opportunity to not only make a fortune but to also extend his influence and prestige into a new arena. Atlantic City, once a glamorous resort town, had fallen into decline by the 1970s, but with the advent of legalized gambling, there was a chance for a revival—and Trump wanted to be at the center of it.

Trump's first foray into the casino business came in 1984 with the opening of Harrah's at Trump Plaza, a joint venture with the Harrah's corporation. Situated at the heart of the Atlantic City Boardwalk, Trump Plaza was designed to be a glittering palace of gaming, complete with high-end restaurants, luxury suites, and of course, a casino floor filled with slot machines and gaming tables. From the beginning, Trump was heavily involved in the project, making sure that it reflected his signature style of opulence and grandeur. However, the partnership with Harrah's was short-lived. Trump, ever the dealmaker, soon bought out his partners and rebranded the property simply as Trump Plaza, giving him full control over the operation.

Trump Plaza was an instant success, drawing in high rollers and tourists eager to experience the excitement of Atlantic City. Trump's flair for self-promotion played a significant role in the casino's early success. He made sure that his name was prominently displayed everywhere, from the massive "Trump Plaza" sign on the building's exterior to the Trump-branded amenities inside. Once again, Trump understood the power of his name as a brand, and he used it to attract visitors who associated the Trump name with luxury and success. He also capitalized on Atlantic City's proximity to New York and Philadelphia, marketing the casino as an accessible getaway for the region's wealthy and middle-class gamblers.

But Trump wasn't content with just one casino. His next move was even more ambitious: acquiring and developing multiple properties to create a casino empire. In 1985, Trump bought the unfinished and financially troubled Atlantic City Hilton Hotel and Casino for $325 million. He rebranded it as Trump Marina, turning it into another high-profile destination. However, Trump's biggest acquisition came in 1988 when he purchased the Taj Mahal, a colossal casino project that had been started by Resorts International but had stalled due to financial difficulties. The Taj Mahal was designed to be the largest casino in the world, a $1 billion mega-resort that would outshine anything in Las Vegas.

The Taj Mahal was Trump's most audacious gamble yet. The casino was lavish beyond measure, with crystal chandeliers, gold-leaf detailing, and acres of gaming space. Trump marketed it as "the eighth wonder of the world," and the opening of the Taj Mahal in 1990 was a major media event. Celebrities, politicians, and the press gathered for the grand unveiling, and Trump, as always, was front and center, basking in the limelight. The Taj Mahal's opening cemented Trump's image as a casino mogul, and for a time, it seemed like his gamble had paid off.

However, beneath the glittering surface of Trump's Atlantic City empire, trouble was brewing. The costs of building and maintaining the Taj Mahal were astronomical, and the Atlantic City market was becoming increasingly saturated with casinos. Although Trump was bringing in millions of dollars in revenue, the overhead costs and debt from his rapid expansion were overwhelming. The Taj Mahal, in particular, was burdened with more than $800 million in debt. Trump had financed much of the construction with high-interest junk bonds, a risky move that put the entire project in jeopardy.

The financial strain soon became evident. Trump's casinos, while popular, weren't generating enough cash flow to cover the massive debt payments, and by the early 1990s, the cracks in Trump's Atlantic City empire began to show. Despite his public image as a man who could turn anything into gold, Trump's casinos were struggling. In 1991, just a year after its grand opening, the Taj Mahal filed for bankruptcy protection. It was the first of several financial restructurings that Trump's Atlantic City properties would go through over the next decade.

Trump, however, managed to weather the storm. He negotiated deals with his creditors to keep control of his casinos, even as they went through multiple bankruptcies. Trump's ability to negotiate his way out of these financial crises demonstrated his resilience and his skill as a dealmaker, but it also exposed the precarious nature of his casino empire. While Trump portrayed himself as a winner in public, behind the scenes, his Atlantic City ventures were in serious trouble.

Despite the financial difficulties, Trump's casinos remained a key part of his brand. The image of Donald Trump as a casino mogul was firmly embedded in the public consciousness, thanks in no small part to his relentless self-promotion and media presence. Trump Plaza, Trump Marina, and the Taj Mahal became iconic properties, and for a time, Trump was the face of Atlantic City's resurgence. Even as the financial reality of his casino empire became more troubled, Trump continued to maintain the persona of a successful businessman who had conquered the gambling world.

In the end, Trump's Atlantic City ventures were both a triumph and a cautionary tale. They showcased his ability to think big, take risks, and dominate new industries, but they also highlighted the dangers of overextension and excessive debt. Trump's casino empire, while glamorous, was ultimately unsustainable, and by the mid-1990s, it became clear that his grand gamble on Atlantic City had come at a high cost.

For Trump, the rise and fall of his Atlantic City casinos was a pivotal chapter in his career. It revealed both his strengths—his ambition, his boldness, and his skill at negotiation—and his weaknesses, particularly his reliance on debt and his tendency to overreach. Yet, true to form, Trump would emerge from the financial turmoil with his public image largely intact, thanks to his ability to control the narrative and present himself as a winner, no matter the outcome. Atlantic City was, in many ways, a microcosm of Trump's broader approach to business: a mix of audacity, success, and high-stakes risk, with both dazzling victories and painful losses along the way.

The Rise of the Trump Brand—Building a Name Beyond Real Estate

While Donald Trump's real estate developments and casino ventures were central to his career in the 1980s, one of his most enduring legacies from this era was the creation of his personal brand. Trump understood early on that his greatest asset wasn't just the buildings he constructed or the deals he made, but his own name. The "Trump" brand became synonymous with wealth, luxury, and success, transcending real estate and expanding into a vast range of industries. It was this shift—from being a real estate mogul to becoming a brand mogul—that would lay the groundwork for Trump's future dominance in media, business, and eventually, politics.

In the 1980s, branding as a business concept was still in its infancy, particularly in real estate. Most developers focused on the properties they built rather than promoting themselves as individual brands. Trump, however, took a different approach. He didn't just want to build buildings; he wanted to turn his name into a symbol of prestige. To do this, Trump meticulously crafted his public persona as a larger-than-life businessman, one whose name alone carried significant weight. Every project he touched, from Trump Tower to his Atlantic City casinos, prominently bore the Trump name in bold, gleaming letters. This was more than vanity—it was a strategic move to elevate his personal profile and ensure that people associated his name with success and luxury.

Trump's understanding of branding wasn't just limited to real estate; he quickly realized that his name could be applied to a range of products and industries. He began licensing the "Trump" name to various ventures, turning it into a symbol of high-end living. Trump's first major branding deal outside of real estate came in 1987 when he licensed his name for use on a board game called "Trump: The Game." Modeled after Monopoly, the game allowed players to engage in real estate deals and build their own empires. Although the game wasn't a huge commercial success, it marked the beginning of Trump's foray into licensing, an arena where his name would become a highly valuable asset.

In addition to licensing deals, Trump began expanding his empire into industries where his brand could thrive. He launched the Trump Shuttle, an airline that offered premium service for business travelers on the East Coast. While the Trump Shuttle struggled financially and was eventually sold, it further cemented Trump's image as a man who was willing to take risks and expand his reach beyond real estate. Trump also explored luxury consumer products, including cologne, fashion, and accessories, each emblazoned with his iconic name. Even when some of these ventures failed to achieve long-term success, they contributed to the growing perception of Trump as a man whose influence extended far beyond New York skyscrapers.

One of Trump's most successful branding ventures in the late 1980s was his move into the world of hospitality. He had already built a number of luxury hotels in New York and Atlantic City, but his most ambitious project came in 1988 with the purchase of the Plaza Hotel. The Plaza, one of the most iconic hotels in the world, had been a symbol of elegance and high society for decades. Trump's acquisition of the Plaza for $407 million was a bold move, one that he described as a "trophy" purchase. He saw owning the Plaza not just as a business investment, but as a way to further enhance the Trump brand's association with luxury and exclusivity.

Trump's management of the Plaza Hotel was emblematic of his approach to branding. He spared no expense in renovating the property, spending millions to restore the hotel to its former glory. Trump brought in his then-wife, Ivana, to oversee the redesign, ensuring that every detail reflected the opulence and grandeur associated with the Trump name. Under Trump's ownership, the Plaza became a symbol of luxury not just in New York, but globally. Though the Plaza would eventually become financially burdensome, requiring Trump to sell a controlling interest, its role in elevating the Trump brand during the late 1980s cannot be overstated.

At the heart of Trump's branding strategy was his unparalleled ability to command media attention. Trump understood better than anyone how to use the media to amplify his personal brand. He cultivated relationships with reporters, gave countless interviews, and was always willing to put himself at the center of a story. Whether it was the grand opening of a new property or his latest acquisition, Trump made sure that the press was there to capture the spectacle. He knew that by staying in the public eye, he could continually reinforce the image of himself as the ultimate dealmaker and businessman.

Trump's media-savvy approach reached new heights with the publication of *The Art of the Deal* in 1987. The book wasn't just a bestseller—it was a massive branding success. Trump used *The Art of the Deal* to portray himself as not just a real estate mogul, but a business philosopher with insights into success that could be applied to anyone's life. The book was filled with tales of his business triumphs, told in Trump's bombastic style, but its greatest achievement was turning Trump into a household name across America. Millions of readers who had never set foot in New York or Atlantic City were now familiar with Donald Trump, and they began to see him as the personification of the American Dream.

Trump also became a regular fixture on television, appearing on talk shows and in interviews where he played up his image as a self-made billionaire. His charm, brashness, and flair for the dramatic made him a perfect fit for the media, and he became a favorite guest on shows like *The Late Show with David Letterman* and *The Oprah Winfrey Show*. These appearances not only boosted his visibility but also allowed him to shape his brand narrative on a national level. Trump was no longer just a New York real estate developer—he was a bona fide celebrity.

By the late 1980s, Donald Trump had successfully transformed his name into one of the most recognizable brands in the world. The Trump brand, with its associations of luxury, wealth, and power, was a valuable asset that Trump could leverage in almost any industry. Even as his business ventures faced financial struggles, particularly in Atlantic City, the strength of his brand remained intact. This branding success laid the foundation for Trump's later ventures in television and politics, where his name recognition and reputation as a winner would prove crucial.

For Trump, the 1980s weren't just about building skyscrapers and casinos—they were about building a brand that would transcend those physical structures. The Trump name became his most valuable asset, a symbol that could be applied to a variety of industries and ventures. Trump's ability to promote and protect his brand, even in the face of financial adversity, was a testament to his deep understanding of the power of perception. The Trump brand, born in the glitzy world of real estate and nurtured through savvy media strategies, would continue to grow in the decades that followed, turning Donald Trump from a businessman into a global icon.

Chapter 4

Chapter 4: The Media Magnet

Trump's Relationship with the Press

From early in his career, Donald Trump understood the power of the press. In the cutthroat world of New York real estate, attention was currency, and Trump made sure to position himself as a master of self-promotion. While many businessmen preferred to keep a low profile, allowing their work to speak for itself, Trump saw an opportunity to turn media attention into a strategic advantage. His relationship with the press during the 1980s and 1990s helped establish him not only as a real estate mogul but as a public figure whose name was synonymous with wealth, success, and controversy.

Trump's approach to the media was bold and relentless. He made himself accessible to journalists and reporters, always eager to feed them stories about his latest deals or personal milestones. Whether it was the construction of Trump Tower, his high-profile marriages and divorces, or his luxurious lifestyle, Trump understood that every headline—good or bad—helped build his brand. As long as his name stayed in the public eye, he remained relevant, which was crucial in a city where competition was fierce and fortunes could change overnight.

In many ways, Trump's public persona was crafted in the pages of New York's tabloids. The New York Post and The Daily News frequently ran stories about his extravagant lifestyle, his real estate conquests, and the drama surrounding his personal life. Trump's first marriage to Ivana Trump, a glamorous former model, became a favorite topic for gossip columns. Their lavish parties, their presence at elite social events, and the birth of their three children all provided endless fodder for the press. As their marriage began to unravel in the late 1980s, culminating in a very public divorce in 1990, the tabloids followed every twist and turn. Trump, far from shying away from the attention, used the publicity to his advantage, keeping his name front and center.

Beyond the tabloids, Trump also cultivated relationships with more serious media outlets. He regularly gave interviews to respected publications like The New York Times and The Wall Street Journal, positioning himself as a savvy businessman with a Midas touch. These outlets often ran profiles on Trump's latest real estate developments, marveling at the size and scale of his projects. Trump knew how to play both sides, appealing to those who loved the glamour of his personal life and those who respected his business acumen. The result was that Trump was constantly in the news, his image ever-evolving but always larger than life.

One of Trump's key media strategies during this time was his ability to turn controversy into opportunity. Rather than running from scandals, Trump often embraced them, knowing that any attention could be spun in his favor. For instance, when his financial struggles in Atlantic City became public, instead of downplaying the crisis, Trump used it as a platform to negotiate deals with creditors and to present himself as a fighter who could withstand adversity. The press, intrigued by Trump's resilience and his audacity, continued to cover his every move, keeping him in the public consciousness even during periods of financial instability.

Trump's mastery of the media was rooted in his understanding of the press's need for a compelling story. He consistently delivered, whether through his flamboyant personal life or his grandiose business ventures. He gave journalists quotable soundbites, often speaking in hyperbole to make sure his words would be printed. Statements like "I'm the best dealmaker in the world" or "Everything I touch turns to gold" were designed to capture headlines and reinforce his image as a winner. Trump understood that in the media, perception was often more powerful than reality.

One of the most striking aspects of Trump's relationship with the media was his ability to maintain control over his narrative. Even when the press was critical of his ventures or personal decisions, Trump knew how to redirect the conversation to highlight his successes. For example, during his highly publicized divorce from Ivana, much of the coverage focused on the messy details of their separation. Yet, Trump skillfully steered the attention back to his business, often using interviews to talk about his latest projects or upcoming ventures. He was a master at using negative press to generate interest in his business endeavors, understanding that controversy and success were not mutually exclusive.

Throughout the 1980s and 1990s, Trump's media presence was a key driver of his fame. His name became a brand in itself, largely thanks to his ability to keep the press constantly engaged. Whether it was through his real estate deals, his personal life, or his controversial statements, Trump remained in the headlines, ensuring that the public always had a reason to talk about him. The press, in turn, was drawn to his brash personality and the spectacle that often surrounded his life, making Trump one of the most covered figures in New York and eventually, the world.

In many ways, Trump's rise to fame was not just about the buildings he constructed or the deals he closed—it was about how he played the media. He understood that in a world driven by attention, staying visible was half the battle. His relationship with the press during these early decades laid the foundation for the media empire he would later build, and more importantly, it established him as a public figure who could command attention whenever he wanted. This symbiotic relationship with the media would prove invaluable as Trump transitioned from real estate to television, and ultimately, to the political stage.

Television Appearances and Building a Media Persona

As Donald Trump's real estate empire grew, so did his ambition to move beyond being known simply as a businessman. By the 1980s, Trump had already mastered the art of courting the press, but he was not content with the tabloid headlines and business profiles that kept him in the public eye. Trump wanted more—he wanted to be a celebrity. Television offered him the perfect platform to expand his visibility, turning him into a household name not just in New York, but across America.

Television had long been a powerful medium for shaping public perception, and Trump was quick to recognize its potential. He began making appearances on a variety of talk shows, where he wasn't just treated as a business figure but as an emerging pop culture icon. In these appearances, Trump presented himself as the embodiment of the American Dream—a self-made billionaire who had risen to the top through sheer force of will, hard work, and a relentless drive to succeed. These early television spots helped to cultivate the larger-than-life persona that would eventually propel him to fame beyond the boardroom.

One of Trump's first notable television appearances came in 1986 on *The Oprah Winfrey Show*, where he discussed his real estate ventures and his philosophy on success. Sitting across from one of the most powerful media figures in the world, Trump exuded confidence. He spoke about his wealth and business dealings with ease, positioning himself as someone who had cracked the code of financial success. The audience, many of whom were eager for insights into how they could achieve the same, found Trump's bravado both compelling and inspiring. His appearance on *Oprah* gave him access to millions of Americans who had little interest in real estate but were fascinated by the idea of wealth and power.

Trump's TV persona was carefully crafted to appeal to both business-savvy individuals and everyday Americans who were intrigued by his unapologetic pursuit of wealth. He understood how to speak the language of success in a way that was accessible to a broad audience. On *Late Night with David Letterman*, a popular platform for celebrities and public figures alike, Trump demonstrated his wit and charisma, engaging in light banter with the host while still projecting an aura of success. The contrast between Trump's serious business acumen and his ability to charm and entertain made him a unique figure in the media landscape. He wasn't just a businessman—he was becoming a personality.

Trump's media persona also reflected his strategic understanding of branding. In nearly every television appearance, he made sure to mention his latest project or development, subtly promoting his business while entertaining viewers. He always appeared polished, confident, and larger-than-life—traits that became synonymous with his public image. His persona was not built by accident but was a calculated extension of his business brand. Trump wasn't just selling buildings—he was selling the idea of Trump, and television was the perfect platform to showcase that.

Perhaps one of Trump's most important television moments came in 1988 when he appeared on *The Tonight Show* with Johnny Carson. *The Tonight Show* was the gold standard of American late-night television, and appearing on the show signaled that Trump had reached a new level of fame. Sitting across from Carson, Trump spoke about his accomplishments, but what really stood out was his ability to play along with the show's lighthearted tone. He wasn't just a hard-nosed businessman anymore—he was someone who could joke, laugh, and hold his own in a conversation with one of the most iconic entertainers of the time. This blend of business and entertainment was key to Trump's evolving media persona.

By the early 1990s, Trump had become a regular guest on television programs, not only discussing business but offering his thoughts on broader cultural and political issues. Shows like *Larry King Live* and *Donahue* welcomed Trump as a guest who could speak on anything from the state of the economy to the American political landscape. These appearances allowed Trump to further shape his public image as someone who was knowledgeable and opinionated on matters far beyond real estate. He wasn't just a businessman—he was a public figure with influence and insight on the broader issues that mattered to Americans.

Television also gave Trump the opportunity to reach a new demographic: people who were not particularly interested in business but were fascinated by his larger-than-life personality. Trump was more than willing to indulge the media's interest in his personal life, often discussing his marriages, lifestyle, and even controversies with the same ease as he did business deals.

This approach humanized him, making him relatable in a way that many wealthy figures were not. Viewers were not just interested in Trump's business ventures—they were captivated by Trump the man, a figure who seemed to embody the glamour and audacity that characterized the 1980s.

This growing visibility through television appearances helped Trump build a media persona that was both multifaceted and magnetic. He was a businessman, yes, but he was also a showman. Television allowed Trump to carefully craft an image that was dynamic and engaging, combining elements of wealth, success, entertainment, and controversy. His appearances on these programs laid the foundation for what would become one of his greatest strengths: the ability to control and manipulate the narrative around his life and career through media.

As Trump continued to appear on television throughout the 1990s, his media persona became inseparable from his brand. The "Trump" name wasn't just associated with buildings or casinos anymore—it was synonymous with entertainment, celebrity, and spectacle. Every television appearance reinforced his image as a man of power and influence, and every interview added another layer to the persona he had so carefully built. This was the beginning of Trump's transition from a well-known businessman to a media mogul, and television was the perfect stage on which to make that transformation.

Television had allowed Trump to project his image to millions, turning him into a cultural figure whose appeal went far beyond his business acumen. It was here that the seeds of his future media dominance were planted, a dominance that would eventually lead to reality television stardom and, later, an unprecedented foray into politics.

The Apprentice—A Game Changer

Donald Trump's transformation from a successful businessman and media personality to a full-fledged cultural icon reached its apex with the launch of *The Apprentice* in 2004. More than just a reality television show, *The Apprentice* was a platform that redefined Trump's public persona and extended his influence far beyond the world of real estate. This show not only cemented Trump's status as a household name but also gave him a new kind of celebrity: the kind that made him not just admired or envied but seen as a leader who could teach others how to succeed. For Trump, *The Apprentice* was more than just entertainment—it was a powerful branding tool that magnified his image as a decisive, successful mogul, always in control and always one step ahead.

The premise of *The Apprentice* was simple: sixteen contestants, all aspiring business professionals, would compete for a chance to work for Trump in a high-level executive position. Each week, they were given business-related tasks, and at the end of every episode, one contestant would be fired—by Trump himself. While the show followed the typical reality TV format of competition and elimination, what set *The Apprentice* apart was Trump's central role. He wasn't just the host; he was the authority, the arbiter of success and failure. Trump's presence dominated the show, and his decisions carried an air of finality and drama, reinforced by his now-famous catchphrase, "You're fired!"

From the very first episode, it was clear that *The Apprentice* was not just a platform for the contestants—it was a vehicle for Trump to further cement his image as a business titan. His opening monologue, delivered against the backdrop of the Manhattan skyline, was a masterclass in self-promotion. "I've mastered the art of the deal," Trump proclaimed, before explaining how his success in real estate and business qualified him to find and mentor America's next top business leader. The message was clear: Trump was the ultimate dealmaker, the one everyone should aspire to emulate.

Throughout the show, Trump's boardroom persona became iconic. He portrayed himself as a no-nonsense leader with zero tolerance for incompetence. His decisions seemed swift, confident, and rooted in a deep understanding of what it took to succeed. Every week, he evaluated the contestants with a discerning eye, asking pointed questions about their strategies and leadership abilities. While the contestants scrambled to impress him, Trump maintained an aura of control and authority, rarely showing vulnerability or hesitation. To the viewers, he embodied the ideal of American success: smart, sharp, and ruthlessly efficient. The boardroom scenes, where Trump deliberated and ultimately fired someone, became the most watched and talked about part of the show. His blunt delivery of the now-famous "You're fired!" became a pop culture catchphrase, representing the cutthroat world of business.

What made *The Apprentice* unique was that it didn't just entertain—it offered viewers a window into the world of high-stakes business deals and executive decision-making, albeit through a highly dramatized lens. Each episode featured real-world business challenges, from marketing campaigns to product development to running actual companies. Viewers got to see Trump's brand of leadership in action, from his critique of contestants' ideas to his praise for out-of-the-box thinking. The tasks themselves, often sponsored by major corporations, were designed to reflect the kind of work Trump excelled at in real life, such as branding, real estate development, and deal-making. This not only reinforced his business credentials but also made his presence on the show feel authoritative and authentic. In many ways, *The Apprentice* was a weekly showcase of Trump's business philosophy: success came from hard work, bold decisions, and an unshakable belief in one's ability to win.

The contestants themselves became part of Trump's larger narrative. Each season, they arrived on the show eager to learn from him, their goal being not just to win a prize but to gain his approval. Trump often framed his guidance as mentorship, casting himself as a teacher whose knowledge and experience could shape the next generation of business leaders. This dynamic further enhanced his image as an expert in leadership, someone capable of spotting talent and rewarding those who demonstrated Trump-like qualities: confidence, risk-taking, and the ability to think outside the box. At the same time, it allowed Trump to distance himself from the failures of others, as contestants who didn't measure up were quickly dismissed, often with a scathing remark from Trump himself.

While *The Apprentice* became a ratings juggernaut, its impact went far beyond just television viewership. The show significantly expanded Trump's reach into American households. He was no longer just a New York real estate mogul or a tabloid figure; he was now a nationally recognized media personality. Millions of viewers tuned in each week, not just to watch the contestants compete, but to see Trump. His image was everywhere: magazine covers, talk shows, and advertisements. His fame soared to new heights, and his persona as the ultimate businessman became more ingrained in American culture than ever before.

Perhaps the most important legacy of *The Apprentice* was its impact on Trump's brand. The show's success allowed Trump to license his name more broadly, capitalizing on the fame he had cultivated. Real estate projects across the globe began bearing the Trump name, as did products ranging from steaks to bottled water to cologne. Trump's fame had become a business in and of itself, with *The Apprentice* playing a crucial role in elevating his brand to a global level.

More subtly, *The Apprentice* also showcased Trump's ability to resonate with the American public. His portrayal on the show reflected the values many admired—toughness, decisiveness, and an almost mythic understanding of what it takes to succeed in business. Trump became a symbol of ambition, someone who had risen to the top through sheer determination and talent. This carefully crafted persona laid the groundwork for his eventual political run, where these same traits would be used to present him as the outsider capable of "fixing" Washington.

In the end, *The Apprentice* was more than just a television show—it was the catalyst that launched Donald Trump into a new stratosphere of fame and influence. It gave him a platform to project his power and success on a national stage, all while reinforcing the idea that he was the ultimate authority on winning. It was here that the groundwork for Trump's eventual transition from business to politics was laid. *The Apprentice* solidified his public persona, giving him a direct line to the American people and forever altering the trajectory of his career.

Trump as a Media Power Player—Cultivating Control and Controversy

As The Apprentice surged in popularity, Donald Trump's media presence expanded dramatically. Trump, always aware of the importance of visibility, leveraged his growing fame to become a master of manipulating the media. What made this period so significant in his rise to prominence was his ability to blur the lines between business, entertainment, and controversy, and in doing so, Trump elevated himself beyond just a TV star or a businessman. He became a media power player, someone who could command headlines at will and use controversy to his advantage.

Trump's skill at managing the media narrative was unparalleled. He understood, perhaps better than anyone, that the media thrives on spectacle, and he wasn't afraid to be controversial or polarizing if it meant staying in the public eye. In fact, controversy became one of Trump's most valuable tools. Where others might shy away from negative press, Trump embraced it, often turning it into a way to further his own brand. He had an innate understanding of the 24-hour news cycle and how to exploit it to maintain relevance. In a media environment that increasingly valued sensationalism, Trump was the perfect figure: brash, bold, and unafraid of provoking strong reactions.

Throughout the mid-2000s, Trump cultivated a carefully orchestrated persona in the media—one that was at times combative, but always attention-grabbing. His confidence and charisma, often displayed in front of the cameras during The Apprentice boardroom scenes, translated seamlessly into the broader media landscape. Whether on cable news programs, radio shows, or in interviews with prominent magazines, Trump was always prepared to make a statement. He didn't just speak to the press; he dominated the conversation, often making headlines with his candid opinions on everything from business to politics to pop culture.

A key tactic Trump employed was his willingness to engage in public feuds. One of the most famous examples of this came in 2006 when Trump publicly clashed with Rosie O'Donnell, a comedian and co-host of The View, after she criticized him on air. O'Donnell had mocked Trump's decision to give Miss USA Tara Conner a second chance after she was caught in a scandal involving drugs and underage drinking. Trump responded with a personal attack, calling O'Donnell a "loser" and making derogatory remarks about her appearance. The feud escalated in the media, with both sides trading barbs, and it dominated tabloid and entertainment news for weeks.

While some critics decried Trump's tactics as petty or mean-spirited, the public feud with O'Donnell had an undeniable effect: it kept Trump in the headlines. The drama of the back-and-forth exchanges was irresistible to the press, and Trump's ability to navigate and exploit the conflict for attention was masterful. This was emblematic of Trump's broader media strategy—by staying controversial, he ensured that his name remained in circulation, and even when the coverage wasn't positive, it helped solidify his status as a central figure in American pop culture. Trump was always in the news, always being talked about, and always positioning himself as someone who couldn't be ignored.

Trump's approach to media didn't stop at personal feuds. He also became known for his bold, often bombastic statements, particularly about politics and current events. Long before his presidential run, Trump was a frequent guest on cable news networks, offering his unfiltered opinions on everything from the economy to the war in Iraq. While his views were sometimes dismissed as attention-seeking or uninformed, Trump's comments often resonated with a segment of the American public who admired his outspokenness. He wasn't afraid to say things others wouldn't, and in an increasingly polarized media environment, this approach made him a favorite guest for news programs looking to boost ratings.

One of Trump's most significant media controversies came in 2011 when he became one of the most vocal proponents of the "birther" conspiracy theory, which questioned whether President Barack Obama was born in the United States. Trump's public insistence on this unfounded claim dominated the news cycle for months. His calls for Obama to produce his birth certificate were covered relentlessly by cable news outlets, thrusting Trump even further into the political spotlight. While many criticized Trump for fueling a baseless conspiracy, the attention he received was undeniable. The controversy kept his name in the headlines and solidified his image as a populist provocateur unafraid to challenge the political establishment.

Trump's ability to generate controversy and command media attention was a key factor in his rise as a public figure. He knew how to exploit the media's hunger for sensational stories and how to keep himself at the center of the national conversation. Whether through personal feuds, provocative statements, or involvement in high-profile controversies, Trump was able to ensure that he was never far from the public's attention. And in a media environment increasingly defined by the interplay between entertainment and news, Trump's larger-than-life personality made him the perfect figure to dominate the headlines.

Beyond individual controversies, Trump's media dominance was also evident in his mastery of branding. He understood that his name was not just his identity—it was a product that could be marketed, sold, and licensed. Every time he appeared in the media, he was promoting the "Trump" brand, which became synonymous with success, luxury, and power. His television appearances, interviews, and public statements all served as advertising for his business ventures, and the constant media coverage only increased the value of his brand. Trump wasn't just making news—he was making money, using his media persona to attract investors, partners, and consumers to his various projects.

Trump's media strategy during this period was marked by a singular focus: staying relevant, staying controversial, and staying in control. He understood that in the fast-paced world of modern media, visibility was everything. As long as people were talking about him, he had power. And with that power came the ability to shape public perception, expand his brand, and set the stage for even greater ambitions. By the time The Apprentice had reached its peak, Donald Trump had not only become a television star—he had become a media mogul, one who knew how to turn every appearance, every interview, and every controversy into an opportunity to further his influence.

This period of Trump's career laid the groundwork for his future as a political figure. His media persona, carefully crafted through years of strategic appearances and controversies, gave him the visibility and credibility he would later leverage during his presidential campaign. Trump's mastery of the media had turned him into a larger-than-life figure, and with each new controversy, he became more deeply embedded in the American consciousness. The Apprentice may have been the vehicle that brought him into millions of homes, but it was Trump's ability to control the media narrative that truly made him a force to be reckoned with.

The Trump Brand Expands—Turning Fame into Fortune

By the mid-2000s, Donald Trump had mastered the art of blending fame and fortune, turning his public persona into a lucrative brand that extended far beyond real estate. The Apprentice had not only revived his image as a successful businessman, but it also gave him unparalleled visibility. Trump wasn't just a mogul running a business empire—he was a brand unto himself, a name synonymous with luxury, success, and ambition. He realized that his greatest asset wasn't just his properties or his deals, but the Trump name itself, and he leveraged that name to grow his empire in ways that few could have predicted.

At the heart of Trump's success was his ability to transform personal fame into commercial opportunity. He didn't just build buildings—he sold a lifestyle, and his name became the cornerstone of that image. With the constant exposure on The Apprentice, Trump capitalized on the perception of being a master businessman, convincing the public and potential partners that anything bearing the Trump name was inherently valuable. His personal brand—associated with wealth, power, and luxury—became a commodity, something that could be licensed, endorsed, and sold across industries. Whether it was a skyscraper, a golf course, or a bottle of Trump-branded water, the name itself was the selling point.

One of Trump's earliest and most successful ventures into licensing was the Trump International Hotel and Tower in New York. While Trump owned the building, he didn't actually build it. Instead, he lent his name and brand to the project, collecting licensing fees and management revenue without taking on the risk of construction or ownership. This became a model for many of his future deals. Trump discovered that he could lend his name to various real estate projects across the world, receiving fees and revenue based purely on the strength of the Trump brand. His role shifted from developer to marketer, as his presence alone could increase the perceived value of a project. Real estate developers across the globe were eager to slap the Trump name on their buildings, knowing that it came with a built-in promise of luxury and exclusivity.

The Trump brand wasn't limited to real estate, though. Recognizing that his fame and public image had a broad appeal, Trump began licensing his name to a wide array of products, including clothing, fragrances, and even home furnishings. The Trump name appeared on everything from men's ties to mattresses, each product marketed as embodying the same sense of luxury and success that Trump represented. One of the most famous examples of this was the Trump Steaks line, which he aggressively promoted during The Apprentice and in his businesses. Trump Steaks, sold through The Sharper Image and

QVC, were marketed as the finest cuts of meat, with Trump personally vouching for their quality. While the product itself was short-lived, it exemplified his approach to branding: the idea that the Trump name alone could elevate a product's appeal.

At the height of this licensing wave, Trump's business interests diversified further. He launched Trump-branded resorts, casinos, golf courses, and even bottled water. Each of these ventures leaned heavily on the Trump persona, promising consumers access to a luxurious, exclusive lifestyle. Trump World Tower, for instance, wasn't just another luxury high-rise in Manhattan; it was advertised as "the world's most luxurious building," because it bore the Trump name. Similarly, his golf courses were marketed as elite destinations, with Trump personally involved in promoting their exclusivity and grandeur. The consistent message was that the Trump brand represented the pinnacle of success, and those who could afford to be part of it were, in some way, participating in that success.

But Trump's brand wasn't just built on luxury—it was built on his personality. His brash, larger-than-life persona, honed through years in the media spotlight, became inextricably linked to his business ventures. He didn't just sell products; he sold the idea of himself. When people bought Trump-branded goods or invested in Trump properties, they weren't just purchasing luxury—they were buying into the image of Donald Trump as the ultimate winner, the man who never lost. Trump's public appearances, whether on The Apprentice or in interviews, constantly reinforced this image. His famous catchphrase, "You're fired," became shorthand for his decisive leadership style, and it bled into the way his businesses were marketed: Trump made the tough calls, he knew what was valuable, and if something carried his name, it was because it was the best.

The power of Trump's brand was also evident in his ability to weather business failures. Over the years, many of his ventures—Trump Airlines, Trump Vodka, and Trump University, to name a few—ultimately failed, some amid scandal or financial loss. Yet, Trump's brand emerged largely unscathed. Even when his casinos in Atlantic City declared bankruptcy or when Trump Steaks were quietly discontinued, the broader perception of Trump as a winner and a savvy businessman remained intact. This was a testament to Trump's ability to control the narrative around his brand. He framed every failure as a temporary setback, never admitting defeat and always pivoting to the next opportunity. To his supporters and fans, Trump's occasional missteps only reinforced his resilience and entrepreneurial spirit. He was seen as someone who took risks and wasn't afraid to fail, qualities admired in the world of business.

This relentless promotion of his brand paid off in spades. By the late 2000s, Forbes estimated the value of the Trump brand alone at hundreds of millions of dollars. Trump's wealth was no longer tied solely to his real estate holdings or his role on The Apprentice. His name itself was a multi-million-dollar asset, and licensing fees from projects across the globe added significantly to his fortune. What made this even more remarkable was that Trump had built this empire not just through traditional business success, but through his skillful manipulation of media, fame, and public perception. He had turned his celebrity into a revenue stream, and his business acumen, real or perceived, had become a major part of his financial success.

By the time Trump's reality TV fame began to plateau, his business empire had shifted into a new phase—one where his personal brand was the central product. Whether through buildings, golf courses, or bottled water, Trump's face and name were everywhere, and the message was clear: Donald Trump was the embodiment of American success. And this message wasn't just a marketing gimmick—it was the foundation of a business model that allowed Trump to generate wealth and influence on an unprecedented scale.

In many ways, this period of Trump's life was a prelude to his political career. His ability to craft and maintain a public image, no matter the circumstances, would become one of his most powerful assets when he eventually ran for office. But in the mid-2000s, his focus was still squarely on expanding the Trump brand, and by all measures, it was a resounding success. Trump had transformed from a real estate mogul into something much larger—a global brand, a media phenomenon, and an enduring symbol of ambition, wealth, and influence. The stage was set for the next phase of his life, one in which he would leverage this carefully cultivated image to make his most ambitious move yet.

Chapter 5

Chapter 5: The Apprentice—A Star is Born

The Conception of The Apprentice

In the early 2000s, reality television was taking the world by storm, reshaping the entertainment landscape in ways few could have predicted. Shows like Survivor and Big Brother were captivating audiences, offering something unique—real people competing, surviving, and scheming, all under the scrutiny of cameras. This new wave of reality TV was raw, unscripted, and provided a window into the unpredictable nature of human behavior. As networks scrambled to find the next big hit, television producer Mark Burnett had an idea that would eventually change not only the reality TV genre but also the trajectory of Donald Trump's life.

Burnett, already known for creating Survivor, had an innate understanding of how to tap into the zeitgeist. He recognized the public's growing appetite for reality television but saw a gap in the market—there were no shows focusing on business. Burnett envisioned a program where ambitious contestants could compete in real-world business challenges, with the ultimate prize being a job with one of the most powerful and recognizable businessmen in the world. This wasn't going to be just any reality show; it would offer a peek into the high-stakes world of corporate America, with the added drama of fierce competition.

The search for the right business figurehead was crucial. Burnett knew he needed someone larger than life, a personality who could carry the show and hold viewers' attention. Someone whose success was well-documented and whose name evoked a sense of power, prestige, and authority. Enter Donald Trump.

At this point, Trump was no stranger to fame, but his star had dimmed slightly compared to the height of his real estate glory days in the 1980s. The 1990s had been a turbulent decade for Trump. His Atlantic City casinos had suffered financial setbacks, and several of his ventures had declared bankruptcy. While Trump still maintained a high profile, thanks to his name being plastered on buildings and properties, his reputation as a businessman had taken some hits. His lavish lifestyle and bold personality kept him in the spotlight, but his business dealings were seen by some as increasingly risky. What Trump needed was a new platform—a way to reassert himself as a master of success.

Burnett saw in Trump the perfect candidate to lead The Apprentice. Trump's ego, bravado, and sheer presence were tailor-made for television. He was not just a businessman—he was a showman, someone who instinctively knew how to command attention. Burnett approached Trump with the concept of The Apprentice, pitching it as a competition that would showcase Trump's acumen as a business leader and put the spotlight on his ability to mentor and evaluate talent. Trump would sit at the helm of a boardroom, watching contestants navigate weekly challenges, and he would be the one to deliver the ultimate judgment at the end of each episode. It would be a dramatic showdown, culminating in the now-iconic phrase: "You're fired."

Trump initially had reservations. Reality television was still seen by some as lowbrow entertainment, a far cry from the glitz and glamor he associated with his brand. The idea of a businessman appearing on a reality show didn't fit with the traditional image of a corporate mogul. But Trump, always one to recognize an opportunity when he saw one, was intrigued. He knew that Burnett had a track record of success and that Survivor had become a cultural phenomenon. More importantly, Trump saw The Apprentice as a way to reinvent himself in the public eye and reaffirm his status as the ultimate businessman.

In the end, what convinced Trump to sign on was the potential reach of the show. Television offered something that no amount of press conferences, magazine profiles, or business deals could—direct access to millions of households across the country. It was the perfect vehicle for Trump to showcase not just his business empire, but his personality, his decision-making skills, and his unique brand of leadership. The Apprentice would be more than just a show; it would be a platform for Trump to reassert his dominance in both business and media. He would no longer just be a mogul; he would become a media sensation.

The timing was perfect for both Burnett and Trump. Reality television was booming, and audiences were ready for something new. The Apprentice offered a fresh take on the format, combining the drama of competition with the prestige of the business world. It wasn't just about surviving or strategizing—it was about proving oneself in the world of high finance and corporate America, with Donald Trump as the ultimate arbiter of success.

For Trump, the show represented a golden opportunity to rebuild his public image. It was a chance to remind the world that he was still a force to be reckoned with, not just in real estate, but as a cultural icon. His name would be synonymous with success once again, and The Apprentice would serve as the vehicle for that resurgence.

As the concept for the show began to take shape, Trump's involvement generated buzz before the cameras even started rolling. People were fascinated by Trump's involvement in reality television—he was, after all, one of the most recognizable figures in business. The stage was set for what would become a major turning point in Trump's career, and a new chapter in reality television. The launch of The Apprentice wasn't just the beginning of a TV show—it was the birth of a media phenomenon, and, ultimately, the rise of Donald Trump as a cultural and political juggernaut.

The Format and Appeal of The Apprentice

When The Apprentice debuted in January 2004, it was an immediate sensation. The format was simple yet captivating: a group of sixteen aspiring entrepreneurs, from various backgrounds, competed for the chance to win a prestigious position within Donald Trump's organization. Every week, they faced real-world business challenges, and the stakes were high. The ultimate prize wasn't just money or fame—it was a job working directly for Trump, offering a level of access and opportunity that most could only dream of. This was not just reality TV; it was an opportunity to watch the business world unfold in front of millions of viewers.

The show's structure was designed to heighten the drama at every turn. Contestants were divided into two teams, tasked with projects that tested their skills in everything from sales and marketing to event planning and financial management. These weren't hypothetical scenarios; they were real tasks involving actual companies, often featuring major brands and partnerships. Each challenge was intense, with the teams given limited time and resources to prove their worth. From managing budgets to negotiating deals, contestants had to demonstrate their business acumen under pressure, often facing internal conflicts, logistical nightmares, and the ever-present fear of failure.

But the true heart of the show wasn't just the challenges or the contestants—it was Donald Trump himself. At the end of each episode, the losing team would enter Trump's famous boardroom, where the real drama unfolded. Trump, sitting at the head of a long table, would evaluate their performance, asking probing questions about who was to blame for the failure. Contestants had to defend themselves, argue their case, and point fingers at their teammates, all while knowing that one of them would be "fired" before the episode ended.

This boardroom scene became the iconic centerpiece of the show. Viewers were drawn to the tension as Trump, with his steely gaze and authoritative tone, cut through the excuses and bickering, ultimately delivering his verdict. His signature phrase, "You're fired," became a cultural catchphrase, a stark and unforgettable conclusion to each episode's drama. It wasn't just about winning or losing—it was about facing Trump's judgment, which was both terrifying and captivating to watch.

The appeal of The Apprentice went beyond just the competition. The show offered viewers a front-row seat to the world of business, something that had rarely been seen on television in such an accessible way. Watching the contestants struggle through tasks and then justify their decisions to Trump made business feel like a gladiator sport. There were clear winners and losers, and the stakes felt incredibly high. Trump, in his role as the all-powerful judge, embodied the American Dream—a larger-than-life figure who had "made it" and was now holding the keys to success for those bold enough to compete for it.

Viewers were drawn to Trump's persona. On one hand, he was the mentor—someone who had the wisdom and experience to guide the contestants and help them succeed. But on the other hand, he was the ruthless boss who didn't tolerate weakness or incompetence. He expected excellence, and he wasn't afraid to call people out when they fell short. It was this duality that made him such a compelling figure. To win Trump's approval meant something; it symbolized not just surviving the competition but also earning the respect of someone who had mastered the art of business.

The format of the show also struck a chord with audiences because it played into the timeless appeal of competition and ambition. America, after all, has long celebrated the idea that anyone can rise to the top if they work hard enough, take risks, and prove themselves. The Apprentice turned that idea into a spectacle, allowing viewers to live vicariously through the contestants as they fought for success in Trump's world. The challenges were tough, but the ultimate prize—a job working for Trump—was a dream that captured the imagination of millions.

In many ways, the show was perfectly suited to Trump's personality. He was already known for his bold, brash style, and The Apprentice amplified these qualities, presenting him as the ultimate authority figure in business. The show's format allowed him to display his wealth, power, and expertise, while also offering a glimpse into his decision-making process. Viewers tuned in not just to see who would win, but to watch Trump in action—evaluating, critiquing, and ultimately deciding who was worthy of success. Trump's larger-than-life persona was tailor-made for television, and The Apprentice provided the perfect stage for him to shine.

Moreover, the show wasn't just about business—it was about spectacle. The glamorous settings, the high-stakes challenges, the dramatic boardroom showdowns—The Apprentice was as much about entertainment as it was about education. The combination of real business tasks with reality TV drama made the show a hit with a broad audience, from business professionals fascinated by the challenges to everyday viewers who simply wanted to watch the drama unfold.

In its first season, The Apprentice became a cultural phenomenon, drawing millions of viewers and making Donald Trump a household name in a new way. No longer was he just the real estate mogul with skyscrapers bearing his name—he was now the face of one of the most popular shows on television. Trump's role on The Apprentice was a masterstroke of personal branding, and the show's format played perfectly into the mythology of Trump as the ultimate business leader. For many, Trump wasn't just a successful entrepreneur; he was a symbol of the American Dream—someone who had achieved the highest levels of success and was now offering others the chance to follow in his footsteps.

This blend of competition, ambition, and Trump's commanding presence made The Apprentice irresistible to audiences, ensuring its place as one of the most memorable and influential reality TV shows of the decade. And at the center of it all was Donald Trump, whose charisma and business acumen turned The Apprentice into more than just a television show—it became a cultural touchstone.

The Show's Impact on Trump's Public Persona

The Apprentice did more than just entertain viewers—it fundamentally transformed Donald Trump's public image. Before the show, Trump was a well-known figure in the business world, particularly in New York City, where his name adorned towering skyscrapers and luxury hotels. He had long been a symbol of wealth and ambition, someone who embodied the highs and lows of real estate success. However, his reputation was not without blemishes. The 1990s had seen his business empire endure several high-profile bankruptcies, and despite his enduring presence in the media, Trump's image had become somewhat polarizing. While some admired his flashy style and larger-than-life persona, others saw him as a symbol of excess and arrogance.

The Apprentice offered Trump the opportunity to reshape his narrative and extend his reach far beyond the business community. By starring in a prime-time reality television show, Trump was able to reintroduce himself to the American public on a grand scale. No longer confined to the pages of the *New York Times* or *Forbes*, Trump was now in living rooms across the country every week, presenting himself as the ultimate business authority. The show positioned him as a mentor, a guide for those aspiring to success, and a figure whose opinion mattered. It was a platform that allowed him to craft a new version of himself: Donald Trump, the decisive leader and sage of success.

One of the most significant aspects of the show's impact on Trump's public persona was how it elevated him from being a regional figure—primarily known in business and real estate circles—to a national, even global, icon. Millions of viewers who had never heard of Trump before *The Apprentice* quickly became familiar with his name, face, and personality. For them, Trump was no longer just a billionaire developer from New York; he was a pop culture figure, someone who was now as recognizable as any Hollywood star or athlete. His presence on television gave him a celebrity status that transcended his business achievements and allowed him to connect with a much broader audience.

This shift in Trump's public image was profound. On *The Apprentice*, he was depicted not only as a successful businessman but also as someone who had mastered the art of leadership. Each week, viewers watched him make tough decisions, deliver sharp critiques, and offer advice to aspiring entrepreneurs. His demeanor was no-nonsense and often blunt, but this resonated with audiences who admired his confidence and directness. In the boardroom, Trump played the role of the ultimate decision-maker—the person whose approval was the key to success. For millions of viewers, this version of Trump became the dominant image: a man who was not just wealthy, but wise, powerful, and in control.

The show also played into the myth of the self-made man, a narrative that Trump had carefully cultivated throughout his career. While Trump had, in fact, inherited significant wealth and his father's business, *The Apprentice* allowed him to amplify the idea that he was a master of business, someone who had built his empire through sheer talent and hard work. This narrative was appealing to many Americans, particularly those who believed in the values of hard work, ambition, and the possibility of rising to the top. Trump's portrayal as the all-knowing, all-powerful CEO fed into this idea of the American Dream, where success was attainable for anyone with enough drive and determination.

For Trump, *The Apprentice* also provided a much-needed buffer against the negative press that had plagued him in the previous decade. The public had been well aware of his financial troubles, including the high-profile failures of his Atlantic City casinos, but *The Apprentice* offered him a chance to showcase his strengths rather than his weaknesses. The show didn't dwell on his past business failures; instead, it presented him as someone who had learned from his mistakes and was now in a position to teach others. Trump's image was no longer tied to specific real estate deals or bankruptcies—it was tied to his television persona as a successful businessman and leader.

The transformation of Trump's public persona didn't happen by accident. It was a carefully orchestrated process, one that Trump understood and embraced fully. He knew that *The Ap-*

prentice was more than just entertainment—it was an opportunity to redefine how the world saw him. By positioning himself as a mentor and authority figure on the show, Trump was able to reframe his narrative and distance himself from the controversies that had once dogged him. Week after week, viewers saw a version of Trump that was powerful, decisive, and in control—qualities that resonated deeply in a culture that celebrated success and wealth.

Beyond the business world, *The Apprentice* also allowed Trump to tap into a broader cultural conversation about leadership and success. The show came at a time when the U.S. economy was booming, and there was a growing fascination with wealth and power. Shows like *Cribs* and *Lifestyles of the Rich and Famous* had already whetted the public's appetite for glimpses into the lives of the wealthy, but *The Apprentice* took it a step further. It wasn't just about showcasing wealth—it was about demonstrating the qualities that supposedly led to success. Trump's role on the show fed into this narrative, portraying him as a man who had not only achieved great wealth but had also mastered the skills necessary to lead and succeed in any situation.

Ultimately, *The Apprentice* transformed Donald Trump into a pop culture icon. No longer just a businessman, he was now a celebrity in his own right, with a public persona that transcended the real estate world. He became someone whose opinions on success, leadership, and ambition mattered, not just to the contestants on his show but to millions of viewers across the country. This newfound celebrity status would prove invaluable in the years to come, as Trump's television persona laid the groundwork for his eventual political ambitions. The larger-than-life figure that emerged from *The Apprentice* was not just a reality TV star—it was the foundation of a future political candidate who would use his fame and image to reach even greater heights.

The Apprentice and Trump's Brand Expansion

As The Apprentice grew in popularity, Donald Trump seized the opportunity to expand his personal brand in ways that extended far beyond the boardroom. The success of the show was not just about boosting Trump's visibility—it was about creating an entirely new platform for the "Trump" name, a brand that he would leverage to sell a lifestyle, a promise of success, and a symbol of luxury. Trump's mastery of branding had long been a key component of his business strategy, but The Apprentice took it to new heights, allowing him to capitalize on the show's momentum to build a powerful, multifaceted brand empire.

The show itself became a critical marketing tool for Trump's existing businesses. Every episode of The Apprentice was essentially an hour-long advertisement for Trump's wealth, properties, and success. The opening shots of the show featured sweeping aerial views of Trump Tower, luxurious hotels, and sprawling estates, all underscoring Trump's larger-than-life persona. The New York City skyline, with Trump Tower prominently featured, became a recurring motif, serving as both a backdrop and a symbol of the wealth and power associated with the Trump name. For viewers, it reinforced the idea that Donald Trump was synonymous with success, glamour, and prestige.

In addition to reinforcing his image, Trump used the show to directly promote his businesses. Contestants often stayed in Trump-owned hotels, held meetings in Trump properties, and conducted challenges within Trump-branded spaces. This cross-promotion was a genius move, subtly yet effectively turning The Apprentice into a showcase for Trump's empire. The visibility that his properties gained through the show enhanced their cachet, reinforcing the luxury image that Trump had spent decades cultivating. For millions of viewers, staying at a Trump property or purchasing a Trump-branded product became synonymous with participating in the same world of opulence and success they saw on screen.

Beyond the direct promotion of his properties, The Apprentice also opened doors for Trump to expand his brand into new industries. Trump's persona on the show—a shrewd, no-nonsense businessman with the keys to success—resonated with audiences in a way that few other television personalities did. People didn't just watch Trump; they wanted to emulate him. This aspirational aspect of his brand led to a wave of licensing deals and product endorsements, many of which bore Trump's name and capitalized on his association with success.

Trump's ability to license his name became one of his most profitable ventures during the height of The Apprentice. The name "Trump" became its own product, associated with luxury, exclusivity, and ambition. Soon, the Trump brand extended far beyond real estate, appearing on everything from high-end neckties and menswear to bottled water and home furnishings. Trump's name was also licensed for use on developments and properties around the world, including luxury hotels and residential towers that often had little to do with his core business but benefited from the perceived prestige of the Trump brand.

The "Trump University" initiative, launched in 2005, was another direct result of Trump's expanded brand following the success of The Apprentice. Trump University promised to teach participants how to achieve the same level of success in business that Trump had achieved. The program, which included seminars and courses in real estate, entrepreneurship, and wealth creation, capitalized on Trump's image as the ultimate business expert, which had been solidified by his role on The Apprentice. Although the venture would later be mired in controversy and lawsuits, its initial appeal highlighted how The Apprentice had transformed Trump into more than just a businessman—he was now perceived as an authority on success, someone who could teach others how to follow in his footsteps.

What set Trump apart from other reality TV stars was his ability to turn his fame into a brand empire that wasn't just about entertainment but about aspiration. For Trump, every moment on television was an opportunity to reinforce the myth of his infallibility and success. The audience wasn't just watching a show—they were buying into the idea that by consuming Trump-branded products, they too could share in his world of success and luxury. Whether it was staying in a Trump hotel, wearing a Trump suit, or signing up for a Trump seminar, the message was clear: Donald Trump represented the pinnacle of achievement, and by associating with his brand, you could be a part of it.

The genius of Trump's brand expansion during the The Apprentice era lay in how seamlessly the lines between entertainment and business blurred. Viewers weren't just consuming reality television—they were being sold a vision of the American Dream, with Donald Trump as its ultimate embodiment. His brand became aspirational not just because he was rich and successful, but because the show made him appear relatable in a strange way. He was the tough but fair boss, the mentor who knew how to succeed in a cutthroat world, and the embodiment of the belief that anyone, with the right mix of ambition and strategy, could make it to the top.

This ability to transform television fame into brand success extended even to Trump's personal life. He became a fixture in pop culture, regularly making appearances on talk shows, news programs, and in cameos on other television series. His brash, confident persona made him a favorite for interviewers, as he could always be counted on to deliver a memorable soundbite or a controversial opinion. This constant media exposure kept him in the public eye and further solidified his status as a larger-than-life figure, blending the roles of businessman, celebrity, and television star in a way that few others had done before.

As Trump's brand grew, so did his influence. He wasn't just a real estate mogul or a reality TV star—he was a global brand, recognized around the world. His presence on The Apprentice had transformed him into a figure who transcended traditional boundaries between business and entertainment. The show allowed Trump to reinvent himself for a new generation, positioning him as a symbol of success, power, and ambition at a time when Americans were particularly drawn to narratives of wealth and personal achievement.

Ultimately, The Apprentice didn't just boost Trump's fame—it fundamentally reshaped the Trump brand, allowing him to build a multifaceted empire that extended far beyond real estate. It gave him the platform to capitalize on his image, turning his name into a product that could be sold across industries. And in doing so, it laid the groundwork for Trump's future endeavors, setting the stage for the ultimate brand extension—his entry into politics, where the lines between celebrity, business, and influence would blur even further.

The Global Reach and Long-Term Influence of The Apprentice

The impact of The Apprentice extended far beyond the United States, transforming Donald Trump into a global phenomenon. As the show's popularity grew, international versions of The Apprentice began to air in countries around the world, further expanding Trump's influence. From the UK to Brazil to South Africa, the format was adapted for local audiences, but the essence remained the same: a high-stakes competition where aspiring businesspeople battled for success under the watchful eye of a successful mogul. In most cases, these international versions featured local business leaders in the role of "the boss," but Trump's presence loomed large, as he was still seen as the figurehead of the global Apprentice brand.

For international audiences, Trump became a symbol of American capitalism and ambition. His image, already larger-than-life in the U.S., was exported across the globe through these shows, where he was often seen as the embodiment of success, wealth, and power. Even in countries where the local version of The Apprentice featured different business figures, Trump's shadow was unavoidable. He became synonymous with the idea of entrepreneurship and the pursuit of the "American Dream" on a global scale. His persona, marked by confidence and authority, resonated with audiences who admired his success and sought to emulate it in their own lives.

The global reach of The Apprentice further solidified Trump's brand as an international business titan. The show allowed him to connect with audiences far beyond the skyscrapers of Manhattan, bringing his image to homes across Europe, Asia, and the Middle East. In many ways, Trump became a cultural export—a symbol of American business acumen and wealth who transcended national borders. The show's success in foreign markets reflected the universal appeal of the competition for success, a theme that resonated with people from diverse cultural and economic backgrounds.

Beyond television, Trump's influence as a global figure grew through his expanding business ventures. His hotels and branded properties began to appear in international markets, bolstered by the recognition his name now carried thanks to The Apprentice. From Trump Tower in Manila to Trump International Hotel in Vancouver, his name became a global symbol of luxury and exclusivity. While these developments were often the result of licensing deals rather than direct ownership, the power of the Trump brand, amplified by his television fame, allowed him to capitalize on the aspirational allure of his image.

The rise of social media during this period also played a significant role in amplifying Trump's global presence. As Twitter, Facebook, and other platforms gained traction, Trump, ever the media-savvy businessman, embraced these tools to communicate directly with his growing audience. His blunt, often provocative style translated well to social media, where he quickly amassed a large following. The combination of his presence on The Apprentice and his growing influence online created a feedback loop that allowed Trump to maintain relevance and control over his public image, long after the initial episodes of The Apprentice had aired.

In addition to his expanding international influence, The Apprentice also left a lasting legacy on popular culture. The show became a staple of the reality TV genre, spawning countless imitators and solidifying Trump's role as a cultural icon. Shows like Shark Tank, which followed a similar format of business competition and mentorship, built on the groundwork that The Apprentice had laid. The fusion of business education with entertainment was a concept that audiences found both intriguing and accessible, and it quickly became a trend in television programming around the world. Trump, of course, was seen as the pioneer of this blend of business and entertainment, reinforcing his status as a trendsetter.

More importantly, The Apprentice cemented the idea that Trump was not just a businessman but a brand unto himself. The constant presence of his name, face, and voice across multiple media platforms made him more than just a figurehead of his own real estate empire—he became a symbol of success that transcended any single industry. This was critical for Trump as it allowed him to maintain his relevance even as his real estate ventures fluctuated. His name alone became synonymous with wealth, power, and ambition, and The Apprentice had played a key role in creating that association.

The long-term influence of The Apprentice can also be seen in how it laid the groundwork for Trump's future endeavors, particularly in politics. While many viewed Trump as a businessman first, The Apprentice allowed him to build a relationship with millions of Americans that went beyond his business ventures. The show positioned him as a relatable, albeit larger-than-life, figure who could mentor, judge, and ultimately choose who was worthy of success. His weekly presence on prime-time television allowed viewers to feel as though they knew him personally—an important foundation for his later political career.

By the time Donald Trump announced his candidacy for president in 2015, The Apprentice had already done much of the heavy lifting in establishing his public persona. His name recognition was unparalleled, and his image as a decisive, no-nonsense leader was already ingrained in the minds of millions of Americans. For many voters, Trump's time on The Apprentice had proven that he knew how to lead, make tough decisions, and succeed in high-pressure situations. These traits, carefully cultivated over the course of his television career, became key selling points in his presidential campaign.

In hindsight, The Apprentice was more than just a successful reality television show. It was a platform that allowed Donald Trump to craft a powerful and enduring public persona that would resonate with millions of people both in the United States and around the world. The show transformed Trump from a wealthy businessman into a global brand, a cultural icon, and ultimately, a political force. Its impact on his career—and on the world—cannot be overstated. The success of The Apprentice was not just about ratings or celebrity; it was about creating a narrative of success that Trump would ride all the way to the White House.

In conclusion, The Apprentice marked a pivotal chapter in Donald Trump's rise to fame and influence. It catapulted him from a real estate mogul with a flashy reputation to a global icon whose name was synonymous with success. The show's combination of business education, reality television drama, and Trump's commanding presence created a unique and compelling narrative that resonated with audiences around the world. As Trump expanded his brand globally, The Apprentice became the cornerstone of his personal and professional identity, shaping his image as the ultimate arbiter of success—a role that would later play a critical part in his unprecedented journey from the boardroom to the Oval Office.

Chapter 6

Chapter 6: Crafting the Celebrity Persona

The Calculated Persona – Image as Strategy

Donald Trump's rise to celebrity status was no accident. From early in his career, Trump understood that success in modern America wasn't just about business acumen or financial achievement—it was about crafting a public persona that resonated with the masses. This calculated approach to his image became a defining characteristic of his brand, allowing him to transcend the business world and become a fixture in American popular culture. Trump knew that in an era where media exposure could make or break a career, the power of one's image was often as important as the substance behind it. He leaned into this understanding, consciously crafting a persona that was larger-than-life, built on confidence, extravagance, and unshakable self-assurance.

Trump's early years as a real estate developer in Manhattan gave him the perfect stage to begin shaping this public image. The cutthroat world of New York City real estate was already rife with drama and larger-than-life personalities, but Trump quickly stood out among his peers. His initial rise to prominence in the

1970s was marked by a series of high-profile real estate deals that not only made him a major player in the industry but also gave him an opportunity to develop his public persona. Trump wasn't just content with success behind closed doors—he wanted the world to know that he was successful, and he wanted them to see him as a symbol of power and wealth.

The Trump name began to take on a life of its own during this period, becoming synonymous with opulence and ambition. But this wasn't merely the result of Trump's business deals—it was a deliberate branding strategy. Trump understood the value of his name and worked tirelessly to associate it with luxury and success. The skyscrapers he built weren't just real estate projects; they were monuments to his personal brand. Buildings like Trump Tower were designed to stand out not only for their size and grandeur but because they represented Trump's vision of wealth and dominance. These projects became symbols of the Trump brand, and Trump himself became the embodiment of their message.

One of Trump's greatest strengths was his ability to blur the lines between the personal and the professional, making his own identity inseparable from his business empire. He knew that his image as a confident, charismatic leader was just as important as the properties he was building. His public appearances were carefully calculated to reinforce the idea that Donald Trump wasn't just a successful businessman—he was a titan, a mogul who could do no wrong. Every interview, magazine cover, and press conference was an opportunity for Trump to showcase his personality and remind the public of his achievements. His brash, unapologetic style became a trademark, distinguishing him from the more reserved, buttoned-up figures of the business world.

Trump's ability to use his persona as a business tool was most evident in the way he handled the media. Early on, he recognized that the media could be a powerful ally in his quest for fame and influence. Trump didn't shy away from the spotlight—he actively courted it, understanding that the more attention he garnered, the more powerful his brand became. This approach was revolutionary for a businessman in the 1980s, a time when most corporate leaders preferred to stay behind the scenes. Trump, however, flipped this script, turning his life and career into a public spectacle. He wasn't just building skyscrapers; he was building an image of himself as the ultimate success story—a man who could turn anything he touched into gold.

The media, in turn, couldn't resist Trump's magnetic personality. His combination of wealth, confidence, and boldness made him a compelling figure for journalists and television producers alike. Trump understood that by creating headlines and drawing attention to himself, he could control the narrative around his business ventures. Every deal, every building, every project became a reflection of Trump's persona. Even in moments of failure or controversy, Trump's image as a larger-than-life figure remained intact. He didn't hide from setbacks; instead, he embraced them as part of the story, using them as opportunities to showcase his resilience and determination.

By the 1980s, Trump's public persona had solidified. He was no longer just a successful real estate developer—he was a celebrity in his own right. His name appeared in gossip columns, business magazines, and on the covers of major newspapers. His flamboyant style, often featuring lavish displays of wealth and grandiose statements, made him a constant topic of discussion. But all of this was by design. Trump had built an image that was impossible to ignore, and he knew that in a media-saturated world, staying visible was half the battle.

This calculated approach to his image would become one of Trump's most powerful assets. He had positioned himself not just as a businessman but as a brand, one that people associated with success, power, and ambition. Whether they admired him or criticized him, they couldn't deny that Trump had mastered the art of self-promotion. And it was this mastery of image that would continue to propel him to new heights, laying the foundation for his future as both a media personality and, eventually, a political figure. Trump had understood early on that in the world of fame and influence, perception was reality—and he had carefully crafted a persona that could shape the way the world perceived him.

Trump's Mastery of Media Manipulation

Donald Trump's relationship with the media was one of the key drivers of his rise to fame. From the outset of his career, Trump understood that controlling the narrative surrounding him could significantly enhance his power and influence. He wasn't merely a passive subject of media attention—he was an active player who manipulated the press to serve his purposes. Trump's mastery of media manipulation became one of his greatest strengths, allowing him to maintain constant visibility and build his brand through calculated moves that kept him in the public eye.

From his earliest days as a New York real estate developer, Trump recognized the symbiotic relationship between business and media. In a city dominated by cutthroat competition, Trump used the media as a tool to outshine his rivals. He didn't just want to be successful—he wanted to be seen as successful. His ability to generate headlines was unmatched, and he used every opportunity to showcase his wealth, power, and grand ambitions. Trump's approach was aggressive and bold: if he wasn't making news, he would create it. He was an expert at generating buzz, using everything from flamboyant press conferences to larger-than-life public statements to capture attention.

One of the hallmarks of Trump's media strategy was his ability to dominate the news cycle, even in the face of controversy. Trump famously understood that "no publicity is bad publicity," a mantra he followed throughout his career. While most public figures would shy away from negative press or scandals, Trump embraced them, often using controversy to his advantage. Whether he was embroiled in a high-profile legal dispute, making a provocative comment, or clashing with competitors, Trump ensured that the spotlight remained firmly on him. He recognized that in the world of media, attention was currency, and he was determined to remain the focal point of discussion.

Trump's talent for media manipulation was evident in the way he courted the press during both his successes and his failures. When he completed a major deal or opened a new building, Trump would invite journalists, photographers, and television crews to witness the spectacle. His announcements were often laced with hyperbole, designed to create excitement and reinforce his image as a business mogul with an outsized personality. Headlines would trumpet his achievements, and his name would become synonymous with success and ambition. But even when things went wrong—whether it was a financial setback or a legal challenge—Trump never shied away from the cameras. Instead, he would spin the story in his favor, positioning himself as the victim of circumstances beyond his control or as a man determined to fight back against adversity.

A key element of Trump's media strategy was his ability to craft a narrative that suited his interests. He didn't rely solely on traditional media outlets to tell his story; he became the narrator of his own saga. In interviews and press conferences, Trump would paint himself as a self-made man, a brilliant dealmaker who had overcome obstacles through sheer willpower and intelligence. He was always the hero of his own story, and this self-mythologizing approach resonated with many Americans who saw in him the embodiment of the American Dream. Trump's larger-than-life persona was carefully constructed, and he used the media as his platform to broadcast it to the world.

One of Trump's most effective tactics was his use of hyperbole and bold declarations. He often made exaggerated claims about his wealth, his business acumen, or the success of his ventures. While some of these claims were met with skepticism, they served their purpose: to keep people talking about Donald Trump. For instance, when Trump announced that Trump Tower would be the tallest and most luxurious building in New York City, he created an aura of grandeur around the project long before it was completed. This type of exaggerated marketing was a hallmark of Trump's media manipulation strategy. He wasn't just selling real estate—he was selling an image of unparalleled success and luxury, with himself at the center.

Perhaps the most crucial aspect of Trump's media mastery was his ability to create lasting relationships with journalists and media outlets. Trump understood that keeping the media on his side—or at least keeping them engaged—was essential to maintaining his visibility. Over the years, he cultivated connections with influential reporters, editors, and media personalities, ensuring that his name remained a constant presence in print and on television. Even when the coverage wasn't entirely favorable, Trump knew how to leverage the media's hunger for stories about him. He played the press like a chess game, understanding their need for headlines and using that need to his advantage.

The 1980s and 1990s saw Trump become a staple of tabloid journalism, particularly in New York City, where publications like the New York Post and the Daily News chronicled his every move. Trump became a fixture in the gossip pages, with stories about his lavish lifestyle, celebrity connections, and high-profile relationships. These tabloid stories, often sensationalized, only fueled his growing persona as a man who lived life on a grand scale. While many businessmen of his stature might have recoiled from the attention of the gossip columns, Trump embraced it, recognizing that it was all part of maintaining his celebrity status.

Trump's ability to manipulate the media wasn't limited to his business dealings or personal life. He also used the media as a platform for promoting his political opinions, long before he ever ran for office. In interviews, Trump often made provocative statements about the state of the nation, foreign policy, or economic issues. These comments, sometimes controversial, always generated headlines and allowed Trump to position himself as a thought leader and a man with ideas about how the country should be run. Even in the early 2000s, when Trump's political ambitions were still just whispers, he was already using the media to shape public perceptions of him as more than just a businessman.

By the time Trump announced his candidacy for president in 2015, he had spent decades honing his skills as a media manipulator. His ability to command attention, control the narrative, and use controversy to his advantage had been finely tuned over the years. His years of media experience gave him a unique advantage in a political landscape that increasingly valued spectacle over substance. Trump's mastery of media manipulation wasn't just a footnote in his rise to fame—it was one of the fundamental reasons he became a household name, long before he ever stepped onto the political stage.

In an era when celebrity and media exposure had become more powerful than ever, Donald Trump was the master of the game. He didn't just play the media; he shaped it to suit his ambitions, ensuring that his image was always front and center. His ability to turn attention, even negative attention, into a form of power was one of the defining traits of his public life and one of the keys to his enduring influence.

The Role of Scandal and Provocation in Trump's Celebrity

Donald Trump understood something few public figures ever fully embrace: scandal and provocation, when wielded correctly, can be tools for not only maintaining fame but also enhancing it. While many public personalities go to great lengths to avoid controversy, Trump leaned into it, mastering the art of using scandal to stay in the public eye. For Trump, there was no such thing as bad press. In fact, he often thrived on the attention generated by controversy, understanding that every scandal, no matter how damaging it might appear on the surface, served to keep him relevant in the relentless news cycle.

From early on, Trump demonstrated a unique ability to turn negative situations into opportunities for self-promotion. This approach first became clear in the late 1980s and 1990s, when Trump found himself in the middle of various personal and financial scandals. His highly publicized divorce from his first wife, Ivana Trump, was one such example. What could have been a moment of damaging personal exposure for most figures became, for Trump, an opportunity to further solidify his image as a man constantly surrounded by drama and intrigue. The media devoured the details of Trump's love life, his rumored affair with model Marla Maples, and the extravagant fallout from his divorce, splashing it across the headlines. Instead of hiding from the spectacle, Trump embraced it, treating his personal life like a soap opera that the public couldn't turn away from.

This approach was deliberate. Trump knew that the American public had a fascination with scandal, and he also knew that controversy could enhance his celebrity status. In an era where people craved stories about the rich and famous, Trump became a figure that was endlessly intriguing. He played into this fascination by feeding the media with quotes and dramatic details that kept his name circulating. Where other public figures might have faltered under the weight of bad press, Trump thrived, keeping himself at the center of the conversation through his willingness to embrace scandal rather than shy away from it.

One of the most notable examples of Trump using controversy to his advantage came during the 1990s, when his business empire was facing financial difficulties. Trump had over-leveraged himself in the late 1980s, and as the real estate market declined, so did his fortunes. His Atlantic City casinos were hemorrhaging money, and Trump was facing the possibility of bankruptcy—a situation that could have spelled the end of his career as a high-profile businessman. Yet, even in this moment of financial peril, Trump managed to stay in the public eye. Rather than retreat from the media, he used it to frame himself as a survivor and a fighter.

During his financial struggles, Trump played up the drama of his potential collapse, giving interviews and making statements that portrayed him as someone who was fighting tooth and nail to save his empire. The media eagerly followed the story, fascinated by the possibility that Trump, the man who had built an empire on confidence and extravagance, might lose it all. And yet, even as his finances crumbled, Trump's image remained largely intact. He had successfully shifted the narrative from one of failure to one of resilience, turning a potential disaster into a tale of comeback. In doing so, he reinforced his public persona as someone who could never be counted out, no matter how dire the circumstances.

Trump's ability to use scandal didn't just apply to his personal life or financial difficulties; it extended into his public persona as well. He often made provocative and outlandish statements, knowing that such remarks would generate headlines. His willingness to say what others wouldn't—whether it was about politics, business, or culture—became a hallmark of his public identity. These statements often led to outrage and condemnation, but they also ensured that Trump remained a constant topic of discussion. He was always in the news, always on people's minds, and always shaping the narrative around himself.

A key example of this was Trump's infamous feud with New York City Mayor Ed Koch in the 1980s. As Trump was building his real estate empire, he became increasingly vocal about what he perceived as the city's mismanagement under Koch's administration. Trump publicly criticized the mayor, calling him "a moron" and accusing him of ruining the city's economy. The feud quickly became a media sensation, with the press eagerly covering each new insult and jab. While such public spats might have hurt other figures, for Trump, they only enhanced his reputation as a brash, unapologetic businessman who wasn't afraid to take on powerful opponents. The public, whether they agreed with him or not, saw Trump as someone who was willing to speak his mind, even at the risk of alienating important figures like the mayor of New York.

This strategy of provocation extended into Trump's later years as well, particularly in his time on The Apprentice. As the star of the hit reality television show, Trump's persona as a tough, no-nonsense boss was amplified for dramatic effect. His signature phrase, "You're fired," became a national catchphrase, embodying his image as a powerful figure who wasn't afraid to make the tough decisions. But beyond the surface entertainment, Trump's role on The Apprentice reinforced his public persona in a more meaningful way. He wasn't just a businessman; he was a decision-maker, a leader, someone who could swiftly cut through the nonsense and get things done. His persona on the show was larger than life, and it played directly into his strategy of using provocation to build his brand.

Ultimately, Trump's use of scandal and provocation wasn't just about staying in the headlines—it was about reinforcing his brand as a man who was always at the center of the action. Whether it was a high-profile divorce, a business dispute, or a political controversy, Trump thrived on the attention that came with being provocative. He understood that in a world where media attention was fleeting, controversy had the power to keep him in the spotlight. And as long as people were talking about Donald Trump, his influence remained intact.

For Trump, scandal and provocation weren't obstacles to be avoided; they were tools to be used. By embracing controversy, he ensured that he remained a constant presence in American culture, a figure who was always relevant, always in the public eye, and always in control of the narrative. This tactic of using scandal as a form of self-promotion would serve him well throughout his career, helping him maintain his celebrity status even during the most tumultuous moments of his life.

Mastering the Art of Television Appearances

Long before *The Apprentice* made him a reality TV star, Donald Trump understood the power of television as a medium for shaping his public image. His ability to command attention through the small screen was a critical element in his rise as a celebrity mogul, positioning him not just as a businessman, but as a cultural figure recognizable far beyond the business world. Television provided Trump with a stage, a way to communicate directly with the American public, and he used it masterfully to construct and broadcast his larger-than-life persona.

Trump's foray into television began well before reality TV became a mainstream genre. In the 1980s and 1990s, he was already appearing on television talk shows, news programs, and even making cameos in popular TV series and films. His appearances on shows like *The Late Show with David Letterman* and *The Oprah Winfrey Show* in the late 1980s introduced him to a national audience that may have known little about the complexities of New York real estate but were captivated by his charisma and confidence. During these interviews, Trump would often speak in grand terms about his business successes, his vision for America, and his philosophy on leadership, laying the groundwork for the persona he would continue to build over the coming decades.

One of Trump's earliest uses of television to enhance his brand came in the form of televised interviews where he deftly blended humor, charm, and bold statements. On *The Oprah Winfrey Show* in 1988, for instance, Trump was asked whether he would ever run for president. His answer—while delivered with a hint of playfulness—was serious enough to plant the seed in the minds of viewers that Trump wasn't just a businessman but someone with a broader vision for the country. Trump used these opportunities to present himself as more than just a real estate mogul. He carefully crafted an image of himself as a successful, straight-talking, all-American businessman, a man who represented the ideals of capitalism and individual success.

But it wasn't just his interviews that helped solidify Trump's celebrity. His cameos in TV shows and movies in the 1990s were another deliberate step in expanding his brand into popular culture. Trump's brief appearances in films like *Home Alone 2: Lost in New York* and TV series like *The Fresh Prince of Bel-Air* might seem like minor footnotes in his career, but they played an important role in reinforcing his omnipresence in American media. These cameos were always tied to Trump's persona as a symbol of wealth and power. In *Home Alone 2*, for example, his appearance at the luxurious Plaza Hotel (which he owned at the time) subtly reminded audiences that Trump was synonymous with success and high-end real estate. These appearances were short, but impactful, inserting Trump into the pop culture lexicon and expanding his reach far beyond the boardroom.

The pinnacle of Trump's television dominance, however, came with the creation of *The Apprentice* in 2004. By this point, Trump's image as a brash, confident businessman was well-established, but *The Apprentice* elevated it to a new level. The show was more than just a reality competition—it was a stage for Trump to embody and display the traits that had defined his public persona for decades: decisiveness, confidence, and success. Week after week, millions of Americans tuned in to watch Trump judge contestants vying for a chance to work for him, delivering his famous line, "You're fired," with cold finality. This catchphrase quickly entered the cultural zeitgeist, becoming synonymous with Trump's no-nonsense approach to leadership and decision-making.

On *The Apprentice*, Trump wasn't just a passive figurehead; he was the central character. The show reinforced the narrative that he was the ultimate authority on business, a master dealmaker who could make or break a contestant's dreams with a single word. Trump's on-screen persona was carefully calibrated to blend entertainment with his real-life brand. He positioned himself as the embodiment of American capitalism, a mentor-figure to aspiring entrepreneurs but also an unforgiving judge who demanded nothing less than excellence. This role cemented his celebrity, transforming him from a businessman known mainly in financial circles into a household name with mass appeal.

While *The Apprentice* offered entertainment value, it also served as a platform for Trump to market his broader empire. Throughout the show, viewers were constantly reminded of Trump's wealth, power, and success. The lavish settings—whether it was the boardroom at Trump Tower or the contestants' luxurious living quarters—were visual cues that reinforced Trump's image as a man who had achieved the pinnacle of success. He wasn't just a businessman; he was the businessman, the gold standard of success that others aspired to emulate. Every episode was a testament to the idea that Trump knew what it took to make it in the ruthless world of business, and his celebrity grew in direct proportion to that image.

Trump's use of *The Apprentice* to bolster his brand went far beyond the show's weekly episodes. He leveraged the platform to promote his other ventures, including his hotels, casinos, and branded products. Viewers who watched Trump on television were also potential customers for his various businesses. The show acted as a kind of extended commercial for the Trump brand, with each season offering Trump a chance to showcase his properties and lifestyle to a national audience. Trump had effectively turned reality television into a marketing machine that reinforced his status as a successful mogul while providing him with a steady stream of income and attention.

In many ways, *The Apprentice* was a culmination of everything Trump had learned about media manipulation and celebrity culture. He understood the importance of creating a narrative around himself and used television as the ultimate tool to broadcast that narrative to the masses. Where other businessmen might have been content with success in their industries, Trump wanted more—he wanted to be a media star, someone whose influence extended far beyond the corporate world. Through television, he crafted a persona that was both aspirational and entertaining, blending business acumen with showmanship in a way that resonated with millions of viewers.

By the time *The Apprentice* ended, Trump had not only cemented his place as a television icon but had also laid the groundwork for his next, even more audacious act: his entry into politics. The skills he had honed in front of the camera—commanding attention, controlling the narrative, and leveraging controversy—would serve him well as he transitioned from the world of reality TV to the world of presidential campaigns. For

Trump, television wasn't just a medium; it was the ultimate stage for building his celebrity, and it played a crucial role in his journey from businessman to pop culture phenomenon.

Leveraging Media Relationships and Navigating the Press

As Donald Trump's celebrity status grew, so did his understanding of how to strategically cultivate and manipulate relationships with the media. From tabloid coverage in the 1980s to his reality TV stardom in the 2000s, Trump developed a keen awareness of the symbiotic relationship between himself and the press. The media needed figures like Trump—bold, controversial, and always good for a headline. In turn, Trump understood that by offering the press sensational stories, provocative quotes, and endless intrigue, he could remain a fixture in the public eye.

Trump's media-savviness began to take shape in the 1980s, during a time when he was transitioning from a relatively private real estate developer to a flamboyant public figure. As he undertook high-profile projects in New York, such as the construction of Trump Tower, Trump actively sought out media attention. He became a master at generating buzz for his developments, always ensuring that his name was prominently featured in any story about his ventures. He knew that in the world of high-stakes real estate, public perception was as important as financial success. By cultivating a larger-than-life persona through the media, he made himself synonymous with success and luxury.

One of Trump's most effective media strategies was his willingness to speak directly to journalists and offer them exclusive access. He developed close relationships with New York's tabloid reporters, often feeding them stories or quotes that would guarantee his inclusion in the day's headlines. Trump had a remarkable ability to frame his narrative in a way that kept the media—and by extension, the public—focused on him. He understood what made a story newsworthy and was always ready to provide the right sound bite to ensure his presence in the news cycle.

Perhaps the most illustrative example of Trump's media manipulation came during his contentious divorces in the late 1980s and early 1990s. Rather than shy away from the public scrutiny surrounding his split from Ivana Trump, he leaned into it, allowing the press to document every twist and turn of the high-profile breakup. Trump knew that America had an insatiable appetite for scandal, and he used the media circus surrounding his personal life to his advantage. By keeping his name in the papers, he ensured that people remained fascinated by the "Trump story," whether it involved business or personal drama.

During this period, Trump wasn't just a subject of media coverage; he was an active participant in shaping it. There are even stories suggesting that Trump would sometimes call reporters posing as a spokesman named "John Barron" to plant stories that flattered him or inflated his wealth. While such tactics might seem bizarre, they illustrate Trump's willingness to do whatever was necessary to keep the media's attention focused on him. He understood that controlling the narrative—whether by exaggerating his success or feeding tantalizing details about his personal life—was essential to maintaining his celebrity.

As Trump's fame continued to grow, so did his understanding of how to navigate different types of media. He was equally at home giving interviews to business publications like *The Wall Street Journal* as he was appearing on gossip shows like *Entertainment Tonight*. This ability to straddle different media worlds allowed Trump to expand his brand far beyond the confines of real estate. He became a symbol of wealth and power in business circles, while also transforming into a pop culture icon. By being everywhere—on talk shows, in newspapers, on the cover of magazines—Trump created an omnipresence that kept him relevant and recognizable to all types of audiences.

This mastery of media manipulation came into full bloom with the launch of *The Apprentice*. The show itself was a media spectacle, but it was also a platform for Trump to further enhance his public image. Every week, millions of viewers watched Trump in action, and the press eagerly covered both the show and Trump's behind-the-scenes dealings. Trump wasn't just the star of a reality TV show; he was now an essential part of America's cultural conversation. Journalists would analyze his performance on the show, dissect his business decisions, and speculate about his future. Trump's relationship with the media evolved from being one of mutual necessity to one where Trump became a central figure in the press's constant search for compelling stories.

Trump's ability to navigate media relationships was also evident in how he dealt with negative press. Rather than avoiding criticism, he often embraced it, using it as fuel to further stoke the flames of controversy. Whether it was a scathing article about his business failures or rumors about his personal life, Trump understood that all press—whether good or bad—served to keep him in the spotlight. His frequent mantra, "There's no such thing as bad publicity," perfectly encapsulated his approach to handling negative media coverage. Instead of shrinking in the face of scandal, Trump thrived on it, using it to maintain his presence in the media and the public consciousness.

One of the most notable examples of this occurred in the 1990s, when Trump's businesses were struggling, and he faced significant financial difficulties. In the press, stories emerged about Trump's potential bankruptcies and his failing Atlantic City casinos. While such stories could have ended his public career, Trump turned them into another chapter of his narrative. He portrayed himself as a fighter, someone who wouldn't give up, even in the face of overwhelming odds. Trump's tenacity and refusal to fade from the media spotlight during these difficult times reinforced his image as someone who could bounce back from any setback, and in doing so, he kept the media—and the public—engaged.

By the time Trump transitioned from a media celebrity to a political figure in the mid-2010s, his relationship with the press had been honed to near-perfection. He understood how to manipulate headlines, dominate news cycles, and use television to project his image as a strong, successful leader. His approach to the media was always rooted in his understanding that attention equaled influence, and influence was the key to success in any arena, whether it was business, entertainment, or politics.

Ultimately, Trump's media strategy was a critical component of his rise to fame and influence. By cultivating relationships with reporters, playing into the public's appetite for drama, and maintaining a relentless presence in the news cycle, he ensured that he was never far from the public's consciousness. The press, in many ways, became his greatest asset, helping to transform him from a real estate developer into a pop culture icon, and eventually, into a political figure with unprecedented name recognition. In Trump's world, controlling the media narrative was just as important as closing a business deal—and in both arenas, he proved himself to be a master.

Chapter 7

Chapter 7: The Brand Beyond Business

The Trump Name as a Luxury Brand

From the very beginning, Donald Trump understood the power of a name. As he rose in prominence in the world of New York real estate, he wasn't content to simply build impressive structures or complete lucrative deals. He wanted more than just financial success—he wanted his name to be synonymous with luxury, power, and success. This marked the first step in transforming "Trump" into a globally recognized brand, far beyond the confines of real estate.

In the 1970s and 1980s, as Trump began to undertake increasingly high-profile projects in Manhattan, he made sure that his name was front and center. Trump Tower, completed in 1983, was not just an architectural feat; it was a brand statement. Located on Fifth Avenue, the glittering skyscraper became a physical embodiment of the Trump image—opulent, larger-than-life, and in the heart of New York's most prestigious district. Trump understood that it wasn't enough to build an expensive, impressive building. He needed it to be associated with him personally. The gleaming golden letters spelling out

"TRUMP" on the tower ensured that anyone walking by knew exactly who was responsible for the towering luxury development. It wasn't just a building; it was a statement of who Donald Trump was and what his name represented.

In the world of real estate, the Trump name quickly became shorthand for luxury. Trump made sure to cultivate this image, often designing properties with over-the-top amenities, lavish interiors, and exclusive locations. This wasn't just about aesthetics; it was about selling a lifestyle. People weren't just buying apartments or staying at hotels—they were buying into the idea of living the Trump life, one filled with success, power, and opulence. This approach extended to his hotels, casinos, and golf courses, where Trump's name became a critical part of the marketing strategy. Whether it was Trump Plaza in Atlantic City or Trump International Hotel in New York, the name alone conveyed exclusivity.

But Trump didn't stop there. He expanded his brand across industries, with each new venture reinforcing the idea that the Trump name was synonymous with success. His moves into luxury hotels, golf courses, and even resorts abroad allowed him to reach an audience that might never set foot in one of his Manhattan properties but still wanted to associate themselves with the Trump lifestyle. By putting his name on developments in places like Miami, Las Vegas, and Dubai, Trump not only expanded his real estate empire but also extended his brand's reach globally.

Trump was very strategic in protecting the image of exclusivity. Even as his business interests diversified, he maintained a clear sense of what the Trump brand should signify. He was selective about the types of projects that would bear his name, choosing to affiliate only with those that upheld the perception of luxury. This strategic decision meant that the Trump brand could expand without diluting its essence. It was all about maintaining an image that was bigger than real estate—it was about a way of life, where luxury and success were intertwined.

The value of the Trump brand was also tied to Trump's public persona, which was inseparable from the projects he built. His larger-than-life personality, flamboyant lifestyle, and constant presence in the media helped to elevate the Trump name beyond bricks and mortar. Every time Trump was photographed at a high-profile event, every time he was quoted in a business magazine, it added another layer to the brand's narrative. He wasn't just a businessman; he was a symbol of the American dream, a self-made man who had turned his name into a global symbol of achievement. The Trump name, therefore, became a product in itself—one that could be sold, licensed, and expanded into different ventures.

However, Trump's brand of luxury was always a bit more exaggerated than what the traditional elite represented. While other high-end brands aimed for understated elegance, Trump went in the opposite direction, embracing a gaudy, over-the-top aesthetic that many found garish, but others saw as the pinnacle of wealth and success. His developments were often adorned with gold, marble, and bold design choices that screamed opulence. This aesthetic wasn't just a design preference—it was part of the Trump brand. Trump understood that to some, luxury wasn't about subtlety but about visibility, about showing off one's wealth in the most conspicuous way possible. In this sense, the Trump name attracted a specific clientele—those who wanted to flaunt their success, not hide it.

By the time Trump had become a household name in the 1990s, the Trump brand had transcended real estate. His name was now a badge of success, one that could be sold across industries and continents. The Trump name had become more than just a family legacy—it was a global brand, one that symbolized the pursuit of wealth, power, and the American dream.

Through calculated moves and strategic branding decisions, Trump had ensured that his name would stand the test of time, remaining relevant even as the world around him changed.

The evolution of the Trump name into a luxury brand was not an accident. It was the result of careful planning, relentless self-promotion, and a keen understanding of the power of perception. By the time he entered the political arena, Trump had already built a brand that millions of people around the world recognized, and, in many cases, aspired to. Whether in New York, Dubai, or Las Vegas, the Trump name had become more than just a label—it was a lifestyle, an idea, and for many, a symbol of success itself.

Licensing the Trump Name

As Donald Trump's brand of luxury grew more recognizable, he realized that the power of his name extended far beyond the projects he could physically build or manage. This understanding led to one of the most significant and lucrative moves in his career: licensing the Trump name. By the 1990s, Trump had begun to shift away from solely developing real estate to leveraging his name as a commodity—one that other companies and entrepreneurs could use to attract consumers. In licensing his name, Trump discovered a way to monetize his brand without the substantial risk or effort involved in creating a product from scratch. Instead, he would lend the Trump name to a variety of ventures, allowing him to profit while others handled the operations.

The strategy behind licensing the Trump name was brilliant in its simplicity. Companies that wanted to associate their products with luxury, wealth, and success could pay for the privilege of attaching the Trump name to their offerings. In exchange, Trump would receive royalties without having to invest significant resources. This was a low-risk, high-reward approach that enabled Trump to expand his empire quickly and across diverse industries. From skyscrapers and hotels to consumer goods, Trump's name became a seal of opulence, creating instant recognition in any market it entered.

One of the earliest and most successful examples of this strategy was in real estate. While Trump continued to build his own properties, he also began licensing his name to developers who wanted to capitalize on his brand. These developers would pay to use the Trump name on their buildings, from residential towers to hotels, creating the perception that Trump was intimately involved in the project—even if he had no actual role in its design or construction. In return, they benefited from the allure of the Trump name, which often allowed them to charge higher prices and attract a wealthier clientele. Buildings like the Trump International Hotel and Tower in Chicago and the Trump Ocean Club in Panama were products of this model. These developments bore the Trump name but were managed by separate companies, allowing Trump to extend his reach globally.

As the success of these real estate licensing deals became evident, Trump extended the concept into other areas. He licensed his name to a variety of products that he felt aligned with his brand's image of luxury and success. This included high-end consumer goods like Trump Vodka, Trump Steaks, and even Trump-branded men's suits and ties. The strategy was clear: by associating his name with upscale products, Trump reinforced the idea that his brand was a symbol of elite living. His name had the power to attract customers who wanted to buy into the lifestyle that Trump represented.

However, Trump's approach to licensing wasn't limited to traditional luxury goods. He also ventured into more unconventional arenas, always with the same goal of expanding the Trump brand. Trump University, for example, was an educational venture that promised to teach students the secrets of Trump's business success. Although the institution was later embroiled in lawsuits and controversies, it initially attracted people based on the strength of the Trump name. Similarly, Trump licensed his name to developments and products that ranged from home furnishings to energy drinks, always positioning himself as the ultimate dealmaker and success story.

One of the reasons Trump's licensing strategy was so successful was his ability to carefully curate the projects that would bear his name. Although the sheer volume of licensed products and developments was vast, Trump maintained a focus on ensuring that each one contributed to the perception of luxury and success. For instance, he would often reject deals if he felt the product didn't align with his image, or if it didn't promise high returns. This selectiveness helped preserve the exclusivity of the Trump name, even as it became increasingly ubiquitous.

The brilliance of Trump's licensing model was that it allowed him to diversify his brand without spreading himself too thin. While his real estate ventures required his direct involvement and a significant amount of capital, licensing deals provided a steady stream of revenue with minimal effort on his part. By leveraging his name as a commodity, Trump could reap the benefits of global expansion without the risks traditionally associated with large-scale development. This also insulated him from the potential failure of individual projects; if a venture faltered, his personal wealth and reputation were not directly tied to its success.

Another key aspect of Trump's licensing strategy was his ability to use these deals to keep his name in the public eye. Each new product launch or real estate deal bearing the Trump name became an opportunity for media coverage and public attention. Trump, ever the showman, capitalized on these moments to promote himself and his brand. Whether it was a ribbon-cutting at a new Trump Tower or the unveiling of a new Trump-endorsed product, Trump used licensing deals as marketing tools, ensuring that his name remained relevant and top-of-mind in public discourse.

Licensing also allowed Trump to position himself as a global brand. By attaching his name to developments and products in international markets, he expanded his influence far beyond the United States. From luxury towers in Asia to branded products in Europe, the Trump name became a global symbol of American-style success. This international reach was crucial in maintaining the Trump brand's allure, as it created the perception that Trump was not just a domestic real estate mogul, but a global business icon.

Ultimately, the decision to license the Trump name was a turning point in Donald Trump's career. It allowed him to multiply the reach of his brand exponentially, turning "Trump" into a symbol that could be applied to anything from real estate to consumer products. Through licensing, Trump moved beyond being a mere businessman—he became a brand in and of himself. This move would prove essential in the years to come, as Trump transitioned from the world of business to that of media and politics. The Trump name, once a simple marker of real estate success, had evolved into a global icon, ready to be leveraged in any industry Trump chose to enter.

Expanding into Media and Entertainment

Donald Trump's ability to expand his brand beyond traditional business ventures took a dramatic leap forward when he entered the world of media and entertainment. While Trump had always understood the value of publicity, it was in the late 1990s and early 2000s that he fully embraced the power of television and other media platforms to enhance and extend his brand. In doing so, Trump didn't just build a business empire—he transformed himself into a household name that transcended industries. His media ventures played a crucial role in shaping the public's perception of him as not only a real estate mogul but also a pop culture figure, a celebrity, and ultimately, a politician.

Trump's fascination with the entertainment industry wasn't new. Throughout the 1980s and 1990s, he had appeared in television shows, films, and even music videos, often portraying himself or a version of his larger-than-life persona. These appearances, although brief, helped cement his image as a symbol of wealth and success. But Trump knew that fleeting cameos wouldn't be enough to fully capitalize on the potential of media exposure. He needed a platform that would allow him to showcase his personality, business acumen, and larger-than-life attitude to a much broader audience. That platform arrived in the form of The Apprentice.

When The Apprentice debuted in 2004, it marked a turning point for Trump's media presence. The show was more than just a competition to find a promising new business talent—it was a vehicle for the Trump brand. Every episode was a showcase of Trump's business instincts, his authority, and his persona as a decisive, no-nonsense leader. The catchphrase "You're fired" became iconic, and Trump himself became an even more familiar figure in living rooms across America. Week after week, millions of viewers tuned in to watch Trump dispense advice, judge candidates, and ultimately crown a winner. The show wasn't just a success in ratings; it made Trump a staple of American pop culture.

The Apprentice allowed Trump to control the narrative about himself. While his business dealings had always been scrutinized by the media, often in ways he didn't like, the show provided him with a platform to present himself exactly as he wanted: the ultimate dealmaker, someone who could spot talent and success from a mile away. He was portrayed as the embodiment of the American dream—a man who had built an empire and was now sharing his wisdom with others. The controlled environment of reality television suited Trump's need to shape his public image, and he used it expertly to reinforce the core attributes of the Trump brand: luxury, success, and power.

Beyond The Apprentice, Trump continued to expand his presence in media, understanding that entertainment was a critical component of maintaining his public visibility. His name was attached to numerous high-profile events, perhaps none more so than the Miss Universe pageant. Trump purchased the pageant in 1996 and turned it into a global spectacle. Under his ownership, the pageant became more than just a beauty contest—it was a platform for promoting the Trump brand on a global scale. The lavish production, glamorous contestants, and star-studded judges mirrored the Trump brand's ethos of luxury and opulence. The Miss Universe pageant also gave Trump access to international audiences, further expanding the reach of his brand beyond the United States.

Trump's media ventures weren't limited to television. He also became a regular presence in print media, with multiple books bearing his name. His best-selling book, The Art of the Deal, was first published in 1987, long before his foray into television. In it, Trump outlined his approach to business, negotiations, and success, reinforcing the image of himself as a master dealmaker. The book became a blueprint for aspiring entrepreneurs, and its success helped establish Trump as a thought leader in business circles. Trump followed up with several other books over the years, all reinforcing his personal brand. These books served not only as extensions of the Trump business philosophy but also as vehicles for self-promotion. Each new release brought Trump back into the media spotlight, allowing him to further propagate his brand.

One of Trump's most effective strategies was his ability to turn every media appearance, no matter how small, into a branding opportunity. Whether it was appearing on talk shows, giving interviews to magazines, or making guest appearances in movies, Trump knew how to keep his name in the public eye. Even his personal life became part of his brand. High-profile marriages, divorces, and social events were covered in tabloids and gossip columns, adding to the mystique of Donald Trump as a man who lived an extraordinary life. This constant media presence, combined with his business ventures and celebrity persona, ensured that Trump remained relevant in an ever-evolving entertainment landscape.

Another key factor in Trump's media expansion was his ability to blend reality with performance. Although The Apprentice was framed as a reality show about business, much of it was carefully curated to amplify Trump's persona. Contestants were chosen to fit certain narratives, boardroom meetings were edited for maximum drama, and Trump's final decisions were often made with entertainment value in mind. This blending of reality and performance was a hallmark of Trump's approach to media. He understood that in the world of entertainment, perception was just as important—if not more so—than reality. By presenting himself as the ultimate authority figure on the show, Trump reinforced the public perception that he was an unstoppable force in both business and life.

Ultimately, Trump's media ventures were instrumental in transforming his brand into something larger than life. He wasn't just a businessman anymore—he was a celebrity, a reality TV star, and an entertainer. This elevation of his persona through entertainment allowed him to reach an audience far beyond the world of real estate and business. People who had never heard of Trump Tower or his Atlantic City casinos knew him from The Apprentice. Those who had never followed his real estate deals could still quote his famous catchphrases. Trump had effectively turned himself into a character, one that millions of people recognized and, in many cases, admired.

By the time Trump entered politics, his brand had already been solidified through years of media exposure. His reality TV career had made him a familiar face, his books had cemented his image as a successful businessman, and his constant presence in entertainment media had kept him in the public eye. The groundwork for his political rise had been laid, not through traditional political pathways, but through the power of media and entertainment. In many ways, Donald Trump's success in media was a precursor to his eventual run for the presidency. He had learned how to captivate an audience, control his image, and turn controversy into attention—skills that would serve him well as he transitioned from entertainment to the highest office in the land.

Mastering the Media Narrative

Donald Trump's rise as a media magnet was not just about his appearances on television or his ventures into entertainment; it was about his mastery of the media narrative. From the early days of his career, Trump understood that controlling the narrative about himself was key to maintaining and expanding his influence. He wasn't just content to let the media define him—he sought to shape how he was perceived, using every available platform to reinforce the image he wanted to project. This ability to manipulate media coverage and use it to his advantage became one of Trump's most powerful tools in building his brand.

Trump's media strategy was rooted in a simple principle: any attention was better than no attention. He wasn't afraid of controversy, and in fact, he often courted it. Whether it was feuding with celebrities, sparring with journalists, or making bold, sometimes outlandish statements, Trump knew that controversy generated headlines—and headlines kept him relevant. He understood that the modern media ecosystem thrived on drama and sensationalism, and he skillfully fed that appetite. By staying in the public eye, even when the attention wasn't entirely positive, Trump ensured that his name remained on everyone's lips.

One of the key moments in Trump's media manipulation came in the 1980s when he began courting New York's tabloid press. At the time, Trump was still primarily known as a real estate developer, but he had bigger ambitions. He knew that to become more than just a businessman, he needed to be a public figure—someone people talked about. To achieve this, Trump began building relationships with reporters, especially those from the city's infamous tabloids like the New York Post and the Daily News. These papers thrived on gossip, scandal, and larger-than-life personalities, and Trump was more than willing to oblige. He provided them with stories—some true, some exaggerated, some purely for the sake of grabbing attention—and in return, they kept him in the headlines.

In some cases, Trump even acted as his own publicist. He famously used pseudonyms like "John Barron" and "John Miller" to call reporters and plant stories about himself, particularly about his wealth, business deals, and romantic exploits. This tactic allowed Trump to control the narrative without revealing that he was the source of the information. By pretending to be someone else, Trump could create buzz around his persona, further fueling his public image as a wealthy, powerful, and desirable figure. This blend of self-promotion and media manipulation demonstrated Trump's deep understanding of how to exploit the press for personal gain.

Trump's mastery of the media narrative also extended to how he handled criticism and negative press. While most public figures might shy away from bad publicity, Trump embraced it. Rather than avoiding controversy, he often leaned into it, using negative stories as opportunities to gain even more attention. He would spar publicly with critics, knowing that every back-and-forth would keep him in the news cycle longer. Trump's famous feud with The New York Times is a prime example of this strategy. While many public figures would have avoided confrontation with such a prestigious newspaper, Trump engaged in a running battle with the publication, often accusing it of bias or "fake news." This not only kept him in the headlines but also allowed him to frame himself as a victim of unfair attacks, further rallying his supporters and strengthening his public persona as a fighter who wouldn't back down.

One of Trump's greatest strengths in managing the media was his ability to pivot attention. Whenever a story threatened to damage his reputation or brand, he would often create a new controversy or generate a bigger story to distract from the negative coverage. This tactic was especially effective during his time on The Apprentice. If a business deal faltered or a negative report surfaced about his personal life, Trump would often make a bold statement or take a public stance on an unrelated issue, redirecting the media's focus. By constantly shifting the narrative, Trump ensured that the public's attention was always on him, but rarely for the same reason twice.

Trump also mastered the art of turning media appearances into promotional opportunities. In every interview, television appearance, or public event, Trump made sure to mention his projects, his name, and his brand. He understood that every media moment could serve as free advertising for the Trump Organization and his personal brand. Whether he was appearing on late-night talk shows or speaking at a business conference,

Trump was always in promotion mode. Even when he was ostensibly talking about one subject, he would find a way to steer the conversation back to his achievements, his wealth, and his success. This relentless self-promotion kept his brand front and center, ensuring that the Trump name was synonymous with power and success.

Trump's relationship with the media wasn't always combative. In fact, he had a knack for charming certain journalists and media outlets, cultivating favorable coverage when it suited him. He gave exclusive interviews to select reporters, granted access to his luxurious properties, and made sure that media personalities who portrayed him in a positive light were rewarded with more access. This symbiotic relationship allowed Trump to maintain control over his public image, even as he dealt with more critical outlets.

At the same time, Trump wasn't afraid to reinvent himself through the media when necessary. In the 1990s, after a series of financial setbacks, including the near-collapse of his Atlantic City casinos, Trump faced the possibility of being written off as a failed businessman. Rather than retreating from the spotlight, he doubled down on his media presence. He embraced his role as a public figure and used it to stage a comeback, once again positioning himself as a symbol of resilience and success. He appeared on talk shows, gave interviews about his financial rebound, and began laying the groundwork for what would become his future media endeavors, including The Apprentice.

In essence, Trump's ability to control the media narrative was one of the most important aspects of his rise to fame and influence. He knew that in the modern world, perception often outweighed reality, and he skillfully manipulated the media to shape the perception that he was always winning, always in control, and always the ultimate dealmaker. Whether through controversy, promotion, or carefully crafted media moments, Trump ensured that his brand remained strong and visible. This media mastery not only helped him build his business empire but also played a crucial role in his eventual leap into the political arena, where controlling the narrative became even more critical.

Trump and the Social Media Revolution

As traditional media evolved, Donald Trump's ability to adapt and leverage new forms of communication became one of his most powerful tools. In the early 2000s, as social media platforms like Twitter, Facebook, and YouTube emerged, they transformed the landscape of public discourse and media consumption. Trump, always a keen observer of how to shape public opinion, was quick to recognize the potential of social media to bypass traditional gatekeepers like newspapers and television networks. He used these platforms to communicate directly with the public, amplifying his celebrity, reinforcing his brand, and eventually, launching his political career.

Twitter, in particular, became Trump's medium of choice. It offered a direct, unfiltered way for him to express his opinions, respond to critics, and promote his projects. Unlike television appearances or newspaper interviews, which could be edited or filtered through a reporter's lens, social media allowed Trump to control the message entirely. With the push of a button, he could reach millions of followers, influencing public debate and commanding attention in real-time. His tweets, often provocative and combative, quickly became a central part of his public persona.

Trump's approach to social media was unlike that of most public figures. While many celebrities and business leaders used social media for carefully crafted, polished messages, Trump's tweets were raw, often posted at odd hours, and filled with bold, sometimes inflammatory rhetoric. This style resonated with many Americans who felt that Trump was speaking directly to them without the filter of political correctness or the media establishment. His social media presence mirrored the brash, unfiltered persona he had cultivated for years, but now it was magnified by the reach of the internet.

One of the reasons Trump was so effective on social media was his ability to dominate news cycles. In the world of 24-hour news, journalists and outlets were constantly searching for the next big story. Trump understood this hunger for content and fed it with a steady stream of provocative statements and comments on social media. Whether it was a controversial tweet or a heated response to criticism, Trump knew that each post would generate headlines, debates, and reactions from both supporters and detractors. This constant activity ensured that he remained at the center of public discourse, even when traditional media might have moved on to other subjects.

Trump also used social media to brand himself as a truth-teller, positioning himself against what he frequently called the "fake news" media. By casting doubt on traditional news outlets and presenting himself as the only reliable source of information, Trump cultivated a loyal following who saw his tweets as the unvarnished truth. This strategy allowed him to sidestep critical media coverage and reframe negative stories to his advantage. When mainstream outlets reported negatively on his businesses, personal life, or political stances, Trump would often counter these reports with his own narrative on social media, further solidifying his image as a man who wasn't afraid to challenge the establishment.

Another key aspect of Trump's social media strategy was his ability to turn minor incidents into major stories. Trump often picked fights with celebrities, politicians, and media figures on Twitter, knowing that each feud would be covered extensively by the press. These public spats, whether with high-profile figures like Rosie O'Donnell, or political rivals, helped Trump stay in the headlines. More importantly, they allowed him to frame these battles as personal victories, casting himself as a fighter who wouldn't back down from anyone, no matter how famous or powerful they were. This combative persona resonated deeply with his followers, many of whom saw Trump as someone willing to take on the elites and the media in ways that others wouldn't.

Trump's social media dominance was also a key factor in how he framed his business and personal successes. Whether promoting new ventures or responding to setbacks, Trump used platforms like Twitter to present an image of himself as a perpetual winner. He would frequently tweet about his business deals, luxurious properties, and television ratings, all designed to reinforce the notion that the Trump brand was synonymous with success. Even when facing financial challenges or legal disputes, Trump would present these situations as minor hurdles in his broader narrative of triumph. In this way, social media became a tool for managing and enhancing the Trump brand in real-time.

The direct interaction with his followers on social media also played into Trump's long-standing image as a man of the people. While his wealth and luxurious lifestyle set him apart, his social media presence made him feel accessible to ordinary people. Trump's followers could read his unfiltered thoughts, respond to him, and even get retweeted by him, creating a sense of intimacy and connection that traditional media didn't offer. This direct line of communication made Trump appear more authentic to his base, further solidifying their loyalty. In an age where many public figures were seen as distant and out of touch, Trump used social media to cultivate an image of himself as someone who was constantly engaged with the people.

While Trump's social media mastery was evident long before his political career, it became even more pronounced as he transitioned from business to politics. His ability to control the narrative on social platforms played a crucial role in his 2016 presidential campaign, where he bypassed traditional political norms and used Twitter as his primary means of communication. His unorthodox approach, which included attacking rivals, making bold policy announcements, and engaging directly with voters, turned social media into one of the most important tools in modern politics.

Even after achieving political success, Trump continued to use social media in ways that other public figures did not. His tweets were often the subject of news stories, diplomatic discussions, and even global debates, proving that social media had given him a platform that rivaled the reach of traditional media outlets. More than just a tool for communication, social media had become a central part of Trump's brand and influence.

Ultimately, Donald Trump's use of social media was a natural extension of his long-standing approach to media and public relations. Just as he had dominated headlines in the tabloids and controlled the narrative on television, Trump adapted to the digital age by mastering platforms like Twitter and Facebook. His ability to create controversy, frame narratives, and communicate directly with the public ensured that his brand remained not only relevant but dominant in the modern media landscape. In many ways, social media became the culmination of Trump's media strategy, allowing him to maintain control over his image and continue building his brand in ways that few others could. Through social media, Donald Trump solidified his place not just as a businessman or a celebrity, but as a cultural and political force with unprecedented influence.

Chapter 8

Chapter 8: Navigating Public Controversies

The Atlantic City Casino Bankruptcies

In the early 1990s, Donald Trump found himself in the midst of one of the greatest financial crises of his career. At the heart of the storm were his lavish Atlantic City casino ventures, which had been the crown jewels of his expanding empire. These towering monuments of glitz and glamour, including the Trump Plaza, Trump Castle, and the grandiose Trump Taj Mahal, were intended to cement Trump's reputation as the king of Atlantic City's burgeoning casino scene. However, behind the veneer of success lay an unstable foundation built on excessive borrowing and a gambling market that was quickly becoming saturated.

The signs of trouble began to emerge almost as soon as Trump opened the doors to the Taj Mahal in 1990. Billed as the "eighth wonder of the world," the Taj was an audacious bet that Trump had placed on his ability to outshine his competitors and attract high-rolling gamblers to Atlantic City. But the reality was far more complex. Trump had financed the construction of the Taj Mahal almost entirely with junk bonds, carrying a hefty interest rate of 14%. The debt load on the project was enormous, and the casino needed to generate an extraordinary amount of revenue just to stay afloat. Unfortunately for Trump, the casino market was already overextended, and the expected flood of customers never materialized.

By 1991, the Trump Taj Mahal was facing severe financial difficulties. As profits failed to meet projections, Trump's empire began to unravel. With billions of dollars in debt, Trump was forced to make difficult decisions to avoid personal financial ruin. The Trump Organization was in crisis mode, and Trump had to file for Chapter 11 bankruptcy protection for the Taj Mahal and, eventually, for two of his other Atlantic City properties. This move allowed Trump to restructure his debts but came at a significant cost to his reputation.

In the world of business, bankruptcy often carries a stigma of failure, but Trump was determined to rewrite the narrative. Rather than shying away from the situation, he faced it head-on, publicly framing the bankruptcies not as personal defeats but as smart business decisions. He maintained that the bankruptcies were necessary to protect the Trump Organization and argued that they were simply a part of doing business in a volatile market. Trump positioned himself as a savvy negotiator who could turn a bad situation into a beneficial outcome. This ability to control the narrative was central to how Trump managed his public persona during times of crisis.

One of Trump's key strategies in navigating the bankruptcies was to downplay the personal impact. Despite the financial troubles of his casinos, Trump made it clear that his personal wealth was not at risk. He highlighted that his other ventures—such as his real estate holdings in New York City, including Trump Tower, and his international properties—remained profitable and successful. This helped him maintain the image of a larger-than-life mogul who could weather any storm. By distancing his personal fortune from the failing casinos, Trump was able to keep his public image intact and continue projecting confidence.

Trump also leveraged the media to his advantage, a tactic he had perfected throughout his career. Rather than allowing reporters to define the story as one of financial ruin, Trump actively engaged with the press, often framing the bankruptcies as part of his strategic brilliance. In interviews, he would explain that the bankruptcies were necessary tools to reorganize debt and streamline his operations. By controlling the media narrative, Trump was able to soften the blow of what could have been a devastating public relations disaster. His charismatic, unflinching demeanor in the face of these challenges helped to keep his image as a successful businessman intact.

Another aspect of Trump's strategy was his ability to turn the experience into a learning opportunity. Publicly, Trump would later describe the Atlantic City bankruptcies as important lessons in financial management. He portrayed himself as someone who could take risks, learn from failures, and come back stronger. This narrative of resilience became a cornerstone of his brand, reinforcing the idea that even in the face of adversity, Trump was a figure who could adapt and emerge victorious.

Despite the bankruptcies, Trump managed to retain control of his Atlantic City properties through a series of renegotiations with creditors. While his equity in the casinos was reduced, he kept a stake in the businesses and remained at the helm of the operations. This allowed Trump to continue to benefit from his Atlantic City ventures, even as they went through financial restructuring. By the mid-1990s, Trump's casino empire had stabilized, though it never reached the levels of profitability he had initially envisioned. Nonetheless, Trump's ability to manage the fallout from the bankruptcies without suffering a total collapse was a testament to his negotiating skills and media savvy.

The Atlantic City bankruptcies were a defining moment in Trump's career, showcasing both the risks he was willing to take and his ability to bounce back from failure. While other business moguls might have seen their reputations destroyed by such a public financial collapse, Trump turned it into an opportunity to reinforce his image as a tenacious dealmaker. His handling of the crisis set the stage for his future endeavors, including his eventual foray into reality television and politics, where his persona as a resilient, ever-confident winner would be even more critical to his success.

In the end, the Atlantic City bankruptcies did not ruin Donald Trump. Instead, they became part of the larger narrative of his life—one in which setbacks were temporary and even failures could be spun into victories. It was this ability to navigate controversy and emerge with his brand intact that would serve him well in the years to come, as his public profile continued to grow and his influence expanded far beyond the world of business.

Personal Scandals and Divorce

Donald Trump's personal life has always been intertwined with his public image. In the late 1980s and early 1990s, his marriage to Ivana Trump, a Czech-born former model and businesswoman, was part of the glamorous façade that Trump presented to the world. Together, they represented a power couple that dominated tabloid headlines and appeared at the most exclusive events. Ivana wasn't just Trump's wife; she played a crucial role in his business empire, managing several of his properties, including the Plaza Hotel in New York. However, their seemingly perfect marriage began to unravel in the most public and scandalous way possible, making headlines that threatened to overshadow Trump's business accomplishments.

At the center of the scandal was Trump's extramarital affair with Marla Maples, a young actress and beauty queen from Georgia. Rumors of the affair began circulating in 1989, but it wasn't until 1990 that the story broke wide open. The New York tabloids, always hungry for a juicy scandal, covered the affair in excruciating detail. Headlines about Trump's secret meetings with Maples and their alleged romantic trysts dominated the front pages. One particularly infamous headline read, "Best Sex I Ever Had," supposedly quoting Maples about her relationship with Trump. Whether the quote was accurate or exaggerated by the media, it became a defining moment in the public perception of the scandal.

The fallout from the affair was swift and dramatic. Ivana Trump filed for divorce in 1990, citing "cruel and inhuman treatment" in the legal documents. The divorce proceedings quickly became a media spectacle, with reporters and photographers camped outside the courtrooms and family events. Trump's private life was on full display, and the story was too sensational for the public to ignore. For many, it became a soap opera playing out in real life, with Trump cast as the wealthy businessman who couldn't resist temptation, and Ivana as the betrayed wife.

Rather than retreating from the spotlight during this intensely personal and public crisis, Trump did what he always did: he leaned into the media attention. He gave interviews and made appearances, downplaying the affair as a personal matter but never fully stepping away from the tabloid frenzy. In a sense, Trump understood that the scandal, while damaging on a personal level, also kept him in the headlines, feeding the public's fascination with his life. It was this constant attention—good or bad—that Trump understood as a form of power. The media coverage may have been unflattering, but it reinforced his celebrity status.

One of Trump's key strategies during this period was to reframe the scandal. He positioned himself not as the villain of the story, but as a man caught between two women, a victim of the complexities of love and fame. In interviews, he would talk about the pressures of his public life and how difficult it was to manage both a business empire and personal relationships. While Ivana was often portrayed sympathetically in the media, Trump never allowed himself to be cast solely as the antagonist. His charisma and brash attitude helped him maintain a degree of control over the narrative, even as the press continued to scrutinize his every move.

Despite the turmoil in his personal life, Trump's brand remained resilient. The divorce settlement with Ivana was costly—reportedly around $25 million—but it didn't financially cripple him. Ivana received a significant payout, along with various properties, including a mansion in Connecticut and a share of their Florida estate, Mar-a-Lago. However, Trump's business empire, though strained by the concurrent financial crises of his Atlantic City casinos, continued to function, and he maintained his high profile in both business and social circles. Trump's ability to separate his personal scandals from his business dealings was crucial in keeping his brand from collapsing.

The scandal also had a surprising effect on Trump's public image. While some saw him as a playboy billionaire living a reckless life, others were drawn to the very drama that surrounded him. Trump's affair with Maples and the subsequent divorce became part of his larger-than-life persona. In many ways, he embodied the excess and extravagance of the 1980s—a man whose personal and professional lives were marked by high stakes, glamour, and controversy. This aura of unpredictability, while off-putting to some, made him endlessly fascinating to the public.

In 1993, Trump married Marla Maples in a highly publicized ceremony at the Plaza Hotel. The marriage was short-lived, and the couple divorced in 1999, but by then, the scandal had largely run its course. The media had moved on, and Trump had weathered the storm. He emerged from the ordeal not only intact but with his public profile even higher. His ability to turn personal controversies into public fascination, and to stay relevant through the media circus, was a testament to his understanding of fame in modern America. He knew that as long as people were talking about him, he was winning.

Trump's personal scandals, rather than derailing his career, ultimately reinforced his reputation as a figure who thrived in the chaos. He demonstrated a remarkable ability to compartmentalize his public and private lives, using the media to his advantage even when the story was unfavorable. This period of intense personal scrutiny taught Trump valuable lessons about navigating public controversies—lessons he would draw on time and again in the years to come as he continued to build his brand. The divorce, the affair, and the media spectacle surrounding them became just another chapter in the larger-than-life story of Donald Trump, a man who refused to be defined by scandal and who understood that fame, in any form, was its own kind of currency.

Lawsuits, Legal Battles, and Public Disputes

For Donald Trump, lawsuits and legal battles have been an inescapable part of his career, both as a real estate mogul and a public figure. Over the years, he has been involved in a staggering number of legal disputes, ranging from contractor lawsuits to allegations of racial discrimination in his housing developments. Yet, much like with other controversies, Trump managed to transform these legal battles into opportunities to bolster his reputation as a tough, no-nonsense businessman who wasn't afraid to fight back. While most moguls try to avoid the spotlight during legal disputes, Trump often used these public controversies to reinforce his image as a combative, resilient figure who would never back down.

One of the earliest and most significant legal challenges Trump faced was in the 1970s when the Department of Justice sued him and his father, Fred Trump, for racial discrimination in their housing complexes. The suit, filed in 1973, accused the Trumps of refusing to rent apartments to Black tenants, a serious violation of the Fair Housing Act. The case made headlines and put the Trump Organization under intense public scrutiny. For most developers, such a high-profile lawsuit would have been a devastating blow, especially for someone like Donald Trump, who was still trying to build his public persona and establish his business empire.

But Trump, under the mentorship of the notorious lawyer Roy Cohn, took an aggressive stance. Rather than settle quickly or admit fault, Trump countersued the government for $100 million, accusing the Department of Justice of defamation and unfair treatment. While the countersuit was dismissed, Trump's bold, unapologetic approach to the case sent a clear message: he would not be pushed around by the government or anyone else. By adopting an aggressive legal strategy, Trump turned the narrative from one of discrimination to one of him being a victim of overreach by the government. This strategy, though controversial, set the tone for how Trump would handle legal battles for the rest of his career.

The case eventually settled in 1975 with Trump agreeing to comply with the Fair Housing Act and take steps to ensure his properties did not discriminate. Crucially, though, the settlement did not include any admission of guilt or wrongdoing. For Trump, this was a victory. He had managed to navigate a serious legal challenge without tarnishing his brand. The case illustrated a key aspect of Trump's approach to controversy: he rarely, if ever, admits fault. By avoiding admission of guilt, Trump was able to continue presenting himself as a successful, ethical businessman, even when the facts suggested otherwise.

Another major legal battle came in the 1980s when Trump clashed with contractors over the construction of his most iconic property, Trump Tower. The project was a testament to Trump's ambition—a shimmering glass tower that would redefine the New York City skyline and serve as the headquarters of his growing empire. But the project was also mired in legal disputes. Several contractors sued Trump for not paying them for their work. These lawsuits alleged that Trump had withheld payments, leaving contractors and subcontractors struggling to cover their own costs. For a man who prided himself on his business acumen, these lawsuits were potentially damaging, painting a picture of a ruthless businessman who didn't honor his contracts.

Once again, Trump fought back hard. He denied the allegations, claiming that the contractors had not completed their work to his satisfaction or had overcharged him. In Trump's view, he was simply protecting his financial interests and ensuring that the project was completed to the highest standard. While some of the lawsuits were settled out of court, Trump's aggressive stance sent a message to anyone doing business with him: if you come after Trump, expect a fight. His ability to navigate these disputes without suffering lasting damage to his reputation demonstrated his skill at managing public controversies.

Trump's legal battles weren't limited to business. He also became embroiled in numerous personal disputes that played out in the public eye. For instance, in the late 1980s, Trump sued the author of the book *Trump: The Deals and the Downfall*, which painted an unflattering picture of his business practices. Trump claimed the book was full of inaccuracies and sought millions in damages. Although the case was eventually dismissed, Trump's willingness to use the courts to silence critics became a hallmark of his public persona. He frequently threatened lawsuits against journalists, authors, and even business rivals who dared to question his success or integrity. For Trump, lawsuits were not just legal actions; they were a way to control the narrative and protect his brand.

Perhaps one of the most notable examples of Trump's use of legal disputes to his advantage came in his ongoing feuds with the media. Throughout his career, Trump has been a vocal critic of the press, accusing them of spreading "fake news" and unfairly targeting him. He has filed or threatened to file lawsuits against numerous media outlets for defamation. One famous case involved the *New York Times*, which published a story in 2005 suggesting that Trump had overstated his wealth. Trump sued for $5 billion, a staggering amount that drew widespread media attention. Although the lawsuit was dismissed, it demonstrated Trump's willingness to use the courts to challenge any narrative that painted him in a negative light.

These legal battles, while often dismissed or settled, reinforced Trump's brand as a fighter. He positioned himself as a man who wouldn't hesitate to stand up for himself, his businesses, and his reputation, no matter the cost. The sheer number of lawsuits Trump was involved in—both as a plaintiff and a defendant—became part of his larger-than-life persona. To his supporters, these legal disputes only reinforced the idea that Trump was a man who didn't back down, a quality that would later resonate deeply when he entered the political arena.

In the end, Trump's ability to navigate lawsuits and legal challenges without significant damage to his brand was remarkable. Whether he won or lost in court was almost secondary to how he handled the public perception of these disputes.

By consistently framing himself as the victim of unfair attacks, whether from contractors, rivals, or the media, Trump was able to maintain his image as a successful, resilient businessman. His legal battles were just another battlefield in his ongoing quest to build and protect the Trump brand—a brand that would prove resilient through decades of public scrutiny, controversy, and legal challenge.

Feuds with Public Figures and Rivals

Donald Trump's rise to prominence has been marked by a string of high-profile feuds with public figures, celebrities, and business rivals. For Trump, these public disputes weren't just personal; they were part of a calculated strategy to keep himself in the spotlight and cement his persona as a larger-than-life figure who didn't shy away from confrontation. Trump's willingness to engage in public spats—often with inflammatory rhetoric—became a defining feature of his public image and would later fuel his transition from business mogul to political figure.

One of Trump's earliest and most notorious feuds was with New York City Mayor Ed Koch in the 1980s. Trump, still relatively young and building his real estate empire, clashed with Koch over the city's management of various real estate projects, most notably the Wollman Rink in Central Park. The city had spent millions of dollars and years trying to renovate the ice skating rink, but the project had stalled repeatedly. Trump, ever the opportunist, offered to take over the renovation himself, claiming he could complete it faster and cheaper than the city government.

The rivalry between Trump and Koch quickly became personal. Koch, known for his sharp wit and acerbic personality, publicly called Trump "piggy, piggy, piggy" and mocked his grandstanding. Trump, never one to back down from a fight, fired back, calling Koch "a disaster" and accusing him of mismanaging the city. The feud played out in the media, with both men trading insults in the press, but Trump ultimately emerged victorious when he completed the Wollman Rink renovation in just a few months and under budget. This public success reinforced Trump's image as a businessman who could get things done and further solidified his reputation for outmaneuvering bureaucrats.

This battle with Koch set the stage for many of Trump's future public feuds. He thrived on conflict and used it as a way to keep his name in the headlines. Whether the disputes were based on legitimate business disagreements or personal vendettas, Trump knew that a public feud could generate media attention, which in turn fueled his celebrity. By positioning himself as a fighter who wouldn't be bullied by anyone—whether a politician, a rival developer, or a celebrity—Trump managed to turn even negative press into an advantage.

Another infamous feud occurred in the late 1980s when Trump found himself at odds with media mogul Merv Griffin. Griffin, a wealthy television producer and talk show host, was also eyeing properties in Atlantic City, where Trump had already established a presence with his casinos. The two titans of industry went head-to-head in a battle to control Resorts International, a casino company with prime real estate in the area. The public rivalry between Trump and Griffin captivated the media, as both men made aggressive moves to outbid and outmaneuver each other.

The feud escalated when Trump accused Griffin of using unfair tactics to seize control of Resorts International. Trump, always the showman, didn't hesitate to make his opinions known to the press, criticizing Griffin's business acumen and questioning his motives. Griffin, for his part, remained largely silent, choosing to fight his battle behind the scenes. In the end, Griffin won control of the company, but Trump managed to walk away with a significant financial settlement, allowing him to save face and claim some degree of victory. As with many of Trump's rivalries, the battle wasn't just about the business deal—it was about who could control the narrative. Even in defeat, Trump found a way to emerge from the feud with his image as a hard-nosed businessman intact.

Public feuds weren't limited to Trump's business rivals; he also had a knack for getting into high-profile celebrity disputes that played out on a national stage. One such feud occurred in the mid-2000s when Trump clashed with Rosie O'Donnell, the outspoken talk show host and comedian. The feud began when O'Donnell, during a segment on The View, mocked Trump for his handling of the Miss USA scandal, in which one of the pageant winners had been caught engaging in controversial behavior. O'Donnell criticized Trump's decision to give the pageant winner a second chance, accusing him of being a "snake-oil salesman" and calling his character into question.

Trump, never one to let an insult go unanswered, responded with a tirade against O'Donnell. He called her a "loser," "fat," and "a real slob," escalating the feud to a personal level. The media quickly picked up on the story, and the feud dominated headlines for weeks. O'Donnell fired back, accusing Trump of being a misogynist and a bully. The public spat drew enormous attention, not just because of the insults traded, but because it became a proxy for larger cultural conversations about gender, power, and celebrity. Despite the ugliness of the feud, Trump's willingness to engage so openly and viciously only reinforced his brand as someone who never backed down from a fight, no matter how personal it got.

Trump's public disputes extended to other realms as well, including the sports world. One of his more infamous battles came in the mid-1980s when Trump purchased the New Jersey Generals, a team in the United States Football League (USFL), a competitor to the National Football League (NFL). Trump quickly became a vocal critic of the NFL, accusing them of monopolizing the sport and advocating for the USFL to move to a fall schedule to directly compete with the more established league. His aggressive tactics and public attacks on the NFL led to a lawsuit, with the USFL accusing the NFL of violating antitrust laws.

The legal battle ended disastrously for Trump and the USFL. While the court ruled in favor of the USFL, it awarded them only a symbolic $1 in damages, effectively dooming the fledgling league. Yet, despite the failure of the USFL, Trump walked away with his public image largely unscathed. He had taken on the NFL, one of the most powerful organizations in sports, and had not shied away from the fight. For Trump, the battle was more about making headlines and maintaining his public profile than about the actual outcome.

Throughout his career, Trump's public feuds have served as a way to keep his name in the news, even when the stakes were relatively low. Whether it was a spat with a mayor, a media mogul, or a celebrity, Trump knew that conflict generated attention, and attention was the lifeblood of his brand. His combative style, his willingness to go toe-to-toe with anyone, and his flair for the dramatic all contributed to the creation of the Trump persona—a persona built on defiance, resilience, and a refusal to be ignored. These public disputes were never just about winning or losing; for Trump, they were about maintaining his place in the public consciousness, ensuring that his name—and brand—remained at the center of the conversation.

The Trump University Scandal—Brand vs. Reality

One of the most damaging public controversies in Donald Trump's career came in the form of the Trump University scandal. It was a moment that threatened to expose the gap between Trump's carefully crafted public persona of success and the reality of his business practices. The controversy centered around Trump University, a for-profit education company that offered real estate training programs, promising students they could learn the secrets of Trump's business success. The reality, however, was far from what was advertised, and the ensuing legal battles and media coverage forced Trump to confront one of the most significant threats to his brand.

Trump University was launched in 2005, at a time when Trump's public image was riding high. His role as the host of *The Apprentice* had made him a household name, and his brand was synonymous with wealth, power, and success. The university was marketed as a way for ordinary people to learn from Trump himself, with advertisements prominently featuring his image and promises that students would gain the knowledge needed to build their own fortunes. The pitch was irresistible for many aspiring real estate investors who wanted to follow in Trump's footsteps.

The program was not a traditional university—it offered seminars, workshops, and mentoring programs, all for hefty fees. Students were encouraged to enroll in increasingly expensive packages, with some programs costing up to $35,000. The idea was that by paying these fees, students would gain access to Trump's "secrets" and insider knowledge, as well as one-on-one mentoring from experienced real estate professionals. The program's promotional materials made bold promises, featuring testimonials and imagery that suggested success was virtually guaranteed for those who enrolled.

However, by 2010, complaints began to mount. Students alleged that they had been misled by Trump University's marketing and that the courses they received were far from what was promised. Many students claimed they were pressured into paying for more expensive programs without receiving any valuable knowledge in return. They reported that the mentors and instructors were not hand-picked by Trump, as the advertisements implied, and that the program did not offer any real connection to Trump's business strategies. Worse, some alleged that the program preyed on vulnerable individuals, including retirees and those already struggling financially, selling them a false dream of wealth and success.

In 2013, New York's attorney general, Eric Schneiderman, filed a $40 million lawsuit against Trump University, accusing it of fraud. The lawsuit alleged that Trump and his university had engaged in deceptive practices, falsely advertising the program as a legitimate educational institution and misleading students into paying for services they did not receive. The suit, along with other class-action lawsuits filed by former students, painted a picture of Trump University as a predatory scheme designed to exploit Trump's celebrity and fleece consumers of their hard-earned money.

As the lawsuits progressed, Trump took a characteristically defiant stance. He refused to admit any wrongdoing, repeatedly claiming that Trump University had a high satisfaction rate among its students and dismissing the lawsuits as politically motivated attacks. He attacked Schneiderman personally, accusing him of seeking publicity and being part of a broader political effort to undermine his reputation. Despite mounting evidence against Trump University, Trump continued to assert that the program had been a success and that any negative claims were part of a smear campaign orchestrated by his enemies.

The media coverage of the Trump University lawsuits was intense, particularly as Trump's political profile began to rise in 2015 with his presidential campaign. Critics pointed to the scandal as evidence that Trump's business success was built on fraud and exploitation, while his supporters framed the lawsuits as yet another example of the establishment trying to tear him down. Trump's ability to maintain his loyal base of supporters, despite the growing evidence of wrongdoing, demonstrated the power of his brand. Even when faced with serious allegations, Trump managed to convince a significant portion of the public that he was being unfairly targeted.

In 2016, as Trump's presidential campaign gained steam, the Trump University lawsuits became a major issue on the campaign trail. His political opponents, particularly during the Republican primary, seized on the scandal as a way to undermine his credibility. Trump, however, continued to insist that he would prevail in court and that Trump University had done nothing wrong. His refusal to back down or admit fault became part of the broader narrative of his political campaign—he was the outsider taking on a corrupt system that was out to get him.

Ultimately, Trump settled the lawsuits in November 2016, just days after being elected president, for $25 million. The settlement allowed him to avoid a lengthy trial, but it also required him to compensate the thousands of former students who had filed claims against Trump University. Importantly, the settlement did not include an admission of guilt, which Trump framed as a victory. He continued to insist that the lawsuits were politically motivated and that he had chosen to settle simply to avoid the distraction of a court battle during his presidency.

The Trump University scandal was a critical moment in Trump's career because it exposed the fragility of the gap between Trump's public image and the reality of his business practices. For years, Trump had cultivated a persona of wealth and success, positioning himself as the ultimate American businessman who could turn anything into a success. Trump University, however, revealed the extent to which that persona relied on marketing, branding, and, in some cases, exploitation. The program promised students access to Trump's supposed secrets of success, but in reality, it offered little more than generic real estate advice and high-pressure sales tactics.

Despite the damaging details of the scandal, Trump's ability to settle the lawsuits without admitting guilt and maintain his brand's integrity was remarkable. For many public figures, such a controversy would have been a devastating blow. But Trump's handling of the situation—his refusal to back down, his attacks on his accusers, and his insistence that he was the victim of a political witch hunt—allowed him to emerge largely unscathed in the eyes of his supporters. The Trump University scandal became yet another example of Trump's resilience in the face of controversy, reinforcing his image as a fighter who wouldn't be taken down by critics or legal challenges.

In the end, the Trump University scandal reflected the broader themes of Trump's career: the power of branding, the importance of perception over reality, and the way Trump managed to turn even negative press into a tool for reinforcing his persona. For all the criticism and legal battles, Trump's brand remained intact, allowing him to continue his meteoric rise in the worlds of both business and politics.

Chapter 9

Chapter 9: Politics and Power

Early Political Ambitions and Explorations

Donald Trump's political ambitions were not a sudden development, nor were they born in 2015 when he descended the golden escalator at Trump Tower to announce his presidential candidacy. In reality, Trump had been toying with the idea of a political career for decades. Long before his meteoric rise to the presidency, he had expressed a fascination with politics and power, even as he built his real estate empire and established himself as a media personality.

The seeds of Trump's political aspirations were sown in the 1980s, a period when he was already becoming a household name in New York City. His successful real estate ventures, particularly the development of high-profile properties like Trump Tower, had catapulted him into the public eye, and with that visibility came a growing interest in political influence. Trump began to explore the idea of leveraging his business acumen and larger-than-life persona to gain a foothold in the political world. Throughout the 1980s, Trump made headlines with bold statements about the state of American politics, often positioning himself as someone who could "fix" the system with the same ruthless efficiency he claimed to bring to his business dealings.

In a 1987 interview with *The Washington Post*, Trump made one of his earliest public suggestions that he might someday run for president. The interview followed the publication of his first book, *The Art of the Deal*, which had turned him into a national celebrity and a symbol of American success. In the interview, Trump criticized U.S. foreign policy, particularly in relation to Japan, and hinted that he might consider running for office if the country needed him. "I don't want the presidency," he told the interviewer, "but I do want the country to be in better shape. And if it ever got so bad, I would never rule it out."

Trump's statements were typical of his approach at the time—suggestive, provocative, and non-committal. He recognized the power of public speculation and used it to keep his name in the news. Even though he wasn't seriously considering a presidential run in the 1980s, his comments served to build an image of him as a potential political savior, someone who could step in and use his business smarts to rescue America from its problems. This carefully constructed image would later prove to be a cornerstone of his 2016 campaign, but at the time, it was just another way for Trump to enhance his growing brand.

Throughout the late 1980s and into the 1990s, Trump continued to flirt with politics, attending events with political leaders and making sizable donations to both Republican and Democratic candidates. His political donations reflected a pragmatic approach rather than a clear ideological commitment. Trump supported politicians who could help his business interests, regardless of their party affiliation. This bipartisan support allowed him to cultivate relationships with key figures on both sides of the aisle, positioning himself as a power player who could influence politics without formally stepping into the ring.

In 1999, Trump's political ambitions seemed to take a more serious turn when he considered running for president as a candidate for the Reform Party, a third-party movement founded by businessman Ross Perot. Perot's own success in the 1992 presidential election, where he garnered nearly 19% of the popular vote, had demonstrated the potential for an outsider, particularly a businessman, to make waves in American politics. Trump saw an opportunity in the Reform Party, which had become disillusioned with the traditional two-party system. He launched an exploratory committee and began campaigning, advocating for policies such as universal healthcare, a flat tax, and a hard stance on trade with China.

Trump's brief foray into the Reform Party, however, was short-lived. He quickly grew frustrated with the party's internal divisions and the presence of controversial figures like David Duke, a former Ku Klux Klan leader who was also seeking the party's nomination. Trump withdrew from the race in early 2000, declaring that the Reform Party was "self-destructing" and that it was not a viable path to the presidency. His exit from the race was in line with his tendency to back out of situations that did not align with his long-term goals or public image. Even though his flirtation with the Reform Party was brief, it demonstrated his willingness to explore nontraditional routes to power and his awareness of the role third-party movements could play in disrupting the political landscape.

Despite stepping away from the 2000 election, Trump continued to publicly comment on political issues throughout the next decade. His interest in politics remained, though it was often overshadowed by his business ventures and his burgeoning career as a television personality with *The Apprentice*. Nevertheless, the groundwork for Trump's future political career was being laid. His consistent messaging about America's decline, his disdain for the political establishment, and his belief in the power of a strong, independent leader were themes that he would later amplify during his 2016 campaign.

Trump's early political ambitions reveal a man who was not content with success in business alone. He understood that real power in America lay not just in wealth but in political influence. While he may have been unsure about committing fully to a political career in the 1980s and 1990s, his public flirtations with the idea of running for president allowed him to maintain a level of political relevance that he would later capitalize on. His ability to blend business, media, and politics into a coherent brand would become one of his greatest strengths as he transitioned from real estate mogul to political heavyweight. In these early years, Trump was already laying the foundation for the seismic political shift he would lead in 2016, positioning himself as a potential outsider who could shake up the system when the time was right.

Transition from Business Mogul to Political Figure

As Donald Trump transitioned from the 20th to the 21st century, his identity as a businessman began to morph into something broader, more multifaceted, and politically charged. While real estate had been his primary domain, his growing presence in the media—and the way he navigated the spotlight—set him up for a much larger stage. It wasn't just his business dealings or his public persona that drew attention; it was his calculated use of the media and his ability to craft a narrative around his personal brand that made him more than just a businessman. In many ways, Trump had become a cultural phenomenon, someone whose celebrity status blurred the lines between entertainment, business, and politics.

Trump's public life during the early 2000s was defined by his starring role on *The Apprentice*, which launched in 2004 and turned him into a television icon. The show allowed Trump to project an image of a no-nonsense executive, making tough decisions and reinforcing the idea that he was someone who understood success in a way few others did. *The Apprentice* was more than just a hit reality show; it was a platform that gave Trump direct access to millions of Americans, week after week, in their living rooms. With each episode, his catchphrase "You're fired" became a cultural touchstone, symbolizing his authority and control. But beyond entertainment, the show served a more strategic purpose for Trump—it kept him relevant and positioned him as an authoritative figure in the minds of many Americans, not just in business but also in leadership.

At the same time, Trump's media presence began to extend into political commentary. While he had always been outspoken, especially when it came to criticizing politicians or policies that he felt harmed American business interests, his critiques started to take on a more pointed tone in the 2010s. His growing influence on social media, particularly on Twitter, provided him with an unfiltered platform to speak directly to the public. In this era, Trump's tweets were a mix of business promotion, personal boasts, and increasingly, political commentary. His opinions were often polarizing, but they had a way of cutting through the noise and capturing attention.

One of the most pivotal moments in Trump's transition from business mogul to political figure came in the form of the "birther" conspiracy theory, a baseless claim that President Barack Obama had not been born in the United States and was therefore ineligible for the presidency. Trump became one of the most vocal proponents of this conspiracy, demanding that Obama produce his birth certificate to prove his citizenship. While the claim was widely debunked, Trump's persistence on the issue garnered him significant media attention, particularly among conservative circles. For many, it was the first time

Trump had positioned himself not just as a businessman with political opinions but as a political provocateur.

Trump's embrace of the "birther" movement was a calculated move. It tapped into a growing undercurrent of dissatisfaction and mistrust in the government, particularly among voters who felt disconnected from the political elites in Washington. By challenging Obama, Trump positioned himself as a voice for those who felt disenfranchised, and in doing so, he became a symbol of rebellion against the political establishment. His involvement in the "birther" controversy, though widely criticized by many as racially charged and factually false, elevated his profile among a segment of the American electorate that would later become crucial to his political success.

Trump's increasing forays into political controversy, combined with his ongoing media presence, began to build momentum. He was no longer just a businessman commenting on politics; he was becoming a political actor in his own right. His use of social media only intensified this shift. Trump understood the power of direct communication in a way that few politicians or public figures did at the time. While others hesitated to engage with the public in real time, Trump reveled in it. Twitter became his primary tool for shaping the narrative around him, as well as for attacking his rivals—whether they were politicians, journalists, or celebrities.

His messaging was often blunt, combative, and full of hyperbole, but it resonated with people who felt that traditional politicians were out of touch. The directness of his communication style, combined with his willingness to break political norms, helped him build a loyal following. Trump's Twitter presence wasn't just about politics; it was a performance, a constant stream of commentary that kept him at the center of public conversation. His tweets made headlines daily, further blurring the line between celebrity and political figure.

By the time Trump announced his candidacy for president in 2015, he had already built a strong base of support—though it wasn't immediately obvious to the political establishment just how significant that support would be. Trump's celebrity status, honed through his business achievements and amplified through his television and media presence, allowed him to enter the political arena with an advantage most outsiders could only dream of: name recognition and a persona already embedded in the American consciousness. What was initially seen as a long-shot bid for the White House quickly gained traction because Trump wasn't just any businessman or celebrity; he was a master of using the media to control the narrative around his identity.

His political transition was gradual but deliberate. It wasn't that Trump suddenly became a political figure in 2015—he had been building toward it for years. His media savvy, his ability to craft a persona that resonated with millions, and his willingness to say things that others wouldn't all played into his rise as a serious political contender. He had laid the groundwork through years of public exposure, polarizing opinions, and a unique approach to leadership that set him apart from traditional politicians. Trump's journey from real estate mogul to political figure wasn't just about ambition; it was about understanding how to harness the power of media, celebrity, and controversy to create a political movement.

The 2016 Presidential Campaign—Against All Odds

When Donald Trump announced his candidacy for the presidency on June 16, 2015, few people, even within his own party, took him seriously. Standing at the top of a golden escalator in Trump Tower, surrounded by a crowd of supporters, Trump delivered a speech that would set the tone for the next year and a half of his campaign. "We are going to make our country great again," he declared, coining the slogan that would define his campaign. With his brash style, populist rhetoric, and celebrity persona, Trump's entry into the race was seen by many as a spectacle—a billionaire businessman dabbling in politics for attention or perhaps as a way to promote his brand. But what most political analysts and the media didn't anticipate was that Trump's candidacy would tap into something deeper in the American electorate.

At the time, the political landscape seemed to be firmly in the hands of seasoned politicians and traditional candidates. The Democratic frontrunner, Hillary Clinton, was a former secretary of state, senator, and first lady—someone who had been preparing for a presidential run for decades. On the Republican side, a crowded field of 17 candidates, including well-known figures like Jeb Bush, Ted Cruz, and Marco Rubio, was vying for the nomination. Many assumed that Bush, with his family name and deep political connections, was the clear favorite to secure the Republican nomination. Trump, in contrast, was a political outsider with no experience in elected office and a reputation more closely tied to reality television than policymaking.

Yet, from the moment Trump announced his candidacy, it was clear that his campaign would be anything but conventional. His speech that day, in which he controversially referred to Mexican immigrants as "rapists" and criminals, sent shockwaves through the political world. While many predicted that such inflammatory comments would doom his campaign from the start, they instead had the opposite effect. Trump's rhetoric, though divisive, resonated with a significant portion of the American electorate—especially those who felt ignored by the political establishment. His bluntness, his rejection of political correctness, and his unapologetic nationalism struck a chord with voters who had grown disillusioned with career politicians.

Trump's campaign strategy defied all the traditional rules of politics. While other candidates were carefully crafting policy platforms, courting donors, and participating in the usual media circuits, Trump was using his greatest asset: his celebrity. His rallies were massive, energetic, and often unpredictable, with Trump speaking off-the-cuff, railing against his opponents, and mocking the political elites. These events, more akin to entertainment spectacles than political rallies, drew thousands of enthusiastic supporters and garnered non-stop media coverage. Trump dominated the news cycle, and he did so with little to no paid advertising—something unheard of in modern campaigns. The media, initially viewing Trump's campaign as a sideshow, couldn't resist covering his every move, inadvertently fueling his rise. For Trump, there was no such thing as bad publicity; every controversial statement or outlandish claim only kept him in the spotlight.

What made Trump's campaign particularly powerful was how he positioned himself as the ultimate outsider. Unlike his competitors, he didn't claim to be part of the system or to understand the intricacies of Washington politics—he was the antidote to all of that. He framed his wealth and success in business as proof that he was incorruptible, that he didn't need to play by the rules of campaign finance or bow to lobbyists. He sold himself as the man who could shake up the system, drain the swamp, and restore America to greatness. This populist message, combined with his tough stance on issues like immigration, trade, and national security, resonated deeply with working-class voters across the country, particularly in key swing states like Ohio, Pennsylvania, and Michigan.

One of Trump's key tactics during the campaign was his ability to create clear enemies—both within his own party and against the Democrats. He mercilessly attacked his Republican rivals, branding Jeb Bush as "low-energy," Marco Rubio as "Little Marco," and Ted Cruz as "Lyin' Ted." These nicknames, while seemingly juvenile, stuck with voters and helped Trump define his opponents in ways that traditional political strategies couldn't counter. Trump's attacks weren't limited to Republicans, either; Hillary Clinton quickly became his primary target. He coined the moniker "Crooked Hillary," a nickname that would haunt Clinton throughout the general election and reinforce Trump's narrative that she was part of a corrupt political establishment.

Despite facing a crowded Republican field, Trump's unique campaign approach led him to dominate the primaries. He won state after state, capturing the imaginations of voters who were fed up with traditional politics. His lack of policy depth didn't matter to his supporters—what they cared about was his authenticity, his willingness to say what others wouldn't, and his promise to bring back jobs and protect American interests. By the time he secured the Republican nomination, Trump had effectively transformed the GOP in his image, pulling the party away from its more traditional conservative roots and toward a new brand of populism and nationalism.

As the general election approached, Trump faced what many saw as an insurmountable challenge in defeating Hillary Clinton, who was widely expected to win. The polls consistently showed her leading, and the media, once again underestimating Trump, largely predicted a Clinton victory. However, Trump's strategy of appealing to disaffected voters—particularly white working-class voters in the Rust Belt—proved to be his secret weapon. While Clinton focused on maintaining the Democratic coalition and expanding into traditionally Republican areas, Trump zeroed in on the core issues that mattered most to his base: economic anxiety, immigration, and national identity.

In the end, Trump's 2016 campaign was a political masterclass in disruption. By flouting the traditional rules of politics, embracing controversy, and leveraging his celebrity and media savvy, he did what no one thought was possible: he won. His victory shocked the political world and marked a seismic shift in American politics. Trump had redefined what it meant to be a political candidate in the modern age, proving that celebrity, media manipulation, and an outsider message could not only compete with but defeat the well-established political machines of both parties.

The Message of "America First"

As Donald Trump's 2016 presidential campaign gained momentum, his message crystallized around a single theme: "America First." This slogan became more than just a rallying cry—it embodied the core of Trump's populist agenda, aimed at resonating with voters who felt left behind by globalization, trade deals, and the political elites. "America First" was simple, powerful, and appealed to a broad swath of the electorate who wanted to see a return to what they believed were America's glory days, when the country wasn't embroiled in costly international conflicts, and American jobs were not being outsourced to other nations. Trump's ability to simplify complex issues into digestible, emotional appeals made him a master of political messaging, and "America First" became the backbone of his campaign platform.

The origins of the phrase "America First" have a complicated history. Initially popularized in the early 20th century, particularly during World War II by isolationists who sought to keep the United States out of global conflicts, Trump reappropriated the phrase for a new era. While its historical roots were contentious, Trump used it to address modern concerns about America's role in the world. His interpretation of "America First" was centered on economic nationalism and a rejection of the globalist policies that he argued had sold out American workers. Whether discussing trade, foreign policy, or immigration, the underlying message was always the same: America had been taken advantage of, and Trump was the only one who could fix it.

One of the key aspects of Trump's "America First" message was his hardline stance on trade. Throughout the campaign, Trump railed against trade deals like NAFTA (the North American Free Trade Agreement) and the Trans-Pacific Partnership (TPP), which he claimed were disastrous for American workers. Trump argued that these agreements had allowed other countries—particularly China and Mexico—to steal American jobs by undercutting wages and flooding the U.S. market with cheap goods. His promise to renegotiate these deals, or scrap them altogether, struck a chord with many blue-collar workers who had seen their manufacturing jobs disappear over the past few decades. For these voters, Trump's message wasn't just rhetoric—it was personal.

In states like Ohio, Pennsylvania, and Michigan, where industrial decline had left entire communities struggling, Trump's promise to bring back manufacturing jobs and protect American industries resonated deeply. He positioned himself as the champion of these forgotten voters, claiming that under his leadership, American companies would no longer be allowed to outsource jobs or move factories overseas without facing penalties. His attacks on corporations that moved production abroad, coupled with his threats to impose tariffs on imports, were a direct appeal to voters who had lost faith in the political establishment's ability—or willingness—to protect their livelihoods.

Another key pillar of Trump's "America First" platform was immigration. From the very beginning of his campaign, Trump had made immigration a central issue, and his proposals were bold and controversial. His now-infamous pledge to build a wall along the U.S.-Mexico border, and make Mexico pay for it, became a defining feature of his campaign. Trump portrayed immigration, both legal and illegal, as a threat to American jobs and national security. He argued that lax immigration policies had allowed criminals, drugs, and terrorists to flow into the country, while also depressing wages for American workers. His rhetoric often veered into inflammatory territory, particularly when he described Mexican immigrants as "rapists" and criminals during his announcement speech, but for many voters, his tough stance was seen as a much-needed response to years of inaction on immigration reform.

Trump's message on immigration appealed particularly to white working-class voters who felt that unchecked immigration had harmed their communities. His promise to deport millions of undocumented immigrants, implement stricter vetting processes for refugees, and halt immigration from countries that he described as "terror-prone" (later dubbed the "Muslim ban") spoke directly to concerns about national security and cultural identity. Trump tapped into a growing sense of fear and frustration among many Americans who believed that the country's changing demographics, combined with economic stagnation, were eroding their way of life. His promise to put "America First" when it came to immigration was seen as a direct challenge to the bipartisan consensus that had dominated U.S. immigration policy for decades.

Foreign policy was another area where Trump's "America First" platform sharply diverged from the traditional Republican and Democratic approaches. Unlike the interventionist policies of previous administrations, Trump promised to reduce America's involvement in foreign conflicts and focus on rebuilding the nation at home. He criticized the wars in Iraq and Afghanistan, as well as America's military presence around the world, arguing that the U.S. was spending billions of dollars defending other countries while neglecting its own interests. Trump's skepticism of NATO, his questioning of America's role in international alliances, and his calls for allies to pay more for their own defense shocked many in the foreign policy establishment, but they resonated with voters who were tired of endless wars and who questioned why America was footing the bill for global security.

Under the banner of "America First," Trump promised a foreign policy that would prioritize American interests above all else, whether that meant negotiating better trade deals, avoiding costly military interventions, or demanding more from allies. His blunt, transactional approach to diplomacy, combined with his rejection of globalism, made him a radical departure from the internationalist consensus that had defined U.S. foreign policy since World War II. For Trump's supporters, this was precisely the change they had been waiting for—a president who would stop allowing America to be "taken advantage of" by other nations.

Trump's embrace of nationalism, both economically and politically, was a significant factor in his appeal to disaffected voters across the country. He framed his campaign as a movement to restore American pride and prosperity, offering a stark contrast to the policies of the Obama administration and the broader political establishment. While critics accused Trump of stoking fear and division, his message resonated with millions of voters who felt that the system had failed them. For these voters, "America First" wasn't just a slogan—it was a vision for the country's future, one that promised to bring back jobs, secure the borders, and put American interests ahead of global ones.

In the 2016 election, Trump's message of "America First" became the rallying cry for a populist movement that transcended traditional party lines. It was a message that spoke to the heart of the frustrations felt by many Americans who believed that their country had lost its way. By promising to put their concerns at the center of his agenda, Trump not only won their votes—he earned their loyalty.

The Electoral Victory—A Shock to the System

As Election Day 2016 approached, the political landscape seemed to be set. Polls, pundits, and political analysts largely predicted a victory for Hillary Clinton. She was the seasoned politician with decades of experience, and her campaign was heavily funded, well-organized, and supported by a powerful Democratic machine. Meanwhile, Donald Trump's candidacy had been treated by many in the media as a long-shot or even a fluke. Despite his populist message, his campaign was frequently embroiled in controversy, and he had alienated significant segments of the electorate with his blunt rhetoric on race, immigration, and foreign policy. By almost every conventional measure, Clinton's path to the White House seemed inevitable.

However, Trump's campaign had tapped into an undercurrent of discontent in American society, a discontent that was largely underestimated by traditional political analysts. He wasn't running a conventional campaign, and neither was he appealing to traditional voters. Instead, Trump had struck a chord with millions of Americans who felt ignored and left behind by the political establishment. Many of these voters lived in key swing states and were part of a demographic—white, working-class, non-college-educated voters—that had been steadily losing ground in the changing American economy. For them, Trump's message of restoring American jobs, renegotiating trade deals, and curbing immigration wasn't just rhetoric—it was a promise to reverse the decline of their communities and restore their version of the American dream.

In the final days of the campaign, the race tightened. Trump's rallies became more energized and his message more focused. Meanwhile, the Clinton campaign, which had been confident in its lead, began to take on a defensive posture, particularly in the wake of an October surprise: FBI Director James Comey's announcement that the bureau was reopening its investigation into Clinton's use of a private email server during her tenure as secretary of state. Though Comey later cleared Clinton of any wrongdoing just days before the election, the damage had been done. The headlines and the relentless media coverage had reinforced Trump's narrative that Clinton was corrupt, and the scandal served as a reminder to undecided voters of the political baggage she carried.

Despite this, most political observers still predicted a Clinton victory as Election Day arrived. The polls consistently showed her leading in key battleground states, and her campaign had a robust get-out-the-vote operation. Trump, on the other hand, had relied on his celebrity status, social media, and massive rallies to galvanize his supporters, often boasting that his base was "a movement" rather than a traditional campaign. What few predicted, however, was the intensity of the voter turnout among Trump's supporters. While Clinton's campaign was targeting traditional Democratic strongholds and hoping to expand into states like Arizona and Georgia, Trump was laser-focused on the Rust Belt—the industrial heartland of America that had been devastated by decades of economic decline.

As election night unfolded, the results shocked the nation. While Clinton won the popular vote by a significant margin, it was Trump who triumphed in the electoral college—a victory secured by winning key swing states like Pennsylvania, Michigan, and Wisconsin. These states had long been considered Democratic strongholds, part of the so-called "blue wall" that Clinton's campaign had assumed would remain loyal to her. But in these states, Trump's message of economic nationalism and his focus on trade and jobs resonated deeply with voters who had once formed the backbone of the Democratic Party's working-class base.

The voter turnout in rural and exurban areas, particularly in the Midwest, was unprecedented. Trump's campaign had successfully energized voters who had felt ignored by both parties for years, and many of them were voting for the first time in decades, or even the first time ever. Meanwhile, Clinton's turnout among key Democratic demographics—young people, African Americans, and women—was lower than expected. Her campaign had counted on these groups to deliver a decisive victory, but Trump's ability to dominate the conversation and tap into economic and cultural anxieties proved to be more powerful than anyone had anticipated.

In many ways, Trump's victory was a rebuke of the political establishment and the media. His supporters saw him as a truth-teller, someone who wasn't afraid to speak his mind or go against the grain of political correctness. His willingness to defy the norms of politics—to call out his opponents in blunt terms, to question longstanding institutions, and to reject the traditional campaign playbook—was seen as a sign of authenticity. Trump had successfully positioned himself as the ultimate outsider, running against not just the Democratic Party, but also against the Republican establishment, the media, and the Washington elite.

Trump's electoral victory was not just a surprise—it was a seismic event in American politics. It signaled the rise of a new kind of populism, one that blended economic nationalism, nativism, and celebrity culture in a way that had never been seen before in modern American history. For Trump's supporters, his win represented the triumph of the forgotten man, the voter who had been left behind by globalization and ignored by politicians in Washington. For his detractors, it was a troubling sign of the growing divisions in the country—divisions that had been amplified by Trump's own rhetoric throughout the campaign.

As the dust settled after Election Night, the world grappled with the reality of a Trump presidency. The political establishment, both in the U.S. and abroad, had been caught off guard by the power of Trump's message and his ability to upend the traditional rules of politics. His victory showed that in the age of social media, reality television, and a 24/7 news cycle, a candidate could rise to power not by following the playbook, but by ripping it up and writing their own. The election of 2016 was a turning point in American history—one that marked the rise of Donald Trump from celebrity mogul to the most powerful office in the world. The consequences of that victory would be felt for years to come.

Chapter 10: The 2011 Turning Point—Obama and the B

The Beginning of the Birther Movement

In the lead-up to the 2008 presidential election, the United States was buzzing with the historic possibility of electing its first African American president. Barack Obama, a junior senator from Illinois, had quickly risen to prominence with his message of hope and change. But as his popularity soared, so too did the number of rumors and conspiracy theories aimed at undermining his legitimacy. One of the most persistent of these was the claim that Obama was not born in the United States, and therefore ineligible to serve as president.

This conspiracy theory, later dubbed the "birther" movement, started in the murky corners of internet forums and fringe political circles. The core allegation was that Obama had been born in Kenya, the birthplace of his father, and that his Hawaiian birth certificate was either fake or didn't exist. While many of these claims were easily debunked, they nonetheless resonated with certain groups of people who were uncomfortable with

Obama's rapid ascent and his background, which they saw as unconventional for a presidential candidate. His biracial heritage, his time spent living abroad as a child, and even his middle name—Hussein—were all points used by his detractors to paint him as "other" or not fully American.

At first, the birther movement had little mainstream traction. It was largely confined to right-wing blogs and forwarded emails among certain conservative circles. Most of the public, including the media, dismissed the claims as baseless. After all, the state of Hawaii had already certified Obama's birth with a short-form certificate, and there was no credible evidence to suggest otherwise. Mainstream politicians and journalists were wary of touching the issue, afraid of giving credence to what was widely seen as an extreme and xenophobic attack on a legitimate presidential candidate.

Yet, for some, the birther narrative fit neatly into pre-existing suspicions about Obama. The idea that he wasn't "really" American played into fears about his political agenda and concerns about his cultural identity. It also tapped into a broader discomfort about the shifting demographics of the country—an anxiety among some white voters that the rise of minority figures like Obama signaled a decline in their own influence. While many Republicans, including those in leadership, distanced themselves from the birther movement, a vocal minority within the party found the claims compelling, particularly as they aligned with opposition to Obama's progressive policies.

The birther movement simmered on the fringes of public discourse for the next few years. Conservative talk radio hosts and certain right-wing commentators kept it alive, but it struggled to gain a foothold in mainstream political conversations. Few prominent politicians or media figures were willing to openly endorse the theory. But this all changed in 2011, when a brash real estate mogul and reality television star named Donald Trump decided to publicly wade into the controversy.

Trump's decision to engage with the birther issue wasn't just a spur-of-the-moment move. It was a calculated risk, one that would propel him into the national political spotlight in a way he had never experienced before. While Trump had flirted with political ambitions for years—often hinting at a potential run for office—he had never found the right issue to elevate him from celebrity businessman to political player. The birther movement, with its mix of controversy, media attention, and populist anger, presented the perfect opportunity.

What had started as a fringe theory was about to be thrust into the mainstream of American politics, and Trump was the man who would do it.

Trump's Entry into the Birther Debate

In 2011, Donald Trump made a bold move that would forever alter the trajectory of his public image: he became the most prominent voice in the so-called "birther" movement, publicly questioning the legitimacy of President Barack Obama's citizenship. At the time, Trump was already well-known for his real estate empire and his hit television show, The Apprentice, but he had never fully crossed into the realm of serious political discourse. By seizing on the birther conspiracy, Trump found an issue that combined his love for media attention with a burgeoning political brand built on controversy and confrontation.

Trump's entry into the birther debate wasn't accidental—it was strategic. Although his public persona had long been tied to wealth, success, and showmanship, he was now beginning to shape himself as a political outsider unafraid to ask tough questions or take on the establishment. To many, Trump represented a direct challenge to the so-called political elite, a voice for those who felt that their concerns were being dismissed or ignored. His questioning of Obama's birthplace was more than just an attack on the president; it was a calculated play to tap into the skepticism and distrust that many Americans felt toward Washington, the media, and even the legitimacy of government institutions.

From Trump's perspective, the birther issue was the perfect platform to launch his political ambitions. In early 2011, during media appearances and in interviews, Trump began to relentlessly question whether Obama had been born in the United States. He framed his argument as simple curiosity, repeatedly saying that he just wanted to see the birth certificate to "clear everything up." However, Trump's statements were far from neutral. His insistence that something was amiss implied that the sitting president had something to hide, sowing doubt among those who were already predisposed to question Obama's background or qualifications.

In interviews on major news networks like Fox News and The Today Show, Trump presented himself as a crusader for the truth. "I have people in Hawaii right now," he said in a March 2011 interview, claiming he had investigators looking into Obama's birth certificate. "And they cannot believe what they're finding." His rhetoric was deliberately provocative, full of insinuation but lacking hard evidence. Still, the sheer force of Trump's personality and media presence kept the issue alive, making it impossible for the public—and the Obama administration—to ignore.

What made Trump's involvement so effective was his ability to use his celebrity status to amplify the birther movement far beyond the internet's fringes. Prior to his involvement, the issue was largely confined to conspiracy theorists and niche political blogs. But Trump, with his decades of experience in the media, knew how to work the news cycle. He understood that controversy sells, and he capitalized on every opportunity to keep the story in the headlines. Cable news shows, desperate for ratings and drama, invited him on regularly, allowing Trump to turn the birther theory into an ongoing spectacle.

Critics were quick to point out that Trump's focus on Obama's birth certificate was racially charged, playing on fears about Obama's identity as the nation's first Black president. Many argued that Trump's embrace of the conspiracy was not simply about the legal question of Obama's birthplace, but about casting doubt on Obama's legitimacy as an American, tapping into nativist anxieties. In this way, Trump's rhetoric wasn't just a political maneuver—it was an appeal to a deeper, more visceral set of concerns held by some segments of the population who saw Obama as representing a threat to their vision of America.

Yet, for Trump, the controversy was a success. His public statements about Obama's birth certificate dominated headlines, and he saw his poll numbers rise as a result. At the time, Trump was toying with the idea of running for president, and the attention he garnered from the birther issue only seemed to boost his credibility with a certain segment of the electorate—one that was disillusioned with traditional politicians and eager for someone who would take on the establishment.

As Trump leaned further into the birther narrative, he transformed it into more than just a question about Obama's citizenship. It became a proxy for larger cultural and political battles about identity, race, and belonging in America. Trump's insistence on demanding proof, and his repeated claims that something wasn't right, stoked a broader conversation about who gets to be considered "American" and who gets to define that identity. For many, his stance was an unmistakable signal that he was willing to be the champion for those who felt excluded or threatened by the rapid social changes happening in the country.

By 2011, Trump's brand had taken on a new dimension. No longer was he just a flashy real estate tycoon or a reality TV star. He was now a political provocateur, using the birther controversy to position himself as a potential leader for a growing populist movement. This calculated decision would pay off in the years to come, as Trump's name became synonymous with challenging the political status quo and energizing a base of voters who felt unheard. The birther issue was, in many ways, Trump's first major foray into the national political conversation, and it set the stage for the political outsider image that would later define his 2016 presidential run.

Media Firestorm and Public Response

As Donald Trump leaned further into the birther controversy, the media response was swift and all-encompassing. Trump's ability to seize the national conversation and keep himself at the center of it was a testament to his mastery of modern media. What had started as a fringe conspiracy theory suddenly became a mainstay in the national discourse, thanks in large part to Trump's celebrity status and his ability to command attention. In the spring of 2011, cable news networks, talk shows, and political pundits couldn't stop talking about Trump's latest claims regarding President Obama's birth certificate. Trump, who had already spent decades building his reputation as a media-savvy businessman, now found himself in a new role: provocateur-in-chief.

The media firestorm was unlike anything seen in recent political history. Every time Trump made a public appearance or gave an interview, his comments about Obama's citizenship were front-page news. Networks like CNN, MSNBC, and Fox News dedicated hours of programming to the controversy, dissecting Trump's statements and speculating on the possible outcomes. This constant coverage kept Trump in the spotlight, and he used it to his advantage, feeding the narrative with new claims and assertions designed to keep the story alive. He understood that in the media landscape, being talked about—whether positively or negatively—was an asset. Trump's use of provocative soundbites and his talent for stoking controversy ensured that the story had staying power.

For many Americans, Trump's embrace of the birther issue was deeply troubling. Critics, including political analysts, journalists, and civil rights activists, saw it as a thinly veiled attempt to delegitimize the first Black president. They argued that the birther movement, championed by Trump, was rooted in racism and xenophobia, casting doubt on Obama's status as a true American simply because of his race and background. To these critics, Trump was exploiting racial anxieties and pandering to the most extreme elements of the electorate. Newspapers like The New York Times and The Washington Post ran editorials condemning Trump's rhetoric, pointing out the harm it was doing to the national fabric by fueling divisions along racial and political lines.

Yet, while the mainstream media largely condemned Trump's actions, his message resonated with a substantial portion of the American public. Polls taken during the height of the controversy showed that a significant number of Republicans believed there was at least some merit to the idea that Obama might not have been born in the United States. For these voters, Trump wasn't just some attention-seeking celebrity; he was a truth-teller, someone willing to ask the questions that others were too afraid to address. Trump framed the birther issue as a matter of transparency and accountability, repeatedly stating that he was just looking for answers and that Obama could easily put the matter to rest by releasing his long-form birth certificate.

In the era of 24-hour news cycles and social media, Trump's every word was amplified, debated, and analyzed. Cable news, in particular, found Trump's comments irresistible. His bombastic style and willingness to challenge a sitting president made for great television, and networks were eager to give him airtime. Trump's interviews were frequently broadcast live, with pundits providing instant analysis afterward. The more controversial his statements, the more attention they garnered. In one particularly memorable interview on The Today Show in April 2011, Trump doubled down on his claims, stating, "I've been hearing about this for years. I have a real question as to whether Obama was born in this country."

The media's role in perpetuating the birther controversy was complex. While many outlets criticized Trump for promoting a debunked conspiracy theory, they also continued to cover the story extensively, inadvertently giving him a larger platform. Trump's media presence was so dominating that it overshadowed other political issues of the time, turning the birther controversy into a defining moment of the early 2010s. In a way, the media's focus on Trump and the birther issue was emblematic of a broader shift in political journalism, where sensationalism and personality-driven stories often took precedence over substantive policy debates.

The public response to Trump's birther crusade was polarized. On one side were those who viewed Trump as a dangerous demagogue, exploiting racial tensions and sowing discord for his own personal gain. Many saw his actions as an affront to democracy itself, as they undermined the legitimacy of a duly elected president. Obama supporters, in particular, were outraged, viewing the entire birther controversy as an attempt to discredit a historic presidency that had inspired millions of Americans. On the other side, however, were those who saw Trump as a fearless leader who wasn't afraid to challenge the establishment. These individuals believed that Trump was standing up for the common man, raising questions that the political and media elite were too timid or too complicit to ask.

Trump's constant presence in the media during this time not only helped keep the birther issue alive but also elevated his public profile in a new way. No longer was he just a celebrity businessman or reality TV star—he was a political force. The birther controversy allowed Trump to tap into a growing sense of frustration and disillusionment among certain segments of the American electorate. These voters felt that traditional politicians were out of touch with their concerns, and they saw Trump as someone who would speak truth to power. Whether they believed in the birther theory or not, they appreciated Trump's willingness to challenge the status quo.

By the time the birth certificate debate reached its peak, it was clear that Trump had successfully transformed the birther movement into a media spectacle that kept him at the center of American political discourse. His mastery of media manipulation and his ability to exploit controversy for his own gain laid the foundation for his eventual foray into politics, where these same tactics would serve him well in the years to come.

Obama Responds—The Release of the Long-Form Birth Certificate

As Donald Trump's birther crusade reached a fever pitch in the spring of 2011, it became increasingly clear that the issue was not going away. Despite the lack of evidence and repeated debunking of the conspiracy theory, the relentless media coverage and Trump's high-profile attacks on President Obama's legitimacy were creating a narrative that demanded a response.

For weeks, the White House had largely ignored Trump's comments, dismissing them as the ravings of a publicity-seeking celebrity. But as Trump's rhetoric grew louder, and public polls began to show that a significant number of Americans were unsure about Obama's birthplace, the administration decided it had to take action.

On April 27, 2011, President Obama did what Trump had been publicly demanding for months: he released his long-form birth certificate. The document, which confirmed that Obama had indeed been born in Honolulu, Hawaii, on August 4, 1961, was intended to put an end to the controversy once and for all. In a surprise press conference at the White House, Obama stood before the cameras and addressed the nation, his tone measured but tinged with exasperation. He expressed frustration with the fact that such a baseless issue had become a distraction from the more important challenges facing the country, from economic recovery to national security.

In his remarks, Obama made it clear that he viewed the birther controversy as a symptom of deeper divisions in American politics. "We do not have time for this kind of silliness," he said. "We've got better stuff to do. I've got better stuff to do. We've got big problems to solve, and I'm confident we can solve them—but we're going to have to focus on them, not on this." His words were a direct rebuke to Trump and others who had fanned the flames of the birther movement, portraying their obsession with his citizenship as a distraction from the real work of governing.

For Obama, the release of the birth certificate was not just a tactical move to silence his critics; it was also a demonstration of the absurdity of the entire birther debate. By making the document public, he aimed to highlight the lengths to which he had been forced to go to prove something that had already been verified multiple times. The state of Hawaii had already confirmed his birth, and the short-form certificate released in 2008 had been legally sufficient for years. Yet, due to the persistent efforts of Trump and his allies, Obama was compelled to take this extraordinary step, one that no other president had ever been asked to take.

The release of the long-form birth certificate dominated the news cycle for days. Commentators debated whether Obama's decision to release the document would finally put the controversy to rest or whether it would embolden Trump and other conspiracy theorists to move the goalposts and demand further proof. Some argued that Obama had taken the high road, addressing the issue head-on and attempting to move the country forward. Others questioned whether giving in to Trump's demands had legitimized the birther movement in a way that might encourage future conspiracy-driven challenges to authority.

For Trump, Obama's release of the birth certificate was both a victory and a challenge. On the one hand, he claimed credit for forcing the president to act, boasting that his pressure had succeeded where others had failed. In interviews after the release, Trump took a victory lap, telling reporters, "I'm very proud of myself because I've accomplished something that nobody else was able to accomplish." Trump positioned himself as the hero of the story, the man who had compelled the most powerful leader in the world to bend to his will. His supporters saw this as proof of Trump's toughness and tenacity—a key part of the brand he was building as someone who would never back down from a fight.

However, Obama's release of the birth certificate also posed a challenge to Trump's narrative. With the document now public, many expected the issue to fade away. If the central claim of the birther movement—that Obama was hiding something about his birth—had been disproven, where would that leave

Trump? Would he be able to pivot away from the controversy and maintain the political momentum he had built on the back of it? Or would he double down, continuing to sow doubt about Obama's identity even in the face of overwhelming evidence?

Trump's response to the release of the birth certificate was revealing. Rather than acknowledge that the controversy should be over, he immediately began casting doubt on the legitimacy of the document itself. In typical Trump fashion, he suggested—without evidence—that the birth certificate might be a forgery, or that there were still unanswered questions about Obama's background. "We have to look at it, we have to see—is it real?" Trump said in an interview shortly after the document was released. "Does it conform? What's on it? But I'm really proud that I was able to get him to do something that nobody else could."

This response signaled that Trump had no intention of backing away from the birther issue. He had built his brand on questioning Obama's legitimacy, and he wasn't going to let the release of the birth certificate stand in the way of that. By continuing to raise doubts, even after the document was made public, Trump was laying the groundwork for a broader narrative—one in which he positioned himself as the ultimate outsider, challenging not just Obama but the entire political system. The birther controversy, in Trump's hands, had become less about the specifics of Obama's birth and more about questioning the very nature of authority and truth in American politics.

For Obama, the release of the birth certificate was a necessary step to move beyond a distraction that had plagued his presidency. But for Trump, it was just the beginning of a larger campaign, one that would eventually propel him from reality TV star and real estate mogul to the highest office in the land. The birther issue had given Trump a platform and a following, and he wasn't about to give it up. Instead, he would continue to use controversy and media attention to his advantage, turning himself into a political force to be reckoned with. The release of the birth certificate might have ended the immediate birther debate, but it set the stage for Trump's continued rise in American politics.

The Aftermath—Trump's Momentum and the Legacy of Birtherism

After President Obama released his long-form birth certificate, many expected the birther controversy to lose steam, assuming that the definitive proof of Obama's birthplace would silence Trump and his supporters. However, the aftermath played out very differently. Rather than retreating, Trump used the controversy—and its resolution—as a launching pad for his continued media presence and, eventually, his political aspirations. The release of the birth certificate marked the end of one chapter in Trump's public life, but it also ignited a new phase where his influence would grow exponentially.

In the immediate aftermath, the national conversation didn't suddenly shift away from the birther issue, as many had hoped. Instead, Trump found new ways to remain in the spotlight, pivoting from questioning Obama's birthplace to casting doubt on other aspects of his presidency. He started questioning Obama's academic credentials, demanding that the president release his college records, suggesting—again without evidence—that Obama may not have earned his place at prestigious institutions like Columbia University and Harvard Law School. These new attacks were in line with the same strategy Trump had employed with the birth certificate: raising doubts, sowing uncertainty, and presenting himself as the champion of transparency, all while keeping his name in the headlines.

For Trump, the media attention was the real prize. Even when his claims were debunked or dismissed, the relentless coverage kept him at the center of the political conversation. This was the lesson Trump had learned during the birther saga: controversy could be a powerful tool for remaining relevant. Whether people loved or hated him, they were paying attention, and in Trump's world, attention equaled power. He understood the media cycle better than most politicians, knowing that outrageous statements and public feuds kept his profile high. The birth certificate controversy demonstrated that he could control the narrative, even when facts were not on his side. It was a blueprint that Trump would follow again and again, especially during his presidential campaign.

Trump's rise in the polls among potential Republican voters in 2011 was another important outcome of the birther controversy. Although he had not officially announced any plans to run for office, Trump began to be taken more seriously as a potential candidate. Polling data from early 2011 showed that Trump had gained considerable traction among conservative voters, many of whom were disillusioned with traditional Republican leaders. His brash, unapologetic style resonated with a segment of the electorate that felt ignored by the political establishment. Trump was positioning himself as an outsider, someone unafraid to challenge the status quo and ask uncomfortable questions.

This newfound political momentum was fueled in part by the birther controversy, which had amplified his message and introduced him to a wider audience. Trump's base saw him as a truth-teller, a figure who would fight for them against a corrupt political elite. His rhetoric tapped into a broader sense of frustration with the Obama presidency, particularly among conservative and right-wing voters. Although the birther issue itself may have faded over time, the anger and distrust that it stirred up among Trump's supporters persisted, becoming a key element of his political identity in the years to come.

For President Obama, the release of the birth certificate may have quelled the immediate birther furor, but it left a lasting legacy on American politics. The birther controversy was more than just a fringe conspiracy—it was a reflection of deeper divisions in the country, particularly around race and identity. The fact that so many Americans were willing to entertain the idea that Obama, the first Black president, might not be a legitimate citizen highlighted the racial undercurrents that had always been present but were now coming to the surface in more overt ways. Trump had not created these divisions, but he had exploited them for his own gain, using birtherism as a way to challenge Obama's legitimacy without directly attacking his race—though many saw the birther movement as rooted in racial resentment.

The long-term consequences of the birther controversy were profound. It helped set the stage for the kind of post-truth politics that would dominate the Trump era. In a world where facts could be disputed and conspiracies could be mainstreamed, Trump thrived. The birther movement was one of the first major political events of the 21st century where a large portion of the population embraced a narrative that was divorced from reality, guided more by emotion and identity than by evidence. Trump's success in pushing the birther narrative showed that political discourse was no longer bound by traditional norms of truth and decorum.

In hindsight, the birth certificate episode can be seen as a precursor to Trump's eventual presidential campaign and his rise to power. The tactics he used during the birther controversy—challenging the legitimacy of an opponent, questioning basic facts, and dominating media coverage—were the same strategies he would employ during his 2016 campaign. The ability to keep the public focused on his version of events, regardless of their accuracy, would become one of Trump's greatest strengths as a politician. His birther crusade demonstrated that in the modern media age, controversy could be more valuable than credibility.

For Trump, the aftermath of the birth certificate release was not a setback, but a confirmation of his approach to public life. He had successfully forced a sitting president to engage with him, had dominated the national media conversation for months, and had built a political base that saw him as a leader willing to speak uncomfortable truths. The release of the long-form birth certificate might have put the birther conspiracy to bed in the eyes of many Americans, but for Trump, it was only the beginning of his transformation from a reality TV star and businessman into a political powerhouse.

By keeping the focus on Obama's birth certificate, Trump had not only challenged the president but had also tapped into a broader discontent with the political system. This discontent would soon coalesce into the populist movement that propelled Trump to the White House in 2016. The birther controversy, then, was more than just a conspiracy theory—it was a testing ground for Trump's political philosophy and the first major step in his journey from celebrity mogul to political phenomenon. It showed that in Trump's world, there was no such thing as bad publicity, and that in politics, winning the narrative could be just as important as winning the argument.

Chapter 11

Chapter 11: Transition to Politics—A New Arena

Flirting with Politics—Trump's Early Political Aspirations

Long before Donald Trump formally entered the political arena in 2016, he had flirted with the idea of running for office on several occasions. His public persona as a wealthy businessman, combined with his keen sense of media influence, positioned him as a figure who was always able to keep one foot in the political conversation, even if he never fully committed. Trump's early aspirations for higher office, dating back as far as the 1980s, reflect both his ambition and his strategic thinking, as he often used political speculation to boost his profile and maintain relevance in the public eye.

Trump's initial forays into the political world can be traced back to the late 1980s, during the Reagan administration. At that time, Trump was already a high-profile real estate mogul with growing national fame. He was known for his bold developments in Manhattan and his larger-than-life personality, both of which caught the attention of the media. Trump capitalized on this exposure to hint at political ambitions. In 1987, he took out full-page ads in major newspapers such as *The New York Times* and *The Washington Post* to criticize U.S. foreign policy, particularly regarding Japan and the Persian Gulf. These ads, which were widely seen as a precursor to a possible political career, positioned Trump as someone who was not only a businessman but also an outspoken critic of American leadership.

Although Trump did not officially declare any candidacy during the 1980s, the speculation surrounding his political ambitions never truly went away. He continued to engage in political discourse, offering opinions on national issues and maintaining relationships with influential political figures. In 1999, Trump took his flirtation with politics a step further by considering a presidential run on the Reform Party ticket, a third-party movement founded by Ross Perot. The Reform Party had gained traction during the 1992 and 1996 elections, and Trump saw an opportunity to enter the race as a centrist candidate. He announced that he was forming an exploratory committee to consider a run, and for a brief period, the media and political pundits took the possibility seriously.

However, Trump's potential Reform Party candidacy never gained significant momentum. Internal party disputes and a lack of clear direction within the Reform movement led Trump to abandon the idea before it fully materialized. Still, the experience provided Trump with valuable insights into the mechanics of political campaigning. He learned how to navigate the complexities of a potential run for office and gained a sense of how the media would cover him in such a context. Despite pulling out of the race, Trump left a lasting impression, solidifying his position as a political outsider who wasn't afraid to challenge the establishment.

During the 2000s, Trump continued to cultivate his political persona, building relationships with both Democratic and Republican figures. Notably, he was not ideologically rigid during this period. In fact, he donated to candidates from both parties and maintained connections with politicians across the political spectrum. This flexibility reflected Trump's pragmatism—he was more interested in positioning himself as a power player within the political world than aligning himself strictly with one party or another. His connections to figures like the Clintons, who attended his wedding to Melania Knauss in 2005, demonstrated that Trump was comfortable navigating the upper echelons of political society, regardless of party affiliation.

Trump's willingness to toy with the idea of a political career became even more apparent during the 2012 presidential election cycle. As President Barack Obama's first term came to an end, Trump began to increase his public appearances and rhetoric, leading many to speculate that he might run as a Republican candidate. He became one of the loudest voices in the "birther" movement, publicly questioning Obama's citizenship and demanding that the president release his long-form birth certificate. This strategy, while controversial, earned Trump significant media attention and raised his profile among conservative voters who were disillusioned with the Obama administration.

Ultimately, Trump decided not to run in 2012, but his political presence had been significantly elevated. The media, the public, and the political establishment all took note of his ability to command attention and drive national conversations, even without holding public office. It was during this period that Trump realized the power of controversy and media spectacle in shaping public perception—tools he would later use to devastating effect in his 2016 campaign.

Through these early political flirtations, Trump learned how to leverage his celebrity status and media savviness to keep his name in the headlines and maintain relevance in the political conversation. Though he never fully committed to a run before 2016, these experiences gave him the foundation to understand the dynamics of modern American politics. Trump's early ventures into politics were not just idle musings; they were part of a calculated approach to staying in the spotlight and positioning himself for a future, more serious bid for power. His ability to use speculation and media manipulation to his advantage would later become one of his most potent weapons on his path to the presidency.

Building a Political Base—Trump's Alignment with Conservative Values

As Donald Trump continued to explore the idea of entering politics, the shifting political landscape of the early 21st century provided him with an opportunity to align himself with the growing wave of conservative discontent. Throughout the 2000s, and especially during the Obama administration, Trump's political rhetoric began to reflect a more pronounced alignment with the values of the Republican Party and, more specifically, the concerns of grassroots conservative voters. This was a departure from his earlier years of political flexibility, where he had straddled both parties and engaged in donations to candidates on both sides of the aisle. By the time he seriously considered running for president, Trump had identified a powerful base of disillusioned conservative voters, particularly among those who felt neglected by the political establishment.

Trump's alignment with conservative values didn't happen overnight. Instead, it evolved gradually as he began to identify key issues that resonated with the Republican base. One of the earliest signs of this shift was his growing criticism of free trade agreements, particularly NAFTA (the North American Free Trade Agreement) and China's entry into the World Trade Organization. Trump framed these deals as catastrophic for American workers, especially those in the manufacturing and industrial sectors. His strong stance against these trade agreements struck a chord with blue-collar workers and rural conservatives, many of whom felt that globalization had gutted American industry and left them economically vulnerable.

Trump's anti-globalization message became one of the central tenets of his political identity. He argued that both Democrats and establishment Republicans had sold out American workers in favor of multinational corporations and foreign interests. In doing so, Trump positioned himself as a populist champion of the working class, a narrative that resonated deeply with voters who had felt ignored by traditional conservative elites. His rhetoric on trade and economic nationalism gave voice to a growing frustration within the GOP base—particularly in regions hit hard by the decline of American manufacturing—and allowed Trump to forge a new coalition of voters who were eager for a candidate who would fight for their interests.

Another key issue where Trump's views began to align with conservative values was immigration. While immigration had been a contentious issue for years, Trump's approach was particularly aggressive. He argued that the United States had lost control of its borders and that illegal immigration posed a threat not only to American jobs but to national security and cultural identity. In the years leading up to his presidential run, Trump began to emphasize his concerns about immigration more publicly, advocating for stronger enforcement measures and tighter restrictions. He was especially vocal about building a wall along the U.S.-Mexico border—a bold and provocative policy proposal that would become the cornerstone of his 2016 campaign.

Trump's hardline stance on immigration tapped into the anxieties of many conservative voters who believed that the country's immigration system was broken. For these voters, the issue was not just about economics, but about maintaining the cultural and social fabric of the nation. Trump's rhetoric about the dangers of illegal immigration resonated with those who felt that their way of life was under threat from unchecked migration and the perceived failure of the government to enforce the law. His promise to "build the wall" became a symbol of his commitment to restoring order and security to the country, a message that resonated deeply with his growing base of supporters.

In addition to trade and immigration, Trump began to adopt a more traditional conservative stance on issues like law and order, national security, and the military. During the Obama administration, Trump became an outspoken critic of what he saw as the administration's failure to project strength on the world stage. He repeatedly emphasized the need for a strong military and a more assertive foreign policy, positioning himself as a hawk on national security issues. He also took a tough stance on crime, advocating for stricter law enforcement policies and expressing support for police officers in the face of rising tensions between law enforcement and communities of color.

As Trump's views on these key issues became more clearly aligned with conservative values, he also began to distance himself from his earlier relationships with Democratic politicians. His ties to figures like Bill and Hillary Clinton, which had once been a symbol of his political flexibility, became less important as he focused on solidifying his appeal to Republican voters. Trump's ability to pivot away from his past affiliations and position himself as a champion of conservative causes was a testament to his keen sense of timing and his understanding of the political moment. He recognized that the GOP base was hungry for a candidate who would take a strong stand on the issues they cared about, and he was more than willing to fill that role.

By the time Trump began seriously considering a run for president in 2016, he had effectively aligned himself with a set of conservative values that resonated with a large portion of the Republican electorate. His positions on trade, immigration, law and order, and national security placed him squarely in the center of the GOP's populist wing, which had grown increasingly disenchanted with the party's leadership. Trump's ability to identify and amplify the concerns of these voters was a key factor in his eventual rise to power. He had built a political base that was not only loyal to him but deeply invested in the issues he championed.

This growing alignment with conservative values set the stage for Trump's eventual entry into the political arena. He had carefully crafted a message that resonated with the Republican base, positioning himself as a political outsider who was unafraid to take bold stances on controversial issues. As he moved closer to announcing his candidacy, Trump's ability to connect with conservative voters would prove to be one of his greatest strengths, allowing him to break through the crowded field of Republican candidates and emerge as a serious contender for the presidency.

The Media Power Play—Using the Bully Pulpit

As Donald Trump continued to align himself with conservative values, one of his greatest assets in transitioning to the political stage was his mastery of the media. Trump had long understood the importance of media in shaping public perception—his entire career had been built on using the press to his advantage, whether promoting his real estate ventures, his television show, or his personal brand. However, as he began his transition into politics, Trump's relationship with the media took on a new significance. No longer just a businessman or a reality TV star, Trump was becoming a political figure, and he knew that controlling the narrative would be key to his success.

Trump's ability to dominate the media landscape was not accidental. For decades, he had cultivated relationships with journalists, editors, and television producers, making sure that his name stayed in the news. This instinct for staying in the spotlight only intensified as he inched closer to the political arena. Trump had a natural talent for understanding how news cycles worked, how to generate controversy, and how to keep his name at the top of headlines—all of which would serve him well in his eventual presidential campaign.

Perhaps more than any other public figure of his time, Trump understood that media attention, even negative attention, could be leveraged to build his brand. This insight guided his approach to politics. He wasn't concerned with being universally liked; rather, he wanted to be talked about. Whether people were praising or criticizing him didn't matter—what mattered was that his name remained in constant circulation. In this way, Trump turned what many politicians considered a liability (bad press) into an asset. His willingness to engage in controversial rhetoric and make bold, often inflammatory statements kept him in the media spotlight, driving endless news cycles and giving him unparalleled visibility.

A key example of Trump's ability to manipulate the media came in 2011, when he took on the issue of President Barack Obama's birth certificate. By publicly questioning whether Obama had been born in the United States, Trump tapped into a conspiracy theory that had been circulating among some fringe groups. While many political observers dismissed the "birther" movement as baseless and damaging, Trump saw it as an opportunity. He understood that by championing the cause, he could both elevate his profile and connect with a segment of the Republican base that was deeply skeptical of Obama's presidency.

The birth certificate controversy became a media firestorm, and Trump was at the center of it. He made public demands for Obama to release his birth certificate, claiming that the president had something to hide. The media, sensing the provocative nature of Trump's claims, covered the story relentlessly, giving Trump hours of free airtime and millions of dollars' worth of exposure. While many pundits criticized him for promoting a conspiracy theory, Trump's focus was on the attention. He didn't need the claims to be true; he needed them to resonate with a certain portion of the electorate, and more importantly, he needed to remain in the spotlight.

The birth certificate controversy was a turning point in Trump's media strategy. It demonstrated his ability to dominate the national conversation and force the press to follow his lead, even when the issue at hand was widely regarded as frivolous or conspiratorial. Trump's success in keeping the story alive for as long as he did was a testament to his media instincts. He understood that controversy drove ratings, and ratings drove attention—something that would prove essential when he eventually launched his presidential bid.

In addition to his strategic use of controversy, Trump also mastered the art of direct communication with his audience. While traditional politicians relied heavily on carefully crafted speeches and statements vetted by teams of advisors, Trump took a more improvisational approach. His unscripted speeches, filled with ad-libs and off-the-cuff remarks, felt raw and authentic to his supporters. This unfiltered style was amplified by his use of social media, particularly Twitter, which allowed him to bypass traditional media outlets and communicate directly with millions of followers.

Trump's Twitter account became a political weapon. It allowed him to shape the news cycle, react instantly to events, and control the narrative without the need for press conferences or media intermediaries. Whether he was attacking political opponents, lambasting the press, or announcing major policy positions, Trump's tweets were designed to provoke strong reactions. Each tweet was a calculated move, designed to create maximum impact with minimal effort. For Trump, Twitter was more than just a social media platform—it was a way to command the news cycle and keep the focus squarely on him.

As Trump's media dominance grew, so too did his political influence. His ability to command attention gave him an advantage over more traditional politicians, who struggled to keep up with his pace. He didn't need to spend millions on advertising; the media gave him free coverage because he was constantly generating news. This allowed Trump to build momentum leading up to his formal entry into the 2016 presidential race.

While Trump's relationship with the media was often contentious—he frequently criticized journalists and referred to certain outlets as "fake news"—he understood that the media was essential to his success. Trump's mastery of the media allowed him to control the narrative and dictate the terms of political debate. His ability to generate controversy, dominate the news cycle, and speak directly to his base made him a force to be reckoned with as he prepared to enter the political arena in earnest.

In the end, Trump's media strategy was one of the most important elements of his transition to politics. He used the media not just as a platform for communication, but as a tool for building his brand and cementing his political identity. His ability to command attention, no matter the cost, would prove to be one of his greatest strengths as he moved closer to declaring his candidacy for the presidency. This media savvy, combined with his alignment with conservative values and his growing base of support, positioned Trump as a political figure unlike any other—one who understood the modern media landscape better than anyone else in the game.

Testing the Waters—Trump's Initial Forays into Politics

As Donald Trump prepared for a possible run for president, he began to make calculated moves to test his political viability. His shift from businessman and media personality to potential political figure didn't happen overnight. It was a gradual process, shaped by years of public speculation, and marked by a series of attempts to gauge whether the American public—and the political establishment—would take him seriously as a candidate. Trump's early flirtations with politics were strategic, designed to elevate his profile while allowing him to measure the pulse of the electorate without fully committing to a campaign.

Trump had toyed with the idea of running for office for years before he made any serious moves. As early as 1987, he had begun floating the idea of running for president. That year, he took out full-page ads in several major newspapers, including *The New York Times* and *The Washington Post*, criticizing the U.S. government's foreign policy and declaring that "America should stop paying to defend countries that can afford to defend themselves." Though he didn't explicitly announce a run for president, the ads were widely interpreted as a signal that Trump was testing the waters for a political future. His bold and controversial statements captured attention, and for the first time, Trump was seen as a potential political player.

Throughout the 1990s and early 2000s, Trump's political ambitions remained in the background, occasionally surfacing in interviews and media appearances. His flirtations with politics during this time were often ambiguous, as he remained firmly entrenched in the world of business and entertainment. But Trump kept himself relevant in political discussions by making public comments on national issues, endorsing candidates, and keeping a close eye on the shifting political landscape. His ability to navigate the media ensured that his name stayed in the mix, even if he wasn't actively pursuing office.

In 1999, Trump made his first real move toward a presidential bid by briefly considering running for president on the Reform Party ticket. The Reform Party, founded by Ross Perot in 1995, was a third-party alternative that focused on issues like fiscal responsibility, economic nationalism, and government reform. Trump saw an opportunity to break into politics without the constraints of the Republican or Democratic establishments. He even formed an exploratory committee and began laying the groundwork for a potential campaign. However, internal divisions within the party and Trump's own doubts about its viability led him to pull back. The flirtation with the Reform Party was short-lived, but it demonstrated that Trump's interest in politics was more than just talk.

Trump's brief foray into the Reform Party revealed key aspects of his political approach that would later define his 2016 campaign. First, it showed his willingness to challenge the traditional two-party system and present himself as an outsider, unencumbered by political norms. Second, it highlighted his ability to tap into populist sentiment. Even in 1999, Trump was positioning himself as a candidate who would "shake things up" and represent the interests of ordinary Americans over those of the political elite. Though his campaign didn't materialize, these themes would reemerge in full force more than a decade later.

Throughout the 2000s, Trump's political ambitions remained simmering beneath the surface. He continued to be a public figure who opined on political issues, but he wasn't yet ready to commit to a run for office. During this time, Trump made headlines with his critiques of President George W. Bush's handling of the Iraq War, his opposition to free trade agreements, and his harsh rhetoric on immigration. These positions, which were sometimes at odds with the Republican establishment, helped Trump build a following among conservatives who felt disenfranchised by their own party.

In 2012, Trump again considered running for president, this time as a Republican. The lead-up to the 2012 election was a crucial period in Trump's political evolution, as it allowed him to further test the waters without fully diving in. Trump made several public statements about his interest in running, conducted polling to assess his chances, and even began making speeches in key battleground states like New Hampshire. Once again, Trump's political ambitions were serious, but ultimately, he decided not to run. The timing wasn't right, and he was still building the infrastructure he would need to mount a serious campaign.

Despite pulling back from a formal campaign in 2012, Trump's influence on the election was still felt. He used his platform to attack President Barack Obama relentlessly, focusing on issues like trade, foreign policy, and the economy. Trump also doubled down on the "birther" controversy, continuing to cast doubt on Obama's citizenship. Though these tactics were controversial, they kept Trump in the media spotlight and helped solidify his appeal to a segment of the Republican base that was increasingly frustrated with the establishment.

By 2014, as the midterm elections approached, Trump was more serious than ever about running for president. He had spent years building his brand, refining his political positions, and cultivating a following among conservative voters. His repeated forays into the political arena, from the Reform Party to the 2012 election, had taught him valuable lessons about how to connect with voters and navigate the political landscape. More importantly, Trump had learned how to command media attention and use it to his advantage, a skill that would prove critical in the months to come.

In hindsight, Trump's decision not to run in 2012 was a strategic one. By waiting, he gave himself more time to refine his message, build his base of support, and capitalize on the growing frustration within the Republican Party. The political environment of 2016 would be far more favorable to an outsider candidate like Trump than 2012 had been. When he finally did announce his candidacy, Trump would be able to present himself as a political outsider with a proven track record of challenging the status quo.

These early political forays were essential in shaping Donald Trump's eventual run for president. They allowed him to test the waters, refine his message, and understand the dynamics of a modern political campaign. More importantly, they set the stage for his entrance into the 2016 race, when Trump would take everything he had learned from his years in the public eye and turn it into one of the most unconventional and successful presidential campaigns in American history.

Laying the Groundwork for the 2016 Campaign—Building the Political Brand

By 2015, Donald Trump had positioned himself as a larger-than-life figure in both business and media, but his sights were now set squarely on politics. After decades of speculation, flirtations with presidential bids, and a growing presence in the conservative political discourse, the groundwork for his 2016 campaign was ready. Trump's move into the political arena wasn't just a decision made in the heat of the moment; it was the culmination of years of brand-building, carefully calculated moves, and a keen understanding of what American voters—especially those feeling alienated by the political establishment—were looking for in a leader.

One of the key elements of Trump's preparation for the 2016 campaign was his relentless cultivation of a brand that resonated deeply with a wide swath of Americans, particularly within the Republican Party. Over the years, Trump had successfully crafted an image of himself as a self-made billionaire who was tough, unafraid to take risks, and always willing to fight for what he believed was right. This persona, cultivated over decades through media appearances, television, and his public dealings, was the foundation of his political brand. The "Trump" name had become synonymous with success, confidence, and winning, qualities that he would later emphasize in his campaign.

Trump also positioned himself as a political outsider—someone who wasn't beholden to special interests or the political class. This outsider status, combined with his immense wealth, allowed him to argue that he couldn't be bought and would always put "America First." He had watched from the sidelines as career politicians in both parties made decisions that, in his view, weakened the country—whether through trade deals that hurt American workers, foreign interventions that drained U.S. resources, or lax immigration policies that failed to protect the borders. Trump's criticism of these issues struck a chord with many voters who felt left behind by globalization and the rapid changes in American society.

One of the most pivotal components of Trump's 2016 groundwork was his mastery of messaging. Trump had long understood the importance of keeping his language simple, direct, and memorable. During his time in the media, he learned that people resonated with clear, bold statements, and that controversy often fueled media coverage, even if the coverage was negative. He translated this strategy directly into his political rhetoric. Phrases like "Make America Great Again" and "Build the Wall" were easy to remember, emotionally charged, and served as rallying cries for disillusioned voters. Trump's ability to craft memorable slogans became one of the defining features of his campaign.

At the heart of Trump's political strategy was his ability to identify and exploit a deep dissatisfaction among voters, particularly within the Republican base. He had his finger on the pulse of a large segment of Americans who felt that the political elites had ignored their concerns for too long. His focus on issues like immigration, national security, and the economy was not new to political discourse, but Trump's approach was. He spoke about these issues in blunt, often confrontational terms, refusing to adhere to the norms of political correctness that had come to define much of the mainstream discourse. This unfiltered style made Trump stand out, and his message resonated with millions who felt that traditional politicians were too detached from their daily struggles.

As he prepared for his 2016 campaign, Trump also took careful steps to build alliances with key figures in the conservative media and political ecosystem. He recognized early on that media platforms like Fox News, talk radio, and conservative websites like *Breitbart* had tremendous influence over Republican voters. Over the years, Trump had built relationships with conservative pundits and personalities who would later become some of his most vocal supporters. This media support was crucial in amplifying his message and legitimizing him as a serious contender, even as many political elites continued to dismiss him.

In addition to his media allies, Trump also sought to forge connections with grassroots conservative organizations and movements, most notably the Tea Party. Although Trump had not been an active figure in the Tea Party during its rise in the early 2010s, he recognized that the movement represented a significant force within the Republican Party. The Tea Party's focus on limited government, opposition to President Obama's policies, and dissatisfaction with the Republican establishment aligned with many of Trump's positions. As he began laying the groundwork for his campaign, Trump increasingly aligned himself with the frustrations of the Tea Party base, capitalizing on their discontent with the GOP's leadership.

One of the final steps in preparing for his run was the refinement of his position on key issues that would define his candidacy. Trump had always been vocal about certain topics, but as he geared up for the 2016 election, he took steps to ensure that his platform would appeal to a broad spectrum of conservative voters. His opposition to free trade agreements, which he argued were unfair to American workers, resonated with voters in Rust Belt states that had been devastated by deindustrialization. His hardline stance on immigration, which focused on building a wall along the southern border and enforcing stricter immigration laws, struck a chord with voters who were concerned about national security and job competition. Trump's platform was a mix of populism, nationalism, and conservatism that set him apart from the rest of the Republican field.

With his platform established, his media presence solidified, and his brand stronger than ever, Trump was ready to launch his 2016 campaign. His early political forays—testing the waters in previous elections, honing his message, and building connections with conservative figures—had all contributed to his preparedness. The groundwork had been laid, and Trump's entry into the political arena was no longer a matter of if, but when.

In June 2015, when Trump descended the golden escalator at Trump Tower to announce his candidacy for president, it marked the culmination of years of preparation. What followed was one of the most unexpected and unconventional presidential campaigns in American history. The groundwork Trump had laid—through his mastery of the media, his cultivation of a powerful brand, and his understanding of the electorate's frustrations—would soon propel him to the highest office in the land, forever changing the political landscape in the process.

Chapter 12

Chapter 12: The Celebrity Candidate

Leveraging Fame for Political Gain

Donald Trump's entrance into the 2016 presidential race was unlike any candidacy the nation had ever seen. From the moment he descended the golden escalator at Trump Tower to announce his bid for the White House, it was clear that this was no ordinary political campaign. What set Trump apart from the other candidates was not just his wealth or his brash, unfiltered style, but the fact that he was already one of the most recognizable figures in America. As a celebrity real estate mogul and television star, Trump had spent decades building a public persona that would prove to be a crucial asset in his campaign. In many ways, his fame was his greatest political currency.

Unlike most politicians who have to spend months, if not years, introducing themselves to voters, Trump came into the race with near-universal name recognition. For over a decade, he had been the face of The Apprentice, a top-rated reality TV show that aired weekly in prime time. The show not only elevated Trump's brand as a successful businessman but also allowed millions of Americans to feel like they "knew" him. To them, Trump wasn't just a billionaire; he was the tough, no-nonsense executive who knew how to get things done. Each week, viewers watched as he made bold decisions in the boardroom, delivering his now-famous catchphrase, "You're fired," with authority. This image of Trump as a decisive leader who demanded excellence was burned into the public consciousness, long before he ever stepped into the political arena.

This celebrity status gave Trump a head start that no other candidate in the 2016 field could match. While his competitors worked to build recognition and craft narratives about their backgrounds and qualifications, Trump was able to skip that phase entirely. Voters already had a clear, pre-formed idea of who Donald Trump was—whether they admired him or loathed him, they knew him. In fact, for many, Trump had become synonymous with success and power. The Trump name was emblazoned on skyscrapers, hotels, and casinos around the world. His name alone evoked an aura of wealth, luxury, and ambition, and in a country that often equates financial success with competence, Trump's wealth became a key part of his appeal.

Moreover, Trump's celebrity status allowed him to bypass the traditional gatekeepers of political influence. Whereas other candidates needed to rely on endorsements from party elites or major donors to gain legitimacy, Trump could rely on the power of his own brand to propel him forward. His wealth, fame, and media connections gave him a direct line to voters that bypassed traditional political machinery. He didn't need the backing of established Republican power brokers; instead, he turned to the people, positioning himself as a voice of the "silent majority" that had grown frustrated with career politicians. His fame allowed him to reach millions directly, and he leveraged it to build a following long before the race even began.

Trump understood better than anyone that in politics, as in business, perception is reality. He recognized that in a crowded field of experienced politicians, his unique status as a celebrity outsider gave him an edge. While his opponents tried to prove their qualifications through years of public service and policy expertise, Trump's appeal was simpler: he was already famous for being a winner, and he sold that image to voters. "We don't win anymore," Trump would often say at his rallies, promising to restore America to its former greatness. His message was rooted in the same narrative that had defined his business career—success, winning, and strength. To his supporters, Trump wasn't just another politician; he was a force of nature, a man who had spent his life at the top and was now offering to bring that same success to the country.

In this way, Trump's fame became a key tool in his political strategy. He didn't need to conform to the rules of political campaigning because he was already a brand unto himself. His celebrity insulated him from the need to explain his positions in the same way his competitors did. While others debated policy specifics, Trump's fame allowed him to speak in broad strokes, painting a picture of America's future that was simple, memorable, and rooted in his brand of bold, unapologetic leadership.

Ultimately, Trump's fame became both a shield and a weapon. It shielded him from the traditional obstacles that trip up most political newcomers—like lack of name recognition or a weak network of political contacts—and it became a weapon he wielded against his opponents, many of whom struggled to compete with his outsized presence. In a race where media coverage, public perception, and emotional connection with voters mattered more than policy expertise, Trump's celebrity was a political asset unlike anything the nation had seen before. He wasn't just a candidate; he was the product, and millions of Americans were ready to buy what he was selling.

Media Manipulation—Owning the News Cycle

One of Donald Trump's most effective strategies during his 2016 presidential campaign was his ability to dominate the news cycle. Trump's innate understanding of how media works, honed over decades in business and entertainment, enabled him to capture headlines and command attention in a way that no other candidate could. His mastery of media manipulation was a key reason why, despite starting out as a political outsider, he quickly became the focal point of the entire election. Trump's approach to media was not just unconventional—it was revolutionary, turning the traditional rules of political communication on their head.

From the earliest days of his campaign, Trump understood that in the media-driven age of politics, visibility mattered more than anything else. Political candidates typically spend millions of dollars on advertising to introduce themselves to voters and promote their messages. But Trump, armed with his celebrity status, needed no introduction. Instead, he capitalized on the 24-hour news cycle by making himself the story, day after day. He didn't have to pay for ads because the media couldn't stop talking about him. From his provocative statements to his unscripted, off-the-cuff speeches, Trump knew how to say things that would generate headlines, stir controversy, and keep the spotlight firmly on him.

Trump's genius lay in his understanding that the media, especially television news, thrives on conflict and spectacle. Cable news networks, in particular, are always hungry for content that drives ratings, and Trump provided them with an endless stream of it. Whether he was attacking his opponents, deriding the media itself as "fake news," or making bold proclamations about what he would do as president, Trump was a constant source of material that the networks could not ignore. He effectively turned the news cycle into his own personal platform, where his every word and action was magnified, broadcast, and dissected, ensuring that his message reached millions of voters without the need for traditional campaign ads.

A key part of Trump's media strategy was his use of controversial, sometimes inflammatory rhetoric. While other candidates might carefully craft their statements to avoid offending potential voters or attracting negative press, Trump seemed to thrive on controversy. Every time he made a shocking statement—whether it was about immigration, his opponents, or foreign policy—it would dominate the news for days. What made this even more effective was Trump's refusal to back down or apologize when his comments sparked outrage. Instead of trying to walk back his remarks, Trump would often double down, turning what could have been a damaging situation for another candidate into an opportunity to reinforce his image as a straight-talking, politically incorrect outsider.

The media, both traditional and social, played a pivotal role in amplifying Trump's message. His ability to exploit this environment reached new heights through his use of Twitter, a platform that gave him direct access to millions of followers and allowed him to bypass traditional gatekeepers of political discourse. With a single tweet, Trump could set the day's news agenda, forcing networks to react to whatever he said. His tweets were often deliberately provocative, sparking immediate media coverage and debate. Trump used Twitter as a tool not just to communicate with his base, but to dominate the conversation. Whether he was attacking his political rivals, criticizing the media, or commenting on world events, Trump's tweets kept him at the center of public attention.

What was remarkable about Trump's media strategy was the sheer volume of coverage he generated. Studies conducted during the 2016 campaign found that Trump received significantly more free media coverage than any of his rivals. One analysis estimated that by March 2016, Trump had received close to $2 billion in free media coverage—far more than the other candidates, including those who were spending heavily on paid advertisements. This relentless exposure helped solidify his image as the frontrunner, making it difficult for other candidates to gain traction.

But Trump's relationship with the media was not one of simple cooperation. In fact, he often positioned the media as one of his chief adversaries, regularly accusing outlets like CNN, The New York Times, and The Washington Post of bias and dishonesty. His attacks on the press resonated with many of his supporters, who felt that the media was out of touch with the concerns of ordinary Americans. By turning the media into a foil, Trump simultaneously fed into the public's distrust of mainstream outlets while ensuring that those very outlets continued to cover him obsessively. The more the media tried to fact-check or criticize him, the more his base rallied around him, seeing Trump as a victim of a biased establishment.

In essence, Trump mastered the art of media manipulation by understanding how to turn every situation to his advantage. His ability to create news, even when the news was controversial or negative, kept him at the forefront of the race. His constant presence in the media meant that he didn't have to rely on traditional political advertising or carefully orchestrated public appearances. Instead, he used the power of the media itself to fuel his campaign, making sure that no matter what happened, all eyes were always on him.

Ultimately, Trump's success in owning the news cycle helped redefine the role of media in political campaigns. His ability to control the narrative, keep himself in the headlines, and bypass traditional political messaging was a testament to his deep understanding of the modern media landscape. It wasn't just that

Trump was in the news; he was the news, and in the world of politics, that was the ultimate advantage.

The Rally Machine—Building a Direct Connection with the People

While Donald Trump's media manipulation gave him unprecedented visibility, it was his rallies that forged a deep, emotional connection with his supporters. In 2016, Trump's campaign rallies became one of the most potent weapons in his political arsenal. They were not just events where voters could hear from the candidate—they were spectacles, gatherings that allowed Trump to solidify his base, spread his message unfiltered, and create a sense of momentum that was unmatched by any other candidate in the race. Through these rallies, Trump built a direct, almost personal relationship with his supporters, bypassing traditional forms of communication and establishing himself as a leader of a movement.

Trump's rallies were unlike any typical political event. While most candidates adhered to tightly scripted speeches delivered in controlled environments, Trump's rallies were raw, unscripted, and filled with energy. Held in stadiums, arenas, and even airfields, these events attracted thousands of enthusiastic supporters, many of whom had never been involved in a political campaign before. The sheer size and passion of the crowds became a defining feature of Trump's candidacy, reinforcing his image as a political outsider with widespread grassroots appeal. To those attending the rallies, Trump was more than just a candidate—he was a symbol of their frustrations, their hopes, and their desire for change.

At the heart of Trump's rally strategy was his ability to communicate directly with his supporters. In an era when many politicians spoke in carefully measured language, Trump's freewheeling style felt refreshing to his audience. His speeches often lasted for over an hour, during which he would speak extemporaneously, riffing on current events, making jokes, and feeding off the energy of the crowd. This informal, conversational style made his rallies feel more like an intimate gathering than a traditional political speech, even when they were attended by tens of thousands of people. Trump's ability to read the mood of the crowd and adjust his tone accordingly made each rally feel unique, creating a sense of authenticity that resonated with many voters.

The themes of Trump's rallies were consistent and deeply emotional. He railed against illegal immigration, political correctness, and what he saw as the failures of past administrations. He promised to "drain the swamp" of corrupt politicians and special interests, to bring back jobs to American workers, and to restore the country to greatness. These themes tapped into the anxieties and frustrations of many voters who felt left behind by globalization, cultural change, and the political establishment. Trump's message was simple, direct, and often visceral, which made it easy for supporters to grasp and rally around.

In addition to his message, the structure of Trump's rallies was designed to foster a sense of community and shared purpose among his supporters. The chants that became staples of his campaign—"Build the wall," "Lock her up," and "Make America Great Again"—were not just slogans; they were rallying cries that unified the crowd and gave them a sense of collective identity. At each rally, Trump supporters felt as though they were part of a larger movement, bound together by a shared desire to take the country back from elites, immigrants, and other groups they saw as threats. This sense of belonging and empowerment was crucial to the success of Trump's rallies and helped turn them into a vital tool for his campaign.

The rallies also allowed Trump to present himself as a political outsider fighting on behalf of ordinary Americans. His off-the-cuff remarks, his willingness to criticize both Republicans and Democrats, and his attacks on the media all reinforced the idea that he was not part of the Washington establishment. Trump frequently positioned himself as the underdog, telling his supporters that the media and political elites were conspiring to stop him from winning. This narrative of being the anti-establishment candidate gave his rallies an added layer of urgency and emotional intensity. Trump portrayed his candidacy as a battle not just for the presidency, but for the soul of the nation.

Moreover, the size and frequency of Trump's rallies contributed to a sense of momentum that became self-reinforcing. As his rallies grew larger and more enthusiastic, they generated more media coverage, which in turn helped him attract even bigger crowds. Each event became a spectacle that drew attention from both supporters and critics alike. The media, despite often being the target of Trump's attacks, couldn't ignore the massive crowds and the fervor they displayed. This continuous cycle of rallies, media coverage, and growing momentum created an impression that Trump was an unstoppable force, making it difficult for his opponents to keep up.

Trump's rallies were also effective in shaping the narrative around his campaign. His repeated focus on issues like immigration and trade at these events kept those topics at the forefront of the national conversation. While other candidates might have focused more on policy details, Trump used his rallies to hammer home his core messages in a way that was simple, memorable, and emotionally charged. These events allowed him to define the terms of the debate, forcing his rivals to respond to his framing of the issues.

In many ways, Trump's rallies were more than just campaign events—they were a reflection of his entire approach to politics. They were about spectacle, emotional connection, and tapping into the frustrations of a large segment of the electorate. By holding rally after rally, often in key battleground states, Trump built a direct and loyal connection with his supporters that was immune to the attacks of his opponents or the criticism of the media. His rallies became a source of energy and enthusiasm that sustained his campaign, helping him maintain momentum all the way to the White House.

In the end, Trump's ability to mobilize massive crowds and create a sense of emotional urgency at his rallies was one of the defining features of his candidacy. His mastery of the rally format allowed him to communicate his message in a way that resonated deeply with his base, ensuring that his campaign was driven not just by policies, but by the powerful connection between candidate and supporter. This direct, unfiltered communication became a hallmark of Trump's political strategy and would continue to define his relationship with his followers throughout his presidency.

Harnessing Social Media—Amplifying the Celebrity Candidate

While Donald Trump's rallies created a powerful connection with voters on the ground, his mastery of social media amplified his message to millions more, creating a direct line of communication with the public. Throughout the 2016 campaign, Trump's use of social media—particularly Twitter—became a central feature of his strategy, allowing him to bypass traditional media outlets and speak directly to voters in real time. This approach was not just about disseminating information; it was about shaping the narrative, controlling the conversation, and keeping himself at the center of public attention.

Trump's use of social media was unprecedented in modern politics. Whereas previous candidates had used platforms like Twitter, Facebook, and Instagram to broadcast carefully crafted messages, Trump used them as tools of immediacy and authenticity. His tweets were raw, unfiltered, and often controversial, making them impossible to ignore. By posting directly to millions of followers, Trump was able to circumvent the press, presenting his thoughts and opinions without the filter of media interpretation. This allowed him to speak to his base in a way that felt personal, direct, and unmediated—an incredibly powerful tool in an era of growing distrust of traditional media.

From the outset of his campaign, Trump's Twitter feed became a constant source of headlines. He used it to comment on everything from policy issues to personal attacks on his opponents, often in the blunt, provocative style that had become his trademark. Whether he was tweeting about immigration, the economy, or foreign affairs, Trump's posts were designed to provoke a reaction. They were short, punchy, and often inflammatory—perfectly suited to the fast-paced, attention-driven nature of social media. Trump understood that in the age of social media, simplicity and boldness often outweighed nuance and detail. His tweets cut through the noise, generating coverage not just online but across television and print media as well.

One of the key ways Trump used social media to his advantage was by framing the terms of the debate. While his opponents were often bogged down in policy discussions or defensive responses to attacks, Trump would set the agenda with a single tweet. Whether it was calling for a ban on Muslims entering the U.S. or mocking his rivals with demeaning nicknames, Trump's posts dominated the conversation. By the time other candidates or the media reacted, Trump had already moved on to the next topic, leaving his opponents constantly playing catch-up. His ability to set the terms of the debate kept him in control of the narrative, even when his statements sparked outrage or controversy.

This strategy was particularly effective in shaping the media's coverage of the campaign. Traditional news outlets found themselves in a constant state of reaction, covering Trump's latest tweet or public statement rather than focusing on other candidates or issues. Cable news networks, in particular, became obsessed with Trump's social media presence, often devoting entire segments to analyzing his tweets. This relentless focus on Trump ensured that he remained the dominant figure in the race, even when other candidates were working hard to gain attention. His ability to keep the media fixated on him—through both positive and negative coverage—was a key factor in his success.

But Trump's use of social media was not just about grabbing attention—it was also about reinforcing his brand as an outsider and a fighter. His tweets often portrayed him as someone willing to take on the establishment, the media, and his political opponents without fear or hesitation. By attacking the media directly, calling them "fake news" and accusing them of bias, Trump cast himself as a victim of an unfair system, a narrative that resonated deeply with many of his supporters. His relentless criticism of the media became a rallying cry for his base, who saw his attacks as proof that he was willing to stand up to powerful elites on their behalf.

Trump's social media strategy also allowed him to maintain constant engagement with his supporters. Unlike traditional political communication, which is often filtered through spokespeople or campaign surrogates, Trump's tweets came directly from him, making his followers feel as though they were hearing from the candidate in real time. This sense of immediacy and directness created a bond between Trump and his supporters that was difficult for other candidates to replicate. His posts were often conversational, speaking in the same blunt, straightforward language that he used at his rallies. This helped reinforce the image of Trump as a man of the people—someone who wasn't afraid to speak his mind, even if it was politically incorrect.

Another key aspect of Trump's social media presence was his ability to weaponize it against his opponents. Throughout the campaign, Trump used Twitter to launch personal attacks on his rivals, both Republican and Democrat, often coining nicknames or labels that would stick. His monikers like "Low Energy Jeb" for Jeb Bush, "Little Marco" for Marco Rubio, and "Crooked Hillary" for Hillary Clinton became part of the political lexicon, damaging his opponents' brands in a way that traditional political attacks rarely do. These tweets, while often dismissed as juvenile or inappropriate, were incredibly effective in shaping public perceptions of his opponents, reducing their campaigns to the caricatures he created.

Furthermore, Trump's social media allowed him to build and reinforce a loyal online following. His supporters, often referred to as the "Trump Train," were highly active on platforms like Twitter, Facebook, and Reddit, where they would share his posts, amplify his message, and attack his critics. This created a feedback loop in which Trump's online supporters not only consumed his content but became part of the messaging machine themselves. The sense of community that developed among Trump's online base mirrored the energy and camaraderie of his rallies, turning his social media presence into a digital extension of his ground campaign.

Trump's social media strategy was not without its risks. His frequent use of inflammatory language and his willingness to engage in public spats with anyone who crossed him led to numerous controversies throughout the campaign. However, these controversies often worked to his advantage, as they kept him in the headlines and reinforced his image as someone who wasn't afraid to break the rules. For Trump, the goal was not necessarily to win every news cycle, but to dominate it—and social media gave him the tools to do just that.

In the end, Trump's use of social media during the 2016 campaign was a game-changer. It allowed him to communicate directly with millions of voters, control the narrative, and keep his opponents and the media on the defensive. His unorthodox, aggressive style may have shocked the political establishment, but it resonated with voters who were looking for something different. By harnessing the power of social media, Trump was able to amplify his message, expand his reach, and ultimately win the presidency in a way that no one had anticipated.

The Power of Provocation—Controversy as a Campaign Tool

As much as Donald Trump's social media presence helped him connect with supporters, his deliberate use of controversy became one of the most potent tools in his campaign arsenal. Trump seemed to understand that in the age of 24-hour news and viral content, staying in the public eye required more than just policy proposals or conventional speeches—it required the ability to provoke strong reactions, both positive and negative. For Trump, controversy wasn't just something to be managed or avoided; it was an opportunity. By consistently creating headlines, he made himself the focal point of the 2016 election, drawing attention and energy that his opponents couldn't match.

Trump's willingness to stir the pot, often in provocative or inflammatory ways, was a hallmark of his candidacy. Whether he was tweeting insults at political rivals, making bold, seemingly outrageous statements about immigration, or attacking the media with a ferocity not seen in modern politics, Trump was always pushing the boundaries of what was considered acceptable for a presidential candidate. But this was no accident. Trump understood that every controversy kept him in the spotlight, and as long as he was the center of attention, his message—no matter how polarizing—would continue to reach millions.

One of the earliest and most memorable examples of this strategy came in the form of his announcement speech in June 2015, when he labeled Mexican immigrants as criminals and rapists. This incendiary remark set off a firestorm of criticism from the media, political pundits, and even some members of the Republican Party. Many believed that this would be the end of Trump's fledgling campaign, but instead, it had the opposite effect. His base, made up of voters frustrated with political correctness and what they saw as uncontrolled immigration, rallied around him. Trump's supporters admired his willingness to speak what they believed was the uncomfortable truth, and the controversy only solidified his standing with this group.

The media, unable to ignore the uproar, gave Trump massive amounts of coverage. Whether they were condemning him or simply reporting on his remarks, they were talking about him—and in the world of celebrity politics, that was all that mattered. Trump's provocative statements became a form of free advertising, allowing him to dominate news cycles without having to spend millions on traditional campaign ads. In this way, controversy was a cost-effective way for Trump to keep his name in headlines, ensuring that he was always the subject of conversation, whether it was praise or outrage.

Another critical aspect of Trump's use of controversy was his ability to frame himself as the victim of unfair attacks. Whenever he said something that sparked outrage, whether it was a personal insult aimed at a political rival or a broad statement about immigration or trade, he would often claim that the media or the "political establishment" was twisting his words or taking him out of context. This narrative of victimization resonated with his supporters, who already felt that they, too, were being unfairly targeted by political correctness and elite institutions. Trump portrayed himself as a fighter, not just against his political rivals but against a broader system that was stacked against him and his followers. This "us versus them" mentality became a defining feature of his campaign, allowing him to turn controversy into a rallying cry for his base.

One of the most telling examples of this came during the Republican primary debates, where Trump's opponents frequently tried to use his controversial statements against him. Instead of backing down, Trump would double down, using the attacks to fuel his outsider persona. When former Florida governor Jeb Bush or Texas senator Ted Cruz attacked him for his positions on immigration or foreign policy, Trump would respond by labeling them as weak or part of the failed establishment. This tactic worked brilliantly in the context of a Republican Party base that was increasingly disillusioned with traditional politicians. Trump's refusal to play by the normal rules of political decorum only endeared him further to his supporters.

Even as the general election approached and Trump's controversies grew in both size and scope, his strategy remained the same. His attacks on Hillary Clinton, labeling her "Crooked Hillary" and calling for her to be jailed over her handling of emails as Secretary of State, dominated media coverage and energized his base. While many in the media and political elite decried Trump's rhetoric as damaging to democratic norms, his supporters saw it as a necessary pushback against a system that had failed them. To them, Trump's willingness to say what other politicians wouldn't was proof that he was different—that he was on their side.

The infamous release of the "Access Hollywood" tape, in which Trump was recorded making lewd and offensive comments about women, was another moment when controversy threatened to derail his campaign. The media and political pundits declared that this would be the final straw, the controversy that would end Trump's bid for the presidency. Yet Trump's response followed the same pattern as before: he acknowledged the remarks but framed the backlash as part of a broader, unfair attack by a biased media and political system. He quickly pivoted the conversation back to Clinton and the issues that mattered most to his base. While the tape did damage Trump's standing with some voters, particularly suburban women, his core supporters remained loyal, further cementing the idea that Trump could weather any controversy as long as he maintained their trust.

Ultimately, Trump's ability to harness controversy as a campaign tool was a key factor in his rise as a celebrity candidate. He understood that in the world of modern media, attention—whether positive or negative—was the most valuable currency. His mastery of this principle allowed him to dominate the 2016 election in ways that no other candidate could. By embracing controversy, framing himself as the outsider fighting against an unjust system, and doubling down in the face of criticism, Trump kept himself in the headlines and, more importantly, kept his base energized and engaged.

In the end, what might have derailed a traditional candidate only fueled Trump's momentum. His unapologetic style, his willingness to provoke, and his instinctive understanding of the media landscape enabled him to turn every controversy into an opportunity. For Trump, controversy wasn't a liability—it was a weapon, one that he wielded with remarkable skill throughout his campaign. And as 2016 unfolded, it became clear that this approach, while unconventional, was exactly what many voters wanted in a candidate.

Chapter 13

Chapter 13: Building a Populist Brand

The Roots of Trump's Populist Appeal

Donald Trump's populist appeal did not emerge out of nowhere; it was deeply rooted in a particular moment in American history, a period when vast swaths of the population felt left behind by both political parties. Throughout the late 20th and early 21st centuries, globalization, technological changes, and a rapidly shifting economy had created winners and losers. While the elite prospered, middle- and working-class Americans, especially in manufacturing hubs, saw their jobs disappear, wages stagnate, and opportunities fade. Trump sensed this growing disillusionment and channeled it into a powerful political message that would come to define his populist brand.

At the core of Trump's populist appeal was his ability to frame himself as the voice of the "forgotten men and women" of America. From the very start of his 2016 campaign, he identified a key demographic—largely white, working-class voters in Rust Belt states—who felt that the political establishment no longer represented them. These voters were often overlooked by both Republican and Democratic leadership, who were more focused on globalization, technology, and urban progress. In contrast, Trump zeroed in on their economic anxieties, job losses, and growing sense of cultural alienation.

Trump's focus on job losses tied to globalization became a cornerstone of his populist message. In state after state, from Ohio to Michigan to Pennsylvania, communities that had once thrived on manufacturing and industry had seen factories close and jobs disappear as companies relocated production overseas. Trump tapped into the resentment caused by these changes, particularly against political elites and corporations who, in his view, had sold out the American worker in favor of cheap foreign labor and increased profits. He positioned himself as someone who understood their plight, despite his status as a billionaire real estate mogul. His frequent refrain—"I'm fighting for you"—struck a chord with voters who felt abandoned by a system they believed was rigged against them.

Another significant aspect of Trump's populism was his sharp critique of free trade deals. For years, both Republican and Democratic administrations had promoted free trade agreements like NAFTA (the North American Free Trade Agreement) and the Trans-Pacific Partnership (TPP) as boons for the U.S. economy. Trump, however, denounced these deals as disasters for American workers. He argued that free trade had gutted American industries, outsourced millions of jobs, and led to the collapse of entire communities dependent on manufacturing. In speeches and debates, Trump railed against the "globalists" in Washington who, in his view, had betrayed American workers for the benefit of foreign nations and multinational corporations.

By attacking these trade deals, Trump aligned himself with a growing sense of economic nationalism—a belief that the American economy should prioritize the interests of American workers above all else. He promised to renegotiate or scrap these deals, bring back manufacturing jobs, and ensure that American industries would no longer be subject to unfair competition from abroad. While the political class largely dismissed Trump's protectionist rhetoric as outdated or impractical, it resonated deeply with voters who had witnessed firsthand the destruction of their livelihoods by what they saw as careless or greedy trade policies.

Immigration, too, was central to Trump's populist appeal. From the very beginning of his campaign, he framed illegal immigration as not only a law enforcement issue but also an economic one. He argued that undocumented immigrants were taking jobs that should belong to Americans and depressing wages by providing a source of cheap labor. Trump's infamous claim that Mexico was sending "rapists" and criminals across the border played into fears about crime and job competition, but it also positioned him as someone willing to address an issue that many voters felt had been ignored or mishandled for too long. His promises to build a wall along the southern border and institute extreme vetting for immigrants were not just policy proposals; they were symbolic of his commitment to putting Americans first.

Trump's populist rhetoric also extended beyond economic issues to include a broader critique of cultural and political elites. He frequently attacked the "coastal elites"—politicians, media figures, academics, and celebrities—whom he portrayed as out of touch with the realities of everyday Americans. In contrast, Trump positioned himself as the outsider who understood what it meant to struggle, despite his wealth and fame. He used his rallies and speeches to denounce political correctness, a concept that resonated deeply with voters who felt that their voices were being silenced in an increasingly progressive and elite-dominated cultural landscape. By railing against the media, Hollywood, and academia, Trump tapped into a deep-seated cultural resentment, portraying himself as the defender of traditional American values under siege by liberal elites.

Perhaps the most striking aspect of Trump's populist appeal was how he was able to combine economic grievances with cultural anxieties. His voters weren't just concerned about lost jobs or stagnant wages; they also feared that their way of life was slipping away in a rapidly changing country. Trump's campaign spoke to those fears, promising to restore not only economic prosperity but also a sense of national pride and identity. For his base, Trump wasn't just a politician—he was a fighter, someone who would take on the elites, reverse the decline of American industry, and restore the dignity of the American worker.

In this way, Trump built a populist brand that transcended traditional political boundaries. His ability to channel economic anxiety, cultural frustration, and a sense of betrayal by the political class made him a powerful and unique force in American politics. By positioning himself as the champion of the "forgotten" and the enemy of the elite, Trump laid the groundwork for a movement that would ultimately propel him to the presidency.

"Make America Great Again"—A Slogan of Identity

One of the most powerful tools in Donald Trump's rise as a populist leader was his campaign slogan, "Make America Great Again." More than just a catchphrase, it became the rallying cry of his political movement, encapsulating his vision, his promises, and his connection with voters. The slogan tapped into a sense of nostalgia for a bygone era and appealed to millions who felt the country had lost its way. In four words, Trump was able to distill a complex set of grievances into a simple, memorable, and emotionally charged message that resonated with his supporters on a deep level.

"Make America Great Again" implied a return to a time when America was, in Trump's view, stronger, wealthier, and more respected on the global stage. But it also implied that something important had been lost—an unspoken acknowledgment that the present was not as good as the past. For many of Trump's supporters, particularly working-class and rural voters, the phrase evoked a sense of loss and a longing for the America they believed had existed before the forces of globalization, rapid social change, and political elitism took hold. This sense of decline was especially potent in communities that had been hollowed out by the collapse of industries like coal, steel, and manufacturing. To them, "great again" was not just an economic promise, but a cultural one.

The choice of the word "again" was particularly important. It suggested that the greatness Trump spoke of wasn't something entirely new or unprecedented—it was something America had once possessed but needed to recapture. For Trump's supporters, this offered a comforting narrative: that America had been on the right track but had lost its way due to poor leadership, misguided policies, and the influence of outsiders. Trump positioned himself as the candidate who could reverse these mistakes and restore the country's former glory.

The appeal of "Make America Great Again" was broad, but it was especially resonant with those who felt left behind by globalization and the technological advancements that had changed the fabric of American life. In the Rust Belt, where factories had shuttered and jobs had disappeared, the slogan seemed to promise the revival of the American manufacturing sector and a return to a time when a high school diploma and a steady job in the factory could provide a comfortable middle-class life. For farmers, coal miners, and steelworkers, it seemed to signal that their struggles had been noticed and that their livelihoods would be prioritized once again. Trump, by emphasizing the idea of "bringing jobs back," directly appealed to these communities, suggesting that the old economic order could be revived if only the right leader took charge.

On a broader scale, the slogan also spoke to a growing sense of cultural alienation among Trump's base. As American society became more diverse and progressive, many of his supporters felt that their traditional values were under siege. Trump's promise to make the country "great again" was heard by some as a commitment to protect their cultural identity in the face of these changes. For many white, Christian, and rural voters, "great again" wasn't just about economic revival—it was about restoring a vision of America where their way of life, values, and beliefs were central.

Trump's genius lay in his ability to leave the definition of "great" deliberately vague, allowing different segments of his audience to project their own meanings onto the phrase. For some, it meant economic recovery and a return to American manufacturing dominance. For others, it symbolized cultural preservation and a pushback against what they saw as an increasingly liberal and multicultural society. This ambiguity gave the slogan extraordinary power, as it resonated with voters on multiple levels—economic, cultural, and emotional—without boxing Trump into specific policies or promises.

Another aspect of the slogan's appeal was its clear differentiation from Trump's political rivals. While Hillary Clinton's 2016 campaign focused on continuity and incremental progress with slogans like "Stronger Together," Trump's message of radical change was a direct rejection of the status quo. His slogan implied that America's current path was wrong and needed a sharp course correction. In a political climate where many voters felt disillusioned with both parties, "Make America Great Again" cut through the noise with its promise of upheaval and renewal. Trump was presenting himself as the disruptor who would turn back the clock on policies that, in his telling, had weakened the nation.

The slogan also evoked a sense of urgency, a feeling that the window to save America was rapidly closing. This added an emotional intensity to Trump's campaign, encouraging voters to rally around him as a last-ditch effort to restore the country they loved. It wasn't just about improving the present; it was about recovering something that had been lost before it was gone forever. This sense of mission, of fighting to preserve a version of America that was slipping away, gave Trump's campaign a zeal that galvanized his supporters and turned his rallies into fervent expressions of loyalty and belief in his cause.

"Make America Great Again" became more than just a slogan—it became a symbol of identity for Trump's supporters. Red "MAGA" hats were worn not just as political paraphernalia, but as declarations of allegiance to Trump's vision and rejection of the political elite and mainstream culture. To wear a MAGA hat or to chant the slogan at a rally was to declare oneself part of a movement, one that viewed itself as standing up for the "real America" against a political establishment that had lost touch with the values and concerns of ordinary people.

In summary, "Make America Great Again" was a brilliantly crafted slogan that encapsulated Donald Trump's populist brand. It spoke to a wide range of economic, cultural, and emotional anxieties, offering a simple but powerful promise: that Trump could restore the country's greatness by challenging the forces that had undermined it. This message of restoration, combined with its broad appeal and emotional resonance, was key to Trump's success in mobilizing a base of voters who believed they had been forgotten by the political system, and it became a defining feature of his populist movement.

The Outsider's Advantage—Positioning Against the Political Elite

Donald Trump's success as a populist figure was significantly driven by his ability to position himself as an outsider, standing apart from the political elite that many Americans had grown to distrust. This outsider status was not incidental—it was a central part of Trump's identity and appeal, allowing him to capitalize on the growing resentment towards the traditional political establishment. Trump's populist brand was built on the idea that he was not beholden to the same rules, norms, or interests that had come to define Washington politics, and his supporters embraced him precisely because of this difference.

In the years leading up to Trump's presidential campaign, trust in the U.S. government had been steadily declining. Scandals, gridlock, and a perceived disconnect between politicians and everyday citizens had created widespread frustration. Congress's approval ratings were abysmally low, and both Republicans and Democrats were seen as part of a system that served its own interests rather than those of the American people. Trump, in contrast, cast himself as the candidate who was not part of this broken system. He was not a politician; he was a businessman, someone who had succeeded outside the political bubble and could therefore challenge it.

This outsider image was reinforced by Trump's frequent and unfiltered attacks on both the Republican and Democratic establishments. While other candidates sought endorsements from party leaders and adhered to traditional campaign strategies, Trump broke the mold. He openly criticized powerful figures within his own party, such as Jeb Bush and Mitt Romney, portraying them as weak, ineffective, and out of touch with the concerns of ordinary Americans. Trump's refusal to play by the established rules of political decorum only strengthened his populist appeal, as voters saw in him a willingness to challenge the status quo.

Trump's candidacy was, in many ways, a rejection of "politics as usual." His unpolished style, bombastic rhetoric, and willingness to speak his mind—no matter how controversial or offensive—set him apart from the polished, cautious image of career politicians. Where other candidates carefully parsed their words to avoid missteps, Trump seemed to thrive on saying the unsayable. He attacked the media, mocked his opponents, and dismissed political correctness as a straitjacket imposed by elites to silence dissent. This approach endeared him to voters who were tired of politicians they saw as out of touch, overly scripted, and beholden to special interests.

For Trump's base, his wealth was also a key factor in his outsider status. In a system where many politicians relied on donations from corporate PACs, lobbyists, and wealthy donors, Trump frequently reminded his supporters that he was self-funding much of his campaign, a claim that reinforced the idea that he could not be bought or influenced by special interests. While his critics pointed to his wealth as evidence of his elite status, Trump flipped the narrative. Instead of downplaying his success, he highlighted it, framing himself as the ultimate American success story—a billionaire who had achieved the American Dream and now wanted to ensure that others could do the same.

Trump's outsider status also extended to his relationship with the media. Unlike traditional candidates, who courted the press for positive coverage, Trump seemed to relish his adversarial relationship with the media, frequently attacking it as biased, corrupt, and dishonest. His use of the term "fake news" became a rallying cry for his supporters, many of whom felt that mainstream outlets were not only out of touch with their values but actively working against them. By positioning himself against the media, Trump cast himself as the only reliable source of truth in a landscape dominated by what he claimed were lies and distortions. This created a feedback loop in which Trump's supporters dismissed negative coverage of him as evidence of media bias, further solidifying their loyalty to him.

Trump's ability to brand himself as an outsider was also evident in his attacks on the political "swamp" of Washington, D.C. Throughout his campaign, Trump promised to "drain the swamp," a metaphor that resonated deeply with voters who saw the nation's capital as a cesspool of corruption, self-dealing, and inefficiency. By promising to eliminate career bureaucrats, lobbyists, and entrenched political interests, Trump positioned himself as a reformer who would fundamentally change the way the government operated. His supporters didn't just want better policies; they wanted to overhaul the system itself, and Trump's outsider status made him the perfect vehicle for that change.

Another element of Trump's populist outsider image was his rejection of political correctness. In the years leading up to his campaign, there had been growing frustration among many Americans over what they perceived as an increasingly stifling culture of political correctness. This frustration was particularly strong among Trump's core supporters, who felt that their voices were being silenced by elites in academia, the media, and politics who were more concerned with identity politics than with the everyday struggles of ordinary Americans. Trump's refusal to bow to these norms—whether through his incendiary comments on immigration, race, or gender—was seen as a breath of fresh air by those who felt they could no longer speak their minds in public without fear of retribution.

In a sense, Trump's campaign was a reaction to the excesses of both the political and cultural elites. While his critics saw his rhetoric as divisive and dangerous, his supporters viewed it as a necessary corrective to a system that had become too insulated, too self-satisfied, and too disconnected from the realities of American life. For them, Trump's willingness to "tell it like it is," even if that meant offending large swaths of the population, was a sign of his authenticity. He wasn't afraid to break the rules because, in his view, the rules were part of the problem.

Ultimately, Trump's outsider image allowed him to tap into a deep well of resentment and frustration among voters who felt abandoned by both parties and disillusioned with the political process. By positioning himself as the antithesis of the political establishment, Trump was able to harness the anger, fear, and discontent that had been simmering beneath the surface of American life for years. His populist appeal wasn't just about policy—it was about identity, about giving a voice to those who felt voiceless, and about offering a stark alternative to the political system they had come to distrust. In doing so, Trump not only built a political movement but also redefined what it meant to be an outsider in American politics.

The Populist Message—"America First" and the Power of Nationalism

Central to Donald Trump's populist appeal was his ability to distill complex political and economic issues into a simple, emotionally charged message: "America First." This slogan, which became the rallying cry of his presidential campaign, resonated with millions of Americans who felt left behind by globalization, unchecked immigration, and the perceived weakening of American influence on the global stage. It tapped into a deep sense of national pride and insecurity, offering a vision of a revitalized America that would once again dominate the world economically, militarily, and culturally.

The roots of Trump's "America First" message can be traced back to a longstanding strain of American nationalism, one that favors protectionism, isolationism, and a focus on domestic concerns over international entanglements. In Trump's hands, however, this message took on new potency, shaped by the anxieties of an increasingly globalized world in which many Americans felt their country's economic and cultural identity was being eroded. Trump's populism thrived on the idea that America had been taken advantage of—by foreign countries, multinational corporations, and political elites alike—and that it was time to fight back.

Trump's version of nationalism was largely economic. At the heart of his message was the argument that bad trade deals and unfair practices by other countries, particularly China, had hollowed out American manufacturing and decimated working-class jobs. For decades, free trade had been a cornerstone of both Republican and Democratic economic policies, with leaders from both parties arguing that globalization was inevitable and ultimately beneficial. Trump, however, rejected this consensus, claiming that free trade agreements like NAFTA were disastrous for American workers. By emphasizing tariffs, renegotiating trade deals, and promising to bring jobs back to American soil, Trump presented himself as the champion of those who had been hurt by the shifting tides of global commerce.

This economic nationalism struck a chord, particularly in the Rust Belt, where entire industries had been decimated by the outsourcing of jobs to countries with cheaper labor. Cities that had once been booming hubs of manufacturing—places like Detroit, Cleveland, and Pittsburgh—had seen factories shutter, families break apart, and communities wither. For the voters in these areas, Trump's promise to make America great again by restoring these jobs and rebuilding their towns wasn't just an abstract campaign slogan—it was a lifeline. He tapped into their frustration with both the Republican and Democratic establishments, which they saw as complicit in their economic decline.

Trump's message was clear: America had been sold out by its leaders, and only he, a businessman who understood the world's economic levers, could reverse the damage.

But Trump's populism wasn't just about economics—it was also deeply cultural. His "America First" message reflected a broader sense of cultural dislocation felt by many of his supporters. For years, they had watched as demographic shifts, changing social norms, and immigration transformed the country's identity. Trump's rhetoric on immigration, particularly his focus on building a wall along the U.S.-Mexico border, played directly into these fears. He framed immigration not just as an economic issue, but as a threat to American culture and safety. Illegal immigrants, he argued, were taking jobs from Americans, straining social services, and contributing to crime. His promise to crack down on illegal immigration and protect American borders was a key part of his appeal to voters who felt that their country was slipping away from them.

This cultural aspect of Trump's populism was also evident in his frequent attacks on political correctness and the progressive values championed by the left. Trump positioned himself as a defender of traditional American values, railing against what he saw as the excesses of identity politics, cancel culture, and the liberal elites who, in his view, were more concerned with diversity and inclusivity than with the concerns of everyday Americans. He presented himself as a truth-teller, someone who wasn't afraid to say what others were thinking, even if it meant offending various groups. For his supporters, this bluntness was refreshing, a rejection of the perceived censorship imposed by political correctness. Trump's message was clear: America needed to stop apologizing for its past, its identity, and its role in the world. It was time to be unapologetically American.

The "America First" message also extended to foreign policy. Trump was deeply critical of international alliances and agreements that, in his view, benefited other countries at America's expense. NATO, for example, was a frequent target of his criticism. He argued that the U.S. was unfairly shouldering the financial burden of defending wealthy European nations that weren't paying their fair share. Similarly, Trump questioned the value of long-standing alliances in Asia and the Middle East, suggesting that the U.S. should only intervene in global conflicts when it was in America's direct interest. This approach marked a sharp departure from the interventionist policies of previous administrations, both Republican and Democrat, which had been more focused on maintaining a global order and promoting democracy abroad. Trump's stance was a direct appeal to the growing isolationist sentiment within the American public, particularly among those who were tired of seeing American lives and resources spent on wars and conflicts that didn't seem to benefit the country.

Trump's "America First" nationalism was also fueled by a deep distrust of international institutions like the United Nations, the World Trade Organization, and the Paris Climate Accord. He saw these institutions as mechanisms through which the global elite exerted control over individual nations, particularly the United States. His decision to pull the U.S. out of the Paris Accord, for example, was framed as a move to protect American workers and industries from the constraints of international environmental regulations. Trump argued that these agreements were designed to benefit other countries, particularly China and India, at the expense of American jobs and energy independence.

By tying together economic nationalism, immigration, cultural identity, and a more isolationist foreign policy, Trump was able to create a populist brand that appealed to a broad cross-section of the American electorate. His supporters saw in him a leader who wasn't afraid to challenge the elites, both at home and abroad, and who was committed to putting American interests above all else. This message of nationalism and populism became the foundation of Trump's political identity and helped propel him to the presidency. It wasn't just about policies—it was about restoring a sense of pride, power, and purpose to a country that many of his supporters believed had lost its way.

Cultivating a Loyal Grassroots Movement—The Rise of Trump's Base

Donald Trump's populist brand didn't just rely on policy promises or slogans like "Make America Great Again." His campaign thrived because of the passionate, unwavering support of a grassroots movement that saw him not merely as a candidate but as a champion for their values and grievances. Trump's supporters—often referred to as his "base"—were more than just voters; they became part of a fervent political movement, driven by a deep emotional connection to their candidate. Trump, in turn, cultivated this loyalty, recognizing that his political survival and success depended on the enthusiasm and dedication of his core followers.

The bond between Trump and his supporters was forged early in his campaign, and it was solidified through a shared sense of alienation from the political establishment, the media, and even elements of society at large. Many of Trump's supporters felt that they had been ignored or condescended to by both Republican and Democratic leaders for years. They believed that the system—whether in Washington, New York, or Silicon Valley—was rigged against them, that elites had little interest in their struggles, and that their voices were being drowned out by a politically correct culture that marginalized their concerns.

Trump tapped into this resentment with laser precision, offering a direct connection to these voters that no other candidate could match.

Central to Trump's success in building this grassroots movement were his rallies. These events were not just typical campaign stops; they were mass gatherings where Trump supporters could come together, vent their frustrations, and celebrate their shared values. The energy and enthusiasm at these rallies were unlike anything seen in modern American politics. Trump fed off the crowd's energy, and the crowd, in turn, responded to his unapologetic rhetoric and unfiltered style. For many of his supporters, attending a rally wasn't just about hearing a political speech—it was about being part of a movement that made them feel empowered and heard. Trump's rallies became a place where grievances could be aired, the political and cultural elites could be vilified, and Trump himself could reaffirm his commitment to their cause.

One of the key aspects of Trump's populist appeal was his ability to foster a sense of "us versus them." He frequently positioned himself and his supporters as outsiders battling against powerful forces—the media, the political elite, and special interests—that were conspiring to undermine their vision for America. By casting his opponents as corrupt and untrustworthy, Trump made his supporters feel as though they were part of a fight to take back their country from those who had betrayed it. This narrative was incredibly powerful, as it not only reinforced the loyalty of his base but also made any criticism of Trump from the media or political opponents seem like further proof of this conspiracy. The more Trump was attacked by the press or the political establishment, the more his supporters rallied around him, believing that he was being unfairly targeted because he was fighting for them.

Trump's use of social media, particularly Twitter, played a crucial role in maintaining his direct connection with his supporters. Unlike traditional politicians who relied on spokespeople, press conferences, and carefully curated messages, Trump communicated with his followers in real time, often bypassing the media entirely. His tweets were raw, often impulsive, and sometimes incendiary, but that only enhanced his populist appeal. His supporters saw his social media presence as proof of his authenticity—a candidate who wasn't afraid to speak his mind and who didn't need to filter his thoughts through political handlers. Whether he was attacking a political rival, mocking the media, or promoting his policies, Trump's tweets kept his base engaged and energized. For many of his supporters, social media allowed them to feel personally connected to Trump in a way that no other politician could replicate.

This constant communication helped foster a sense of community among Trump's supporters. Online forums, Facebook groups, and Twitter threads became gathering places for his base to share memes, discuss political strategy, and defend Trump against criticism. This online presence, often referred to as the "Trump Train," became an integral part of his grassroots movement. It wasn't just about supporting a candidate; it was about being part of a political revolution. Trump's supporters took pride in their outsider status, relishing the idea that they were going against the grain of the political establishment and mainstream culture. This sense of camaraderie, of being part of something larger than themselves, further solidified their loyalty to Trump.

Trump's ability to cultivate a loyal grassroots movement was also evident in how he handled controversy. Throughout his campaign, Trump faced a barrage of scandals and criticism—his comments on immigrants, the Access Hollywood tape, accusations of fraud involving Trump University, and numerous other controversies that would have sunk most candidates. But Trump's base remained steadfast. For his supporters, these controversies were not disqualifying; rather, they were seen as further proof that Trump was being unfairly targeted by a biased media and a corrupt political establishment. His base believed that these attacks were designed to silence Trump because he posed a threat to the status quo. This sense of loyalty, even in the face of scandal, became one of the defining features of Trump's populist movement.

At the heart of Trump's appeal to his base was his ability to make them feel seen and heard in a way that other politicians had failed to do. His populist rhetoric was not just about policies—it was about identity. Trump framed his campaign as a fight for the soul of America, a battle between the forgotten men and women of the country and the elites who had sold them out. His supporters didn't just see Trump as their candidate; they saw him as their champion, someone who understood their struggles and was willing to fight for them against overwhelming odds. This emotional connection was key to Trump's ability to build a grassroots movement that remained loyal to him, even when the odds seemed stacked against him.

In the end, Trump's grassroots movement was a reflection of the power of populism in modern American politics. His ability to connect with voters on a visceral level, to tap into their frustrations and offer them a sense of purpose, was central to his success. Trump's base wasn't just supporting a candidate—they were part of a movement, one that believed it was reclaiming the country from the elites who had betrayed it. This grassroots movement, forged through rallies, social media, and a shared sense of grievance, became one of the most powerful forces in American politics, propelling Trump to the presidency and reshaping the political landscape in ways that would reverberate for years to come.

Chapter 14

Chapter 14: Leveraging Celebrity in the White Hous

Transforming the Presidency into a Media Spectacle

From the moment Donald Trump took office, he fundamentally transformed the presidency into a media spectacle, something unprecedented in modern American politics. As someone who had spent decades in the public eye, Trump understood better than any of his predecessors how to use the media to his advantage. His presidency was not simply a political office—it was a constant performance, designed to command attention, dominate headlines, and ensure that he was always at the center of the national conversation. In many ways, Trump's time in the White House reflected the era of reality television that had helped make him famous, blurring the lines between politics, entertainment, and spectacle.

Trump's approach to the presidency was deeply rooted in his celebrity status. Unlike previous presidents, who often sought to maintain a sense of decorum and dignity in their public communications, Trump thrived on controversy and unpredictability. He frequently used provocative statements, bombastic speeches, and off-the-cuff remarks to generate media coverage. Whether through impromptu press conferences, fiery speeches at rallies, or unscripted moments in interviews, Trump knew that every word he said would be dissected, analyzed, and replayed across news channels and social media platforms. His strategy was clear: stay in the headlines, even if the attention was negative, because visibility was power.

In Trump's world, media coverage—whether positive or negative—was always valuable. He instinctively understood that in the 24-hour news cycle, being talked about was more important than being liked. Trump's presidency became a constant source of content for news networks, providing endless material for debates, analysis, and commentary. From his first day in office, Trump made himself the dominant figure in American politics, overshadowing even significant legislative developments or international events with his personal dramas and media battles. By focusing the nation's attention on himself, Trump ensured that he remained the most talked-about figure, a strategy that mirrored his previous experience as a reality TV star on The Apprentice, where his larger-than-life personality was the show's main attraction.

Trump also understood the power of live television and spectacle in a way that previous presidents had not. He reveled in events that could be broadcast live, such as his rallies, which were not only political gatherings but theatrical performances. These rallies, carried by cable news networks, allowed Trump to communicate directly with his supporters, bypassing traditional filters and creating a sense of immediacy and connection. His speeches were often freewheeling and unscripted, filled with bombastic claims, attacks on his opponents, and praise for his own accomplishments. They were designed to entertain and energize his base, but they also guaranteed extensive media coverage, often dominating the news cycle for days.

One of Trump's most notable shifts in presidential communication was his use of Twitter to engage with the public in real time. While social media had been used by previous presidents, none had used it with the frequency and directness of Trump. His Twitter account became a key tool for shaping the media narrative. In a single tweet, Trump could set the agenda for the entire day's news coverage, often sparking intense debates, controversies, and reactions from politicians, pundits, and the public. Whether attacking political opponents, commenting on global events, or promoting his own policies, Trump's tweets were designed to provoke a response, ensuring that the media remained focused on him.

This media-focused presidency also extended to Trump's relationship with the press itself. While previous administrations maintained a more cooperative relationship with the media, often relying on journalists to help communicate their policies and achievements to the public, Trump took a combative approach. He frequently attacked the media, labeling outlets like The New York Times, CNN, and The Washington Post as "fake news" and accusing them of bias and dishonesty. These attacks on the media were a calculated move, designed to delegitimize any criticism of his presidency while reinforcing his populist message that he was fighting against a corrupt and out-of-touch establishment.

At the same time, Trump's constant feuds with the media helped him stay in the spotlight. The more he attacked the press, the more coverage he received, creating a cycle in which controversy begets attention, and attention begets more controversy. By positioning himself as a victim of media bias, Trump was able to galvanize his supporters, many of whom shared his distrust of the press. This combative stance reinforced his image as an outsider battling the entrenched elites of Washington, D.C., and the coastal media establishment. His base, already suspicious of mainstream news, saw these attacks as proof that Trump was their champion, fighting against forces that had long ignored or marginalized them.

Trump's transformation of the presidency into a media spectacle also had significant consequences for how the White House functioned. His administration often operated in a state of perpetual crisis, with scandals, personnel changes, and policy shifts constantly making headlines. This chaos, while unsettling to traditionalists, fit perfectly into Trump's strategy. By keeping the media and the public off balance, Trump controlled the narrative on his own terms. Each new controversy distracted from the last, and the sheer volume of news coming out of the White House made it difficult for any single issue to dominate for too long. Trump was a master of creating a "new story" to move past potential setbacks, always staying ahead of the media and public perception.

In many ways, Trump's presidency was a reflection of the celebrity culture he had come from—where attention, spectacle, and entertainment value were paramount. The substance of his policies often took a backseat to the drama surrounding his personality and the ongoing conflicts with his critics. For better or worse, Trump's presidency was defined by his ability to turn the highest office in the land into a media-driven phenomenon, one where every moment was designed to be consumed, debated, and replayed on screens across the country.

In conclusion, Trump's transformation of the presidency into a media spectacle was one of the defining features of his time in office. His unique understanding of the media, his willingness to provoke controversy, and his ability to command attention allowed him to control the narrative like no president before him. For Trump, the presidency wasn't just about governance—it was about performance, visibility, and staying at the center of America's attention. Through this approach, Trump reshaped the role of the president, turning it into a daily spectacle that captivated the nation and ensured that he was always in the spotlight, for better or for worse.

The Power of Social Media—The Twitter Presidency

Donald Trump's presidency will be remembered for many things, but perhaps none as transformative as his use of social media, particularly Twitter. From the day he announced his candidacy to his final days in office, Trump's Twitter account served as a direct line to the American people and a tool for bypassing traditional media channels. His tweets became headline-making events, shaping the national conversation in real time, setting the news cycle, and, at times, creating international incidents. In Trump's hands, social media was not just a tool for communication—it was a weapon that could be wielded to promote his agenda, attack his enemies, and rally his base.

While previous presidents had used social media, none had embraced it with the same fervor or directness as Trump. Barack Obama's administration had cautiously adopted platforms like Twitter and Facebook, but their use was largely managed by teams of social media experts crafting carefully controlled messages. Trump, by contrast, took personal control of his Twitter account, using it to voice his thoughts, frustrations, and attacks without the filters of advisers or the constraints of formal presidential communication. His tweets were raw, often inflammatory, and, in many cases, seemed to be fired off without a second thought. This unfiltered approach was one of the key elements of his appeal—his followers saw it as proof of his authenticity, while his critics saw it as reckless.

Throughout his presidency, Trump's Twitter feed became a primary source of news and controversy. Major policy announcements, firings, and even attacks on foreign leaders were often delivered in 280 characters or less, catching not only the media but also members of his own administration off guard. One of the most striking examples of Trump's reliance on Twitter came in March 2017, when he accused former President Barack Obama of wiretapping Trump Tower during the 2016 election campaign—a baseless claim that set off a media firestorm and prompted investigations. The tweet, sent early in the morning, was emblematic of Trump's ability to shape the national conversation with a single post, regardless of its veracity.

Trump's use of Twitter also allowed him to bypass traditional media outlets, which he often derided as "fake news." Rather than relying on press conferences, interviews, or official statements, Trump could communicate directly with millions of Americans through his social media platforms. His followers didn't have to wait for the evening news or sift through what they saw as biased reporting—they could hear from the president himself, unfiltered and immediate. This direct communication gave Trump unprecedented control over his public image and the narrative surrounding his presidency, as he no longer needed to rely on journalists or pundits to interpret his words.

At its core, Trump's Twitter strategy was about control. By using social media to speak directly to his base, Trump circumvented the traditional gatekeepers of information. He could reach his supporters with messages that resonated with their frustrations, fears, and hopes, without the risk of his statements being diluted or reinterpreted by the press. His tweets were often provocative and controversial, but that was part of the appeal—they kept him in the spotlight and ensured that his voice remained dominant in the national conversation. Whether he was tweeting about domestic policy, international affairs, or personal grievances, Trump's use of social media ensured that he could dictate the terms of political debate.

But Trump's use of Twitter wasn't just about policy; it was about spectacle. His social media presence turned political communication into a daily reality show, where each tweet could become the day's top story. He often used Twitter to create drama, teasing major announcements, attacking political rivals with nicknames like "Sleepy Joe" or "Crooked Hillary," and sharing conspiracy theories that would inflame his base. This constant stream of content kept his supporters engaged and his critics on the defensive. Trump understood that in the age of social media, attention is currency, and he was a master at generating it.

The implications of Trump's social media strategy were profound. By using Twitter as his primary communication tool, he blurred the line between official presidential communication and personal opinion, creating confusion about what constituted formal policy and what was merely Trump's personal musings. This ambiguity often left his administration scrambling to clarify or walk back statements made on Twitter, as in the case of his tweets about North Korea's leader Kim Jong-un, which raised concerns about escalating tensions between the two nations. In one tweet, Trump referred to Kim as "Little Rocket Man" and warned that the U.S. would use military force if necessary. While the tweet captured headlines, it also unnerved diplomats and defense officials, who worried that Trump's flippant language could have serious consequences on the international stage.

Yet, despite the chaos that often followed his tweets, Trump's social media presence proved to be one of his most effective tools for rallying his base. His tweets were direct, often bypassing the complexities of policy to speak in blunt, emotional terms that resonated with his followers. Whether he was attacking the media, criticizing Democrats, or promoting his accomplishments, Trump's Twitter feed was a constant reminder to his supporters that he was fighting for them and standing up to the establishment. His base saw his use of Twitter as a rejection of the traditional political system—an unvarnished, unfiltered president who wasn't afraid to say what he thought, no matter how controversial.

However, Trump's reliance on Twitter also had its drawbacks. His tweets often alienated potential allies, created unnecessary crises, and fueled his opponents' criticisms of his presidency. While his base remained loyal, many moderate voters and political leaders were put off by his constant tweeting, viewing it as unpresidential and undisciplined. His social media habits also contributed to a deeply polarized political climate, as his incendiary rhetoric on Twitter often inflamed tensions and deepened divisions within the country.

In the end, Trump's presidency will be remembered, in large part, for how he redefined the use of social media as a political tool. He turned Twitter into a platform for governing, bypassing the traditional filters of the press and using it to maintain a direct line of communication with his base. His tweets were often controversial, provocative, and even dangerous, but they kept him at the center of public attention, ensuring that his voice was always the loudest. In many ways, Trump's use of social media was emblematic of his presidency: unconventional, chaotic, and deeply polarizing, but undeniably effective in shaping the narrative of his time in office.

The Trump Brand in the Oval Office

When Donald Trump entered the White House, he didn't just bring his political agenda—he brought with him the powerful Trump brand that had been cultivated over decades as a real estate mogul, television star, and celebrity. Throughout his presidency, the blending of his personal brand with the office of the president was not only unprecedented but also central to how Trump approached governance. His presidency was an extension of the Trump brand: success, wealth, toughness, and, above all, winning. It was this fusion of celebrity and politics that made Trump's time in the Oval Office so distinctive, and at times, controversial.

From the beginning of his presidency, Trump made it clear that his identity as a successful businessman and media personality would define how he operated in the White House. He frequently touted his experience in business as proof that he could "make deals" and fix the problems that, in his view, career politicians had failed to address. In speeches, interviews, and even tweets, Trump leaned into his image as the ultimate dealmaker—the person who had built an empire with his name on it and who could now do the same for America. He framed his presidency as a business venture, where efficiency, profit, and strength were the guiding principles.

This mindset was reflected in how Trump structured his administration. Early on, he appointed key business figures to prominent positions, people who, like himself, came from the corporate world rather than the political establishment. Whether it was appointing CEOs to cabinet posts or inviting corporate leaders to the White House, Trump believed that successful businessmen were best equipped to run the country. He frequently referenced his corporate experience in decision-making processes, equating running the government to running a business. This business-first mentality was a direct reflection of his brand—an emphasis on profit margins, economic growth, and the bottom line.

Perhaps more than any other president, Trump made sure that his personal brand remained front and center. His name, synonymous with luxury and wealth, became intertwined with the image of his presidency. Even the physical space of the White House itself took on Trump's flair, with gold curtains and more opulent touches reminiscent of the lavish decor found in his Trump properties. His family, too, played an unusually large role in the administration, further blending the personal with the political. Ivanka Trump and her husband Jared Kushner, both of whom had prominent roles in the Trump Organization, became senior advisors, symbolizing the fusion of Trump's family and business empire with the executive branch. Critics frequently raised concerns about conflicts of interest, noting the blurred lines between Trump's business dealings and his political role, but for Trump, this was business as usual—his family had always been central to the Trump brand, and the White House was no different.

The most visible and direct way Trump integrated his personal brand with his presidency was through his constant self-promotion. Trump frequently touted his achievements—whether real, exaggerated, or aspirational—as proof of his success. Whether discussing the stock market, job creation, or foreign policy, Trump's language often centered around superlatives: the best, the greatest, the biggest. He positioned himself as the embodiment of American success, framing his presidency as the ultimate expression of his business prowess. In this sense, Trump treated the presidency like an extension of his business empire, using his platform to bolster not only his political standing but his brand's reputation as well.

Another significant way Trump leveraged his brand in the Oval Office was through his approach to the media. As someone who had spent years in the spotlight, Trump understood the power of perception and the importance of controlling the narrative. His administration was often more focused on optics than policy, with much attention given to how events, meetings, and decisions were presented to the public. He staged grand signing ceremonies, held press conferences in settings designed to evoke strength and power, and used the White House as a backdrop for high-profile summits. Trump wanted every moment of his presidency to reflect the image he had spent years cultivating—one of a leader who was in control, making bold moves, and delivering wins for the country.

Trump's brand also manifested itself in how he interacted with foreign leaders and approached diplomacy. Much like in his business ventures, Trump approached world affairs with a transactional mindset. He viewed relationships with other countries through the lens of deals, often emphasizing personal relationships and direct negotiations over the traditional channels of diplomacy. This was perhaps most famously illustrated in his dealings with North Korea's leader Kim Jong-un. Trump, breaking with decades of U.S. diplomatic norms, embraced a high-profile personal summit with Kim, a move that was as much about spectacle as it was about substance. For Trump, the summit represented a brand-building opportunity—he was the leader who could bring the world's most volatile leaders to the table, making deals that no one else could.

This focus on personal diplomacy extended to his relationships with other world leaders. Trump often emphasized his personal rapport with figures like Russian President Vladimir Putin and Turkish President Recep Tayyip Erdoğan, framing his interactions with them as part of his dealmaking expertise. In Trump's view, these personal relationships were more effective than the bureaucratic processes that had governed international relations in the past. His critics, however, argued that this approach undermined America's global standing and weakened alliances. But for Trump, the ultimate metric of success was not the long-term strength of alliances but the immediate impact of his deals and the perception of strength and decisiveness that they projected.

Throughout his presidency, Trump also used his platform to promote his personal successes and frequently took credit for achievements—whether economic growth, low unemployment, or foreign policy victories. This constant self-promotion reflected the marketing strategy he had long used in his business ventures, where the Trump name itself was the product being sold. Trump knew that his presidency, much like his businesses, thrived on attention and the projection of success. Whether he was cutting regulations, meeting with world leaders, or announcing new initiatives, Trump ensured that his involvement was front and center, reinforcing the notion that his personal brand was at the heart of his administration's achievements.

However, the blending of Trump's brand with the presidency also led to numerous ethical concerns and accusations of self-dealing. Throughout his term, there were frequent questions about whether Trump's policies and decisions were influenced by his financial interests, especially regarding his hotels and resorts. Critics pointed to instances where foreign governments or lobbyists booked rooms at Trump properties, raising concerns about conflicts of interest and potential violations of the emoluments clause of the Constitution. While Trump repeatedly denied any wrongdoing, these controversies were emblematic of the blurred lines between his personal brand and his political role.

In the end, Trump's presidency was inseparable from the Trump brand. His approach to governance, diplomacy, and public relations reflected the same values and tactics that had defined his business career: self-promotion, a focus on optics, and a transactional view of relationships. For Trump, the presidency was not just about leading the country—it was about reinforcing his image as the ultimate dealmaker, the man who could fix what others had broken and do it all while keeping his brand intact. This fusion of personal and political identity made his presidency unique, and it remains one of the defining features of his time in office. The Trump brand, for better or worse, became synonymous with the Trump presidency.

Controversy as a Political Tool—Using Scandal to Stay in the Spotlight

Donald Trump's presidency was marked by near-constant controversy, much of it fueled by his own actions, rhetoric, and deliberate provocations. However, unlike traditional politicians who might try to avoid or downplay scandals, Trump often used controversy as a tool to his advantage. He understood that in the age of 24-hour news and social media, controversy generated attention, and attention kept him in the spotlight. For Trump, visibility was power, and he leveraged the media's fixation on scandal to maintain control over the national conversation. His presidency was a masterclass in using controversy not as a liability but as a political weapon to energize his base, dominate the media cycle, and consolidate his image as a fighter against a hostile establishment.

From the outset of his political career, Trump showed a unique ability to turn scandals into opportunities. Early in his campaign, he made headlines with a string of inflammatory comments—on immigration, Muslims, and political opponents—that would have sunk the candidacy of a conventional politician. Yet for Trump, these controversies only seemed to enhance his appeal among his core supporters. His willingness to say what others wouldn't, to defy political correctness, and to double down in the face of criticism became a central part of his brand. Rather than apologize or backtrack when faced with backlash, Trump would often escalate the rhetoric, further inflaming the controversy and ensuring that he remained the focal point of public attention.

Trump's first major scandal as president—the investigation into Russian interference in the 2016 election and the possibility of collusion between his campaign and Moscow—could have severely undermined his presidency. Instead, Trump weaponized the investigation to rally his supporters and discredit his critics. He repeatedly referred to the inquiry as a "witch hunt" and an attempt by the "deep state" to undermine the will of the people. This narrative played perfectly into his populist message that he was an outsider battling corrupt forces within the government. The investigation, rather than damaging Trump, helped reinforce the idea that he was a victim of an establishment conspiracy—an image that galvanized his base, who viewed the probe as proof that Trump was shaking up the status quo.

One of Trump's most striking uses of controversy as a political tool was his handling of the first impeachment trial, which centered on his dealings with Ukraine and his alleged attempt to pressure the Ukrainian president into investigating Joe Biden, his potential 2020 election rival. The impeachment could have been a defining scandal for his presidency, but Trump used it to solidify his grip on the Republican Party and further energize his supporters. Throughout the process, Trump maintained that the impeachment was a partisan attack, an effort by Democrats to undo the results of the 2016 election. He turned the impeachment into a rallying cry for his base, framing himself as a victim of the political establishment. His defense team, echoing Trump's language, portrayed the trial as an attempt to subvert democracy, a message that resonated deeply with Trump's supporters. By the time the Senate acquitted him, Trump had not only survived the impeachment but had emerged even stronger within his own party, his dominance over the GOP cemented.

Even the most damaging scandals of Trump's presidency—such as the release of the *Access Hollywood* tape during the 2016 campaign, in which Trump was caught on tape bragging about sexually assaulting women—did not have the same impact as they would have on a conventional politician. Trump responded with defiance, issuing a brief apology but quickly shifting the focus to his opponents. His base, already distrustful of the media and political elites, largely dismissed the tape as an attempt by the press to derail his candidacy. Trump's ability to survive—and even thrive—amid scandals of this magnitude was a testament to his strategy of controlling the narrative, keeping the focus on his perceived enemies rather than on the allegations themselves.

Trump's approach to controversy was rooted in his longstanding understanding of the media. As a businessman and reality TV star, Trump had spent years cultivating his public image through controversy. He knew that media outlets are drawn to sensationalism, and that even negative coverage could be beneficial as long as it kept him in the public eye. As president, Trump applied this same principle to politics. By generating constant controversy—whether through his combative tweets, inflammatory speeches, or clashes with the press—Trump ensured that he was always at the center of attention. The media, compelled by the endless stream of stories coming out of the White House, devoted wall-to-wall coverage to Trump's every move. This relentless focus on Trump not only overshadowed his political opponents but also made it difficult for any single scandal to dominate the narrative for too long. New controversies constantly replaced old ones, creating a dizzying cycle that kept Trump's presidency in perpetual motion.

In many ways, Trump's ability to thrive on controversy reflected his broader political strategy: the more he was attacked, the more his base rallied around him. His supporters, who already distrusted the media and political elites, viewed the scandals as part of a broader effort to undermine Trump because he was challenging the status quo. Whether it was accusations of collusion with Russia, allegations of sexual misconduct, or criticisms of his handling of the COVID-19 pandemic, Trump's base remained largely unmoved by the controversies, seeing them as part of a larger narrative in which Trump was the victim of an unjust system. Each new scandal only seemed to deepen their loyalty to him, reinforcing the belief that Trump was fighting on their behalf against powerful forces trying to bring him down.

Trump's use of controversy also allowed him to frame his presidency as a constant battle—a fight not just for policy but for the very soul of the nation. He positioned himself as a warrior taking on the entrenched elites, the corrupt media, and the political establishment. This combative posture resonated deeply with his supporters, who felt that they, too, were under attack by the forces of political correctness, globalization, and progressive social change. Trump's ability to cast himself as a victim, even when embroiled in scandal, created a powerful sense of identification between him and his base. They saw their struggles in his battles and rallied to his defense whenever he was under fire.

In conclusion, Trump's presidency was defined by his ability to use controversy as a political tool. Rather than shy away from scandal, Trump embraced it, using it to keep himself in the spotlight, rally his base, and frame his presidency as a fight against the forces of the establishment. His skill in turning negative attention into political capital allowed him to survive, and even thrive, in a presidency marked by constant conflict and drama. In doing so, Trump rewrote the rules of political communication, demonstrating that in the modern media age, controversy could be as powerful a tool as policy when it came to maintaining control of the national conversation.

Celebrity Diplomacy—Navigating the World Stage

Donald Trump's approach to diplomacy was as unconventional as the rest of his presidency, driven largely by his celebrity status, his transactional mindset, and his preference for personal relationships over traditional diplomacy. Unlike previous presidents who relied on carefully cultivated relationships with foreign allies and the expertise of seasoned diplomats, Trump approached international relations with the same bravado and directness that had defined his career in business and reality television. He frequently bypassed established diplomatic protocols, opting instead for dramatic, high-profile meetings with world leaders, often designed as much for media spectacle as for substantive policy discussions. Trump's version of diplomacy was marked by bold gestures, unconventional tactics, and the belief that his personal charisma and dealmaking skills could reshape America's role on the world stage.

One of the most striking examples of Trump's celebrity-driven diplomacy was his unprecedented relationship with North Korea's leader, Kim Jong-un. For decades, the United States had maintained a policy of isolation and strategic patience with North Korea, aiming to limit its nuclear ambitions through sanctions and international pressure. Trump, however, took a radically different approach. After months of escalating tensions and trading insults with Kim—culminating in Trump calling him "Little Rocket Man" on Twitter—the two leaders shocked the world by agreeing to meet face-to-face. Trump's summit with Kim, held in Singapore in 2018, was the first time a sitting U.S. president had met with a North Korean leader.

The summit was as much a spectacle as it was a diplomatic event. The images of Trump and Kim shaking hands in front of a sea of cameras were broadcast around the world, symbolizing a moment of potential rapprochement between two adversaries. Trump framed the meeting as a breakthrough, highlighting his willingness to do what no other president had done: engage directly with North Korea. His critics, however, argued that the summit lacked substance, pointing out that the vague promises made by Kim did not lead to concrete steps toward denuclearization. But for Trump, the optics of the meeting were key. By positioning himself as the leader who could negotiate with the world's most reclusive dictator, he bolstered his image as a dealmaker and risk-taker on the global stage.

This focus on personal diplomacy over traditional channels was a hallmark of Trump's foreign policy. He often boasted of his "great relationships" with world leaders, suggesting that personal rapport was more important than long-standing alliances or geopolitical strategy. This was particularly evident in his dealings with Russian President Vladimir Putin. Throughout his presidency, Trump sought to cultivate a close relationship with Putin, frequently praising the Russian leader's strength and intelligence. Despite widespread concerns about Russian interference in the 2016 U.S. election, Trump repeatedly downplayed or dismissed the issue, choosing instead to focus on building a personal connection with Putin. His critics argued that Trump's overtures to Russia undermined U.S. intelligence agencies and emboldened a hostile foreign power, but Trump saw his personal diplomacy as a way to reset relations and negotiate from a position of mutual respect.

Trump's approach to foreign policy was deeply transactional, shaped by his belief that international relationships should be measured in terms of concrete benefits to the United States. He frequently criticized multilateral agreements and alliances, such as NATO, which he viewed as unfair to American taxpayers. Trump argued that the U.S. was shouldering too much of the financial burden for defending Europe, while other NATO members were not contributing their fair share. His public criticisms of NATO, particularly at summits with European leaders, caused tension within the alliance. Trump's focus on economic contributions rather than shared strategic interests reflected his broader approach to diplomacy: America first, and any partnership or agreement had to deliver tangible benefits to the U.S. or risk being renegotiated or abandoned.

This transactional mindset was also evident in Trump's decision to withdraw the United States from several key international agreements. In 2017, Trump pulled the U.S. out of the Paris Climate Accord, arguing that the agreement was unfair to American businesses and workers. Similarly, in 2018, he withdrew from the Iran nuclear deal, calling it "one of the worst deals ever made" and claiming it failed to address Iran's destabilizing activities in the region. In both cases, Trump's actions were framed as moves to protect American interests, even if they caused significant friction with U.S. allies. His willingness to disrupt long-standing agreements and alliances signaled a break from the multilateral, consensus-driven approach that had defined U.S. foreign policy for decades.

Trump's celebrity diplomacy was also marked by his use of media and public spectacle to shape perceptions of his foreign policy achievements. He often staged high-profile events with foreign leaders, from lavish state dinners at the White House to carefully choreographed meetings on the international stage. These moments were designed to project strength and success, with Trump frequently highlighting his ability to command attention and make bold moves. His administration's decision to move the U.S. embassy in Israel from Tel Aviv to Jerusalem was one such moment. The move, long sought by Israel and its supporters, was a controversial break from decades of U.S. foreign policy, but Trump framed it as a historic achievement that only he had the courage to deliver. The media coverage of the embassy opening, attended by top U.S. officials and Israeli leaders, reinforced Trump's narrative of being a decisive leader willing to take bold steps, even in the face of international criticism.

However, Trump's focus on personal relationships and media-driven diplomacy also had its drawbacks. His emphasis on showmanship and short-term wins often came at the expense of long-term strategy. Critics argued that Trump's reliance on personal diplomacy sidelined experienced diplomats and weakened America's alliances. His erratic approach to foreign policy—where decisions were sometimes made based on personal whims or tweets—created uncertainty among both allies and adversaries. For example, Trump's decision to abruptly withdraw U.S. troops from northern Syria in 2019, following a phone call with Turkish President Recep Tayyip Erdoğan, was widely condemned by military officials and members of Congress from both parties. The move, which effectively abandoned America's Kurdish allies in the fight against ISIS, was seen as a rash decision that jeopardized U.S. credibility in the region.

Despite these challenges, Trump's celebrity diplomacy did achieve some notable successes. His administration brokered the Abraham Accords, a series of normalization agreements between Israel and several Arab states, including the United Arab Emirates, Bahrain, and Sudan. These agreements marked a significant shift in the Middle East's geopolitical landscape and were widely praised as a diplomatic breakthrough. Trump's ability to leverage personal relationships with key leaders in the region, combined with his administration's economic and strategic incentives, played a critical role in securing the accords. This success underscored Trump's belief that his unique approach to diplomacy—focused on personal connections and transactional deals—could deliver results that traditional diplomacy could not.

In conclusion, Donald Trump's approach to diplomacy reflected his larger-than-life celebrity persona and his business-driven mindset. He bypassed the traditional tools of diplomacy, opting instead for bold gestures, high-stakes summits, and personal relationships with world leaders. While his celebrity diplomacy led to some significant achievements, it also raised concerns about the long-term consequences of sidelining traditional alliances and international agreements. Trump's emphasis on spectacle and short-term wins often overshadowed the complexity of global politics, leaving a legacy of both disruption and occasional breakthroughs on the world stage. For Trump, diplomacy was not just about strategy—it was about performance, dealmaking, and ensuring that he remained at the center of attention, both at home and abroad.

Chapter 15

Chapter 15: The Power of the Trump Brand Post-Pres

Reinventing the Trump Brand After the White House

After leaving the White House in January 2021, Donald Trump faced a unique challenge: how to reinvent his brand after four years as president, while no longer holding the reins of power. Trump was no stranger to reinvention. Over the course of his life, he had transformed from a brash New York real estate developer into a global celebrity, a reality TV star, and eventually the 45th president of the United States. But the post-presidency phase of his life would require a different kind of transformation—one that maintained his influence, kept him relevant in American politics, and ensured that the Trump brand remained potent in a rapidly shifting landscape.

From the start, Trump made it clear that he had no intention of fading into the background, as many former presidents had done. Where others chose a quieter, more reflective post-presidency, Trump leaned into his role as a political and cultural icon, continuing to command attention and dominate headlines. His exit from the White House was hardly the end of his public life—it was, in many ways, the beginning of a new chapter in the ongoing saga of Donald Trump. He knew that his most powerful asset was his brand, and he set out to reinvent and expand it by positioning himself as the leader of the conservative movement and the primary voice of opposition to the Biden administration.

In the immediate aftermath of his departure, Trump wasted no time in reminding his base that he wasn't going anywhere. He made Mar-a-Lago, his private resort in Palm Beach, Florida, the new hub of his political and business operations. This luxurious estate became not only his residence but also a gathering place for conservative leaders, Republican donors, and loyal supporters. From Mar-a-Lago, Trump held court, issuing statements, meeting with GOP power brokers, and plotting his next political moves. The estate, long associated with the opulence and exclusivity of the Trump brand, now symbolized his role as a political kingmaker and the de facto leader of the Republican Party.

Rebranding himself as the primary opposition to the Biden administration allowed Trump to keep his name in the headlines and maintain his grip on the Republican base. Throughout 2021 and beyond, Trump remained a vocal critic of President Joe Biden's policies, particularly on issues like immigration, foreign policy, and the economy. He used every opportunity to frame Biden's presidency as a disaster and positioned himself as the antidote to what he characterized as failed leadership. His frequent statements and interviews, many of which were disseminated through conservative media outlets, kept his voice prominent in national debates. Trump's supporters continued to see him as the true leader of the conservative movement, even as he operated from outside the halls of power.

A key part of Trump's post-presidency reinvention involved positioning himself as a populist leader still willing to fight the establishment. He continued to tap into the same themes that had fueled his rise to power—anti-elitism, economic nationalism, and a deep skepticism of the media and political elites. His speeches and public appearances were filled with rhetoric aimed at energizing his base, reinforcing the idea that he was still battling for the "forgotten Americans" who had supported him in 2016 and 2020. By casting himself as a perpetual outsider—despite having been president—Trump maintained his appeal to voters who felt disillusioned with both parties and saw him as their champion.

Trump also reinvented his brand by doubling down on his claims about the 2020 election. He repeatedly asserted, without evidence, that the election had been "stolen" from him through widespread voter fraud. This narrative became central to Trump's post-presidency identity, as he framed himself as a victim of a corrupt system that had denied him a second term. While these claims were widely debunked, they resonated with a significant portion of his base, who believed that Trump had been unfairly ousted. By continuing to push this narrative, Trump was able to maintain the loyalty of his most fervent supporters and keep the idea of a potential political comeback alive.

Moreover, Trump's post-presidency reinvention was marked by a renewed focus on grassroots activism. He returned to holding rallies—signature events that had defined his campaigns and presidency. These rallies, held in states like Ohio, Florida, and Alabama, drew thousands of supporters eager to hear Trump's message. At these events, Trump spoke about the "rigged" election, criticized Biden's policies, and hinted at a possible run for president in 2024. The rallies not only kept Trump in the public eye but also allowed him to energize his base, showing that his movement was still alive and well. For many of his supporters, these rallies reaffirmed their connection to Trump, ensuring that his brand remained a powerful force in conservative politics.

Throughout this reinvention, Trump's ability to maintain relevance hinged on his understanding of media and public perception. Even though he was no longer in office, Trump knew how to generate headlines and keep the media focused on him. His statements—often fiery and provocative—were covered extensively by conservative media outlets, ensuring that his voice continued to shape the national political conversation. Whether through press releases, interviews, or public appearances, Trump made sure that the spotlight never strayed too far from him.

In essence, Trump's post-presidency reinvention was a calculated effort to retain his influence, solidify his role as a leader of the conservative movement, and keep the Trump brand at the forefront of American politics. By positioning himself as the primary opposition to the Biden administration and maintaining his populist appeal, Trump ensured that his departure from the White House was not the end of his political career—but the beginning of a new, potentially even more impactful chapter. As Trump continued to command loyalty and attention, the power of his brand remained undeniable, cementing his place as one of the most influential figures in modern American political history.

Media Empire and the Creation of Trump's Own Platforms

After leaving the White House, Donald Trump faced a significant challenge: how to maintain his direct line of communication with his supporters in the face of social media bans and the traditional media's often critical coverage. In response, Trump embarked on a bold strategy to create his own media platforms, bypassing the mainstream outlets and big tech companies that he had spent years accusing of bias and censorship. This shift was not only an extension of his long-standing disdain for the media but also a key part of his post-presidency reinvention—an attempt to maintain control over his brand, his message, and his loyal following.

One of the most notable developments in Trump's post-presidency media strategy was the creation of Truth Social, a social media platform launched in February 2022. After being banned from Twitter, Facebook, and other major platforms following the January 6, 2021, Capitol riot, Trump and his team set out to build an alternative space where his supporters could engage with his messages without the restrictions of Silicon Valley. Truth Social was positioned as a platform that promoted free speech and rejected the censorship policies of traditional social media. For Trump, the creation of this platform was not just a way to regain his voice but a business opportunity—a way to capitalize on the growing frustration among conservatives who felt silenced by big tech companies.

Truth Social allowed Trump to reestablish his direct connection with his base, which had been central to his success in both politics and business. During his presidency, Trump had used Twitter as his personal megaphone, tweeting policy updates, attacking opponents, and sharing his thoughts in real-time. Truth Social aimed to replicate that level of engagement, but in an ecosystem that was entirely under Trump's influence. While the platform struggled initially with technical issues and slower-than-expected user growth, it remained a symbol of Trump's determination to create a media empire that could rival the traditional platforms he had long criticized.

In addition to launching his own platform, Trump deepened his ties with conservative media outlets that had remained loyal to him during and after his presidency. Channels like *One America News Network (OANN)* and *Newsmax* became essential tools for Trump to communicate with his supporters, especially after his exclusion from mainstream networks. Unlike the more established outlets, which often scrutinized or fact-checked his claims, these conservative networks provided a more favorable platform for Trump to air his grievances, promote his political agenda, and continue asserting that the 2020 election had been rigged.

By aligning himself with these media outlets, Trump ensured that he still had a powerful megaphone, even if he was no longer on Twitter or Facebook. His interviews with *OANN*, *Newsmax*, and similar outlets were frequently replayed and amplified on social media by his supporters, keeping his messages in circulation. These networks also allowed Trump to reach millions of viewers who were already skeptical of the mainstream media, further reinforcing the deep divide in the American media landscape. In many ways, this alignment between Trump and conservative media marked a continuation of the relationship that had fueled his rise to political power in the first place, with the former president using these platforms to shape the narrative around his post-presidency and influence the direction of the Republican Party.

Another element of Trump's media empire was his frequent use of email and press releases to communicate with his supporters and the broader public. After his social media bans, Trump's team began distributing statements and updates directly through his political action committees (PACs), which were then shared by loyalists on social media and picked up by conservative outlets. These press releases, often written in Trump's signature style, allowed him to continue to make headlines, attack political opponents, and weigh in on current events. For Trump, these communications served as an alternative to the tweets and Facebook posts that had once defined his public persona, ensuring that his voice remained an integral part of the national political discourse.

While Trump's creation of Truth Social and his reliance on conservative media outlets were key parts of his media strategy, there was also ongoing speculation about his potential involvement in launching a full-scale media network. Throughout his presidency and afterward, rumors swirled that Trump would start his own television network—a "Trump TV"—that would cater directly to his base. Although no such network materialized during his first year out of office, the idea remained a tantalizing possibility for many of Trump's supporters, who believed that such a venture could rival the mainstream networks and give Trump an even greater platform to influence American politics.

Trump's embrace of alternative media platforms and his efforts to create his own media channels reflected his understanding of the evolving media landscape. He knew that in order to maintain his relevance and keep his base engaged, he needed to control the narrative and have a platform that was free from the constraints of traditional media. By doing so, Trump ensured that his brand remained powerful, not just as a political figure but as a media mogul in his own right. His ability to adapt to new media realities, even after being banned from mainstream platforms, demonstrated his keen sense of how to wield media influence to his advantage.

In essence, Trump's post-presidency media strategy was an extension of the same tactics that had defined his political rise: a relentless focus on controlling the narrative, engaging directly with his base, and using controversy to generate attention. Whether through Truth Social, conservative networks, or direct communications with his supporters, Trump continued to shape the political landscape and ensure that his voice—and his brand—remained at the forefront of the national conversation. In this way, the Trump media empire became not just a vehicle for his political ambitions but a central part of his ongoing influence in American public life, keeping the Trump brand alive and thriving in a polarized media environment.

The Role of Trump's Business Ventures in His Political Brand

Even after leaving the Oval Office, Donald Trump's business ventures remained a vital part of his political identity, serving as both a symbol of his success and a tool for maintaining his influence. Throughout his career, the Trump brand had been synonymous with luxury, wealth, and power, with his name adorning everything from skyscrapers to hotels and golf courses. During his presidency, Trump used this image of a successful businessman to build his political identity, presenting himself as someone who could "run the country like a business" and bring prosperity to the American people. In the post-presidency phase, this connection between his business empire and his political brand only deepened, as Trump continued to leverage his properties and ventures to reinforce his role as a kingmaker in the Republican Party and a central figure in conservative politics.

One of the most visible symbols of Trump's blending of business and politics was Mar-a-Lago, his luxurious resort in Palm Beach, Florida. Throughout his presidency and after, Mar-a-Lago became more than just a private club and home for Trump—it became a hub for conservative activity and political gatherings. From meetings with Republican lawmakers and donors to hosting conservative conferences and fundraisers, Mar-a-Lago transformed into a de facto headquarters for Trump's post-presidency political operations. The resort's opulent surroundings, lavish events, and exclusive guest lists reflected Trump's image as a leader who operated outside the constraints of Washington's political establishment, offering his supporters a glimpse into the world of power and privilege that the Trump brand embodied.

Mar-a-Lago was not just a physical location but a symbol of Trump's continued influence. Political candidates and Republican leaders flocked to the resort, seeking Trump's endorsement and basking in his political and business success. Trump himself often held court at the resort, greeting guests, making speeches, and engaging in strategy sessions with key figures in the GOP. His presence at Mar-a-Lago reinforced the idea that, even out of office, Trump remained a central figure in Republican politics, with the power to make or break political careers. For many of his supporters, visiting Mar-a-Lago or attending an event there was not just a political gesture but a reaffirmation of their loyalty to the Trump brand.

In addition to Mar-a-Lago, Trump's other properties continued to play a significant role in his political and business strategy. His hotels and golf courses, such as Trump International Hotel in Washington, D.C., and Trump National Golf Club in Bedminster, New Jersey, became venues for political fundraisers, events, and meetings. These properties were not just business ventures—they were extensions of Trump's political identity, offering his supporters and allies exclusive access to a world where business, politics, and luxury intersected. Hosting events at these locations allowed Trump to merge his business operations with his political influence, reinforcing the idea that the Trump brand was inseparable from his role as a political leader.

The overlap between Trump's business ventures and his political brand also raised questions about conflicts of interest and ethics. Throughout his presidency, Trump had faced criticism for refusing to fully divest from his business empire, leading to accusations that his policies and decisions were influenced by his financial interests. His properties continued to attract political and corporate clients, with some foreign governments and lobbyists choosing to stay at Trump hotels or hold events at his resorts. Critics argued that this created the appearance of pay-to-play politics, with some suggesting that spending money at Trump properties was a way to gain favor with the former president. However, Trump and his allies dismissed these concerns, arguing that he was simply continuing his business while maintaining his role as a political leader.

Despite the controversies, Trump's business empire remained a critical part of his post-presidency strategy. The properties not only provided a steady stream of revenue but also served as symbols of Trump's success and influence. For his supporters, the Trump name still represented prosperity, strength, and a rejection of the political elite. Trump's ability to blend his business empire with his political brand created a unique dynamic in which his supporters saw his business ventures as a reflection of his leadership abilities. His success in business, they believed, was evidence of his ability to lead the country, and his luxurious properties became part of the larger-than-life image that Trump had cultivated over decades.

Moreover, Trump's business empire continued to attract attention from both supporters and opponents, keeping his name in the news and ensuring that the Trump brand remained relevant in the national conversation. Whether it was through hosting events at his properties, expanding his business ventures, or engaging in new real estate deals, Trump used his business success to maintain his influence and project an image of continued power. His properties were not just places of business—they were symbols of his ongoing presence in American life, blending his roles as a businessman, political leader, and cultural figure.

Trump's business ventures also became intertwined with his post-presidency political ambitions. As speculation about a potential 2024 presidential run grew, Trump used his properties as stages for rallying support and raising funds. His businesses became key venues for building momentum among his base, with Mar-a-Lago and other properties playing central roles in hosting key Republican figures and donors. Trump's ability to merge his business and political brands allowed him to remain a powerful force in the GOP, despite no longer holding office. His business empire provided him with the resources, infrastructure, and platform to maintain his status as a key figure in American politics.

In the end, Trump's business ventures were more than just financial assets—they were essential components of his political identity. By leveraging his properties and brand, Trump was able to create a unique post-presidency role for himself, one in which his business empire and political influence were inextricably linked. His success in maintaining this balance ensured that the Trump brand continued to thrive, both as a symbol of luxury and as a powerful force in American politics. Whether through Mar-a-Lago's political gatherings, his hotels' fundraisers, or his continued media presence, Trump's business empire remained a central pillar of his post-presidency brand, keeping him relevant and influential in the years following his departure from the White House.

Trump as a Kingmaker in the Republican Party

Even after leaving office, Donald Trump's influence on the Republican Party remained undeniable. His role as a kingmaker—a figure capable of shaping the party's future by endorsing candidates and controlling its direction—became one of the most powerful aspects of his post-presidency legacy. While many former presidents retreat from the political spotlight, Trump thrived in it, continuing to assert his dominance over the GOP and maintaining his position as the most influential figure within the party. His ability to rally voters, raise funds, and handpick candidates who aligned with his vision of the Republican Party solidified his status as a kingmaker, and his endorsements became coveted assets for Republicans seeking to win primaries and elections.

Trump's kingmaker status was rooted in the fierce loyalty of his base. Throughout his presidency, Trump cultivated a deep connection with a large and passionate segment of the Republican electorate. These supporters remained steadfast, even after the controversies and turbulence of his time in office. For them, Trump wasn't just a politician—he was a movement, a symbol of their frustration with the political establishment and their champion against what they saw as cultural and economic forces that had left them behind. This loyalty made Trump's endorsement a powerful tool, as candidates seeking office knew that winning the support of Trump's base was often the key to success in Republican primaries.

Throughout 2021 and 2022, Trump's endorsements carried significant weight in Republican races across the country. From gubernatorial elections to Senate and House races, candidates competed for Trump's blessing, knowing that his endorsement could energize voters, unlock fundraising potential, and lend them credibility with the party's conservative base. Trump's influence was particularly strong in key battleground states like Florida, Ohio, and Georgia, where Republican primaries became tests of loyalty to the former president. Candidates who aligned themselves closely with Trump's policies and rhetoric often surged ahead in the polls, while those who distanced themselves from him risked being labeled as part of the "establishment" and losing the support of grassroots voters.

One of the most striking examples of Trump's kingmaker role was the 2022 primary season, where his endorsements played a decisive role in shaping the Republican slate for the midterm elections. Candidates backed by Trump frequently won their primaries, even against more established or well-funded opponents. In states like Ohio, Trump's endorsement of J.D. Vance in the Senate primary turned the race on its head, propelling Vance from a trailing candidate to the front-runner and eventual nominee. Similar patterns played out in other states, where candidates who embraced Trump's "America First" agenda and echoed his populist rhetoric found themselves winning over the Republican electorate, often by significant margins.

But Trump's influence as a kingmaker wasn't limited to endorsing candidates. He also used his platform to shape the broader direction of the Republican Party, continuing to push it toward a populist, nationalist agenda that had defined his presidency. Trump's vision for the party—a hardline stance on immigration, skepticism of globalism, and a focus on economic protectionism—became the litmus test for many Republicans seeking office. Candidates who embraced these positions and voiced support for Trump's claims about the 2020 election found themselves in Trump's good graces, while those who were perceived as moderates or as insufficiently loyal to Trump were often sidelined.

The power of Trump's endorsements was further amplified by his ability to raise significant amounts of money for candidates and causes he supported. Through his political action committees (PACs), Trump remained a formidable fundraising force in the Republican Party, often outpacing other GOP leaders in both small-dollar donations and contributions from major donors. His fundraising prowess gave him the financial resources to support his chosen candidates, helping them build campaign infrastructure, run advertisements, and mobilize voters. In this way, Trump's influence extended beyond the power of his endorsement—he provided tangible financial and logistical support to candidates who aligned with his vision for the party.

However, Trump's role as a kingmaker also highlighted divisions within the Republican Party. While Trump remained popular with the party's base, some Republican leaders and donors were concerned about the long-term consequences of his continued dominance. These Republicans feared that Trump's influence could alienate moderate voters, particularly in swing districts and battleground states, where a hardline Trumpian candidate might struggle to win in a general election. The tension between Trump's faction of the party and more traditional Republicans led to internal power struggles, with some candidates navigating a delicate balance between courting Trump's base and appealing to more centrist voters.

Despite these challenges, Trump's hold on the party remained strong. His endorsement was often seen as a seal of approval that could boost a candidate's chances, and Republican politicians who received his backing were quick to promote it. At rallies, in advertisements, and on social media, Trump-endorsed candidates proudly touted their association with the former president, knowing that it could be the deciding factor in a close race. Trump's presence, even from outside the White House, loomed large over the Republican primaries, and his ability to mobilize voters continued to shape the outcomes of elections across the country.

The loyalty Trump commanded within the Republican Party also made it difficult for potential rivals to challenge his dominance. While some GOP figures, such as former Vice President Mike Pence or Florida Governor Ron DeSantis, were seen as potential 2024 presidential contenders, few dared to openly criticize Trump or position themselves in direct opposition to him. Those who did—such as Rep. Liz Cheney—faced significant backlash from Trump's base and the broader Republican establishment. In Cheney's case, her vocal opposition to Trump's claims about the 2020 election and her role in investigating the January 6 Capitol riot led to her being ousted from her leadership position in the House and eventually losing her primary race. This demonstrated the risks of crossing Trump within the party and underscored his ongoing power as a kingmaker.

In conclusion, Trump's role as a kingmaker in the Republican Party became one of the defining features of his post-presidency influence. By endorsing candidates, shaping the party's agenda, and maintaining a strong connection with the conservative base, Trump continued to wield significant power within the GOP. His ability to pick winners in primaries, raise funds, and steer the party's direction ensured that the Trump brand remained central to the future of Republican politics. Even out of office, Trump's influence over the GOP was profound, and his endorsements became a critical factor in determining the party's candidates and direction.

The Future of the Trump Brand—Speculation on a 2024 Run and Beyond

As soon as Donald Trump left the White House in January 2021, speculation about his potential return to politics began. For his supporters, the question was not if but when Trump would launch another bid for the presidency. Despite his defeat in the 2020 election, Trump remained the most powerful figure in the Republican Party and one of the most influential voices in American politics. His post-presidency was marked by a continual flirtation with the idea of running again in 2024, fueling excitement and uncertainty in equal measure. Trump's hints about a possible campaign kept him at the center of national political discourse, while also giving him leverage over the future of the Republican Party.

Trump's post-presidency fundraising efforts strongly suggested that he was keeping the door open for a 2024 run. Through his political action committees (PACs), particularly Save America PAC, Trump raised millions of dollars, far outpacing other potential Republican candidates. The funds helped him maintain his influence within the GOP, support candidates loyal to him, and build the infrastructure for a potential presidential campaign. Trump's ability to raise vast sums of money demonstrated that his base remained as energized as ever, willing to contribute financially to keep him in the political fight. For Trump, these funds were not only a financial asset but a symbol of his continued relevance and strength within the Republican Party.

Publicly, Trump played coy about his 2024 intentions, keeping both his supporters and his rivals in suspense. At rallies and in interviews, he frequently teased a potential run, dropping hints that he might return to the political stage. "We're going to make America great again—again," he would say, leaving the door wide open for a comeback. These statements were designed to maintain excitement among his base, ensuring that his name remained at the forefront of Republican politics. By refusing to make a definitive statement about his plans, Trump kept the spotlight on himself and retained control over the Republican Party's future, making it difficult for other potential contenders to announce their own presidential aspirations without first gauging Trump's next move.

Behind the scenes, many political observers speculated that Trump's decision to run in 2024 would depend on a number of factors, including the political landscape, the success of the Biden administration, and the performance of Republican candidates in the 2022 midterm elections. Trump's decision-making was also likely influenced by his desire to maintain power and relevance within the Republican Party. A 2024 campaign would give him the opportunity to reassert himself as the undisputed leader of the GOP and potentially vindicate his claims about the 2020 election. For Trump, winning the presidency again would not only solidify his legacy but also serve as the ultimate victory over his political enemies.

At the same time, some speculated that Trump might choose to influence the 2024 election as a kingmaker rather than a candidate. In this scenario, Trump could wield his power by endorsing a successor who aligned with his "America First" vision and carried forward his populist agenda. Figures like Florida Governor Ron DeSantis, who had gained popularity within the Republican Party and often echoed Trump's rhetoric, were frequently mentioned as potential heirs to the Trump mantle. If Trump chose not to run, his endorsement would almost certainly determine the Republican nominee, as few GOP candidates would dare to challenge him directly without his blessing. Even as a non-candidate, Trump's influence over the 2024 race would be immense.

Regardless of whether he ran for president again, the Trump brand continued to dominate American political life. His ability to shape the Republican Party's agenda, influence elections through his endorsements, and command attention in the media ensured that Trump remained a central figure in conservative politics. His rallies, social media posts (on platforms like Truth Social), and public statements kept his base engaged and ready for action. For Trump's supporters, his role as a political and cultural leader went far beyond electoral politics—they saw him as a symbol of resistance against the political establishment, the mainstream media, and the forces of globalization and cultural change that they believed were eroding the fabric of American society.

Even outside the realm of electoral politics, the Trump brand extended into various cultural and economic spheres. His businesses, media ventures, and involvement in conservative activism allowed him to remain a constant presence in American life. Whether through his real estate holdings, golf courses, or potential future media endeavors (such as the rumored "Trump TV"), Trump's name continued to carry weight both financially and politically. His brand, built over decades as a symbol of success and power, was now deeply intertwined with his political persona, making it difficult to separate the businessman from the politician.

Trump's legacy and influence also had broader implications for the future of the Republican Party. His presidency had transformed the GOP into a populist, nationalist party that prioritized working-class voters, skepticism of globalism, and a rejection of political correctness. Whether Trump himself ran in 2024 or not, the party would continue to operate in the shadow of his influence. Candidates seeking office would need to embrace Trump's agenda or risk alienating his base, which had become the core of the Republican electorate. The future of the GOP would be shaped by Trump's vision for years to come, as the party grappled with the tension between its traditional conservative roots and the populist wave that Trump had unleashed.

Ultimately, Trump's post-presidency demonstrated that the power of the Trump brand extended far beyond his time in office. Whether through his continued dominance of the Republican Party, his business ventures, or his potential return to the presidential stage in 2024, Trump remained a force to be reckoned with in American politics. His ability to command loyalty from his base, influence elections, and shape the national conversation ensured that the Trump brand would continue to play a central role in the future of the GOP and the broader political landscape. As long as Trump remained a key figure in American life, the question of his political future—whether as a candidate or a kingmaker—would continue to loom large over the country's political horizon.

Chapter 16

Chapter 16: The Legacy of a Celebrity Mogul

Redefining Political Communication and the Power of Media

One of Donald Trump's most enduring legacies as both a celebrity and a politician is the way he redefined political communication, particularly through his mastery of modern media. Trump's use of platforms like Twitter, along with his ability to command television and generate headlines, allowed him to bypass traditional media outlets and speak directly to the public. This approach fundamentally changed the way political leaders communicate, shifting the balance of power away from the press and toward the politicians themselves. Trump's media strategy was revolutionary, and its effects will continue to shape the way leaders engage with their constituencies long into the future.

Before Donald Trump, presidential communication was often filtered through layers of media relations teams, advisers, and press conferences. Presidents relied on the mainstream media to communicate their policies and messages, often through carefully crafted speeches and interviews. Trump, however, saw the media as both a tool and an adversary. Early in his political career, he recognized the power of bypassing traditional gatekeepers and going directly to the American people. This was especially evident in his use of Twitter, where he could instantly communicate with millions of followers, unfiltered and unmediated by journalists. For Trump, Twitter was not just a platform for announcements; it was his primary tool for shaping the national narrative, responding to criticism, and rallying his base.

Trump's use of Twitter was unprecedented for a political figure of his stature. While previous presidents, such as Barack Obama, had embraced social media, they did so with restraint and careful messaging, using teams to manage their online presence. Trump, by contrast, took personal control of his Twitter account, firing off tweets at all hours of the day, often in response to real-time events. His tweets were not carefully vetted; they were raw, direct, and often provocative. Whether he was attacking political opponents, promoting his policies, or reacting to breaking news, Trump's Twitter feed became the heartbeat of his presidency. For supporters, it was a refreshing break from the cautious, overly managed communications of the past. For critics, it was reckless and undisciplined. But regardless of the perspective, one thing was clear: Trump had changed the rules of political communication.

By leveraging social media in this way, Trump not only controlled the narrative but also forced the traditional media to follow his lead. News outlets, including those critical of him, found themselves unable to ignore his tweets, which often dominated news cycles for days. Each tweet became a headline, analyzed and discussed endlessly on cable news and in print. Trump's ability to manipulate the media ecosystem in this way was a reflection of his years as a television star and media mogul. He knew that controversy and spectacle drove ratings, and he capitalized on this knowledge to keep himself at the center of the national conversation, often regardless of whether the coverage was positive or negative. For Trump, attention was power, and he wielded it masterfully.

Beyond Twitter, Trump used traditional media in ways that broke with presidential norms. His impromptu press conferences, off-the-cuff remarks, and combative exchanges with reporters during briefings all played into his strategy of making the presidency a media spectacle. Rather than shying away from conflict with the press, Trump embraced it. His frequent attacks on the media—whom he famously dubbed the "enemy of the people"—were designed to undermine their credibility, especially among his supporters, while simultaneously ensuring that his feud with the press became another story that kept him in the spotlight. Trump understood that his base distrusted mainstream media, and by positioning himself as a victim of media bias, he strengthened his bond with his followers, who saw him as fighting not just for them, but against a corrupt media establishment.

In many ways, Trump's presidency was a continuation of the media persona he had cultivated during his years as a real estate mogul and reality TV star. From *The Apprentice*, where he honed his skills in delivering dramatic soundbites and commanding the attention of an audience, Trump had always understood the power of image and performance. As president, he brought this understanding to the Oval Office, turning press briefings, rallies, and even state visits into opportunities to project his brand and control the narrative. He was a master of using television and social media to create a constant sense of drama, ensuring that the public was always watching.

Trump's impact on political communication goes beyond his personal use of media. His presidency ushered in a new era in which political leaders are expected to be constantly visible, constantly engaging, and constantly present in the media landscape. Future politicians, whether they supported or opposed Trump, had to reckon with the fact that the rules had changed. The era of scripted speeches and carefully managed media relations was giving way to an era of immediacy, where politicians were expected to engage with voters directly and often in real time. Social media became not just an option but a necessity, and the pace of political communication quickened dramatically.

The long-term effects of Trump's media strategy are still unfolding, but it is clear that his presidency marked a turning point in how political leaders communicate. His ability to control the narrative, generate media attention, and speak directly to his supporters without the filter of traditional media fundamentally altered the relationship between politicians and the press. His legacy in this area will likely be felt for years to come, as future leaders continue to grapple with the new expectations of constant engagement, direct communication, and the power of social media. In many ways, Trump's presidency was less about policy and more about performance, and his mastery of media will remain one of the most significant aspects of his legacy as a celebrity mogul turned political figure.

In conclusion, Donald Trump redefined political communication in the 21st century by using social media and modern media platforms to bypass traditional channels and speak directly to his audience. His direct, often controversial style transformed the way political figures engage with the public, forcing the media to respond to him rather than the other way around. In doing so, he changed the landscape of political discourse, blending the worlds of entertainment, celebrity, and governance in a way that had never been seen before. His legacy as a media-savvy politician will continue to influence how leaders communicate in the digital age, shaping the expectations of voters and the strategies of future political figures.

The Politicization of Celebrity—Blurring the Lines Between Politics and Entertainment

Donald Trump's political ascent was unique not only because of his unconventional approach but also because of the way he blurred the lines between politics and entertainment. His rise from celebrity businessman and reality TV star to the highest office in the land exemplified a new era in American politics where fame and personality could outweigh traditional qualifications and experience. Trump's celebrity status was not an obstacle to his political success; rather, it became one of his greatest assets. His fame gave him instant name recognition, and his ability to perform in front of an audience—honed during his years on *The Apprentice*—allowed him to connect with voters in ways that most politicians could only dream of. In doing so, Trump politicized celebrity in a way that reshaped not only his campaign but also the broader political landscape.

For decades, Trump had been a fixture in the world of New York real estate, tabloids, and television. He was known for his larger-than-life persona, his brash attitude, and his relentless self-promotion. But it was his role as the host of NBC's *The Apprentice* that transformed him from a well-known businessman into a full-blown television star. On the show, Trump played the role of the tough, no-nonsense boss, delivering his famous line, "You're fired," with dramatic flair. Millions of Americans tuned in each week to watch Trump wield his authority, make decisions, and preside over boardroom drama. This television persona shaped the public's perception of Trump as a successful and decisive leader, even though the reality behind his business dealings was far more complicated.

When Trump announced his candidacy for president in 2015, many political insiders and media commentators dismissed him as a joke—a celebrity with no serious political experience. But Trump's fame gave him a head start that few other candidates could match. He didn't need to introduce himself to voters or explain his background; people already knew who he was. His name was synonymous with wealth, success, and power, and he used that to his advantage. His campaign rallies became extensions of his celebrity persona, filled with the same energy, spectacle, and performance that had characterized his television career. Trump understood that modern politics, like television, was about entertaining the audience and keeping them engaged.

Trump's ability to command attention, create drama, and dominate the media cycle turned his candidacy into must-watch political theater. His off-the-cuff remarks, insults, and bold promises made headlines day after day, ensuring that he remained at the center of the national conversation. Trump's campaign rallies were not just political events; they were media spectacles, filled with bombastic speeches, chants from the crowd, and moments designed to go viral. The media, drawn to the controversy and entertainment value of Trump's candidacy, covered him relentlessly, often at the expense of his more traditional political rivals. Trump's ability to blur the lines between politics and entertainment was a key factor in his rise, as he understood that in the age of 24-hour news and social media, attention was the most valuable currency.

Trump's use of his celebrity status also helped him connect with voters in ways that traditional politicians struggled to replicate. He presented himself as a political outsider, someone who was not beholden to the Washington establishment or the special interests that often dominated American politics. To his supporters, Trump's wealth meant that he could not be bought, and his fame meant that he had already achieved success outside of politics. This image of Trump as a self-made billionaire who was now stepping in to "fix" the country resonated deeply with voters who were frustrated with the status quo. Trump's celebrity, far from being a liability, became central to his populist appeal.

The fusion of Trump's celebrity and political identity also reflected a broader trend in American culture, where the lines between entertainment and politics have become increasingly blurred. With the rise of social media, reality television, and 24-hour news, the distinction between celebrity and political figures has become less clear. Trump's candidacy and presidency took full advantage of this shift, leveraging his fame to build a political movement that relied as much on spectacle as on policy. Trump was a master of using the tools of entertainment—catchy slogans, dramatic rallies, and personal branding—to create a political identity that felt more like a television show than a traditional campaign.

Trump's success in blending politics and entertainment has had lasting effects on the political landscape. His presidency opened the door for other celebrities to enter politics, showing that fame and media savvy could be more important than experience or policy expertise. Figures like Kanye West and Dwayne "The Rock" Johnson have publicly toyed with the idea of running for office, and the trend of celebrities turning to politics shows no signs of slowing down. In a media-driven age, where personal branding and the ability to command attention are paramount, Trump's legacy as the first reality TV star to become president has set a precedent for future political candidates.

Moreover, Trump's presidency highlighted the increasing importance of personality in politics. For many of his supporters, Trump's policies were secondary to his persona. He was seen as a fighter, someone who was willing to take on the elites, the media, and the establishment, regardless of the consequences. This emphasis on personality over policy marked a shift in American politics, where voters were drawn to candidates who could entertain, provoke, and disrupt, rather than those who adhered to traditional norms of political decorum and experience. Trump's ability to project strength, even in the face of scandal or criticism, was key to his appeal. His supporters admired his bravado, his willingness to speak his mind, and his rejection of political correctness, even when it came at a cost.

The merging of politics and celebrity that Trump pioneered will continue to shape future elections. The expectations for political candidates have shifted, with voters now looking for figures who can engage, entertain, and connect on a personal level. Trump's ability to command the media's attention and dominate the public conversation set a new standard for how political figures can use fame and spectacle to their advantage. In this new era, being a celebrity isn't just an asset—it's often the foundation for a successful political career.

In conclusion, Donald Trump's legacy as a celebrity mogul turned president has permanently blurred the lines between politics and entertainment. His rise to power demonstrated the power of celebrity in modern politics, where personality, media presence, and spectacle often take precedence over traditional political credentials. Trump's success has opened the door for future celebrities to follow in his footsteps, reshaping the American political landscape in ways that will reverberate for years to come. The politicization of celebrity, pioneered by Trump, has created a new political reality where fame, media savvy, and personal branding are as important—if not more so—than policy expertise and governing experience.

Shifting the Political Landscape—Trump's Impact on Populism and Nationalism

Donald Trump's presidency not only changed the Republican Party but also fundamentally shifted the political landscape in America and across the globe. His rise to power marked a resurgence of populism and nationalism, challenging the dominance of globalism and liberal democracy that had characterized much of the post-Cold War era. Trump's brand of populist nationalism was defined by a rejection of global trade deals, skepticism of international alliances, a focus on strict immigration policies, and an "America First" agenda that prioritized national sovereignty over multilateral cooperation. This political philosophy resonated with millions of Americans who felt left behind by globalization and disconnected from the political elites in Washington. Trump's success in harnessing these sentiments reshaped the political discourse in the United States and inspired similar movements around the world.

At the heart of Trump's populist appeal was his ability to channel the anger and frustration of ordinary Americans who believed that the political establishment had failed them. For years, globalization had been promoted as a driver of economic growth, but the benefits of global trade, technology, and immigration had not been evenly distributed. Manufacturing jobs disappeared, wages stagnated, and whole communities—particularly in the Rust Belt—were left behind. Trump's message spoke directly to these voters. He promised to restore American manufacturing, bring jobs back from overseas, and renegotiate trade deals that he argued had decimated American industries. By positioning himself as the champion of the "forgotten men and women" of America, Trump built a political movement that thrived on populist anger.

One of Trump's central themes was economic nationalism. Throughout his campaign and presidency, Trump framed globalism as a threat to American workers, accusing multinational corporations and international trade deals of selling out the country's interests. NAFTA (the North American Free Trade Agreement) and the Trans-Pacific Partnership (TPP) became frequent targets of his ire, with Trump arguing that these agreements had outsourced American jobs to Mexico, China, and other countries with lower labor costs. His decision to pull the United States out of the TPP and renegotiate NAFTA (which was replaced by the USMCA) were key moments in his effort to redefine America's relationship with the global economy. For Trump, trade was not about cooperation—it was about winning, and he believed that the U.S. had been losing for far too long.

Trump's economic nationalism extended to his approach to immigration, which became one of the most defining and controversial aspects of his presidency. From the moment he launched his 2016 campaign, Trump made immigration a central issue, promising to build a wall along the southern border and crack down on illegal immigration. He framed immigration not just as a security issue but as an economic one, arguing that immigrants—both legal and illegal—were taking jobs from American workers and driving down wages. His administration's hardline stance on immigration, including the travel ban targeting Muslim-majority countries, the family separation policy at the border, and the push to end the Deferred Action for Childhood Arrivals (DACA) program, reflected his belief that immigration needed to be tightly controlled to protect American workers and national security.

Trump's message on immigration resonated deeply with his base, particularly among white working-class voters who felt that their cultural identity and economic security were under threat from the changing demographics of the country. His willingness to engage in openly nationalistic rhetoric—emphasizing borders, sovereignty, and the preservation of traditional American values—set him apart from both Republicans and Democrats who had largely embraced a more globalist, multicultural vision of the United States. For many of Trump's supporters, his hardline stance on immigration was not just about policy; it was about reclaiming a sense of national identity that they believed was being eroded.

Trump's brand of populist nationalism also extended to foreign policy. His "America First" doctrine marked a sharp departure from the interventionist policies of previous administrations. Trump was deeply skeptical of international alliances like NATO, which he viewed as outdated and unfair to American taxpayers. He frequently criticized NATO members for not paying their "fair share" and questioned whether the U.S. should continue to bear the financial burden of defending Europe. Trump's approach to foreign policy was transactional—he viewed alliances, treaties, and partnerships through the lens of what they could deliver for America. This worldview led to a more isolationist stance, with Trump pulling the U.S. out of international agreements like the Paris Climate Accord and withdrawing from key diplomatic efforts, such as the Iran nuclear deal.

While Trump's critics argued that his isolationist policies undermined America's standing in the world, his supporters saw these moves as necessary corrections to a foreign policy that had been too focused on globalism at the expense of national interests. Trump's presidency, in many ways, reflected a broader backlash against the liberal international order that had been in place since the end of World War II. His rhetoric about "bad deals" and "America First" resonated with voters who believed that international institutions, multinational corporations, and global elites were more concerned with advancing their own interests than protecting the interests of ordinary Americans.

Trump's populist nationalism did not exist in a vacuum—it was part of a broader global trend. Around the world, populist movements were gaining traction, many of them echoing Trump's rhetoric about immigration, trade, and national sovereignty. In Europe, leaders like Marine Le Pen in France, Matteo

Salvini in Italy, and Viktor Orbán in Hungary embraced similar messages, positioning themselves as defenders of national identity and critics of the European Union's globalist policies. Trump's presidency emboldened these leaders, providing them with a model of how populism could win at the ballot box. The rise of these populist movements represented a fundamental shift in global politics, as more countries grappled with the challenges of globalization, immigration, and the erosion of traditional national identities.

Trump's impact on populism and nationalism extended beyond his presidency. Even after leaving office, the ideas and policies he championed continued to shape political discourse in the United States and abroad. The populist wave that he helped unleash showed no signs of slowing down, as more politicians adopted the language of nationalism and protectionism to appeal to voters who felt left behind by globalization. Trump's legacy as a leader of this movement ensured that populism and nationalism would remain central themes in political debates for years to come.

In conclusion, Donald Trump's presidency marked a turning point in the rise of populism and nationalism, both in the United States and around the world. His rejection of globalism, his embrace of economic nationalism, and his hardline stance on immigration reshaped the political landscape, creating a new populist base that rejected the policies of both the Democratic and Republican establishments. Trump's influence extended beyond America, inspiring similar movements across Europe and beyond. His legacy as a champion of populist nationalism will continue to shape politics for years to come, as the forces he unleashed remain a powerful force in American and global politics.

The Transformation of the Republican Party

One of Donald Trump's most profound and lasting legacies is the complete transformation of the Republican Party. Before Trump's rise, the GOP was traditionally known for its advocacy of free markets, limited government, strong national defense, and a commitment to conservative social values. However, Trump's entry into the political arena in 2015 ushered in a seismic shift, reshaping the party's ideology, voter base, and internal dynamics. Under Trump's influence, the Republican Party evolved from a coalition of economic and social conservatives into a populist, nationalist movement that prioritized issues like immigration control, trade protectionism, and an "America First" approach to foreign policy. Trump's transformation of the GOP has left a deep imprint on its future, creating both opportunities and challenges for the party in a post-Trump political landscape.

From the very beginning of his presidential campaign, Trump upended the traditional Republican orthodoxy. He challenged long-standing GOP positions on trade, foreign policy, and immigration in ways that shocked the party establishment but resonated deeply with a new group of voters. Trump rejected free trade deals like NAFTA and the Trans-Pacific Partnership (TPP), which had been pillars of Republican economic policy for decades. He argued that these agreements had devastated American manufacturing and cost millions of jobs, particularly in the Rust Belt. His calls for renegotiating trade deals and imposing tariffs on foreign goods marked a stark departure from the party's long-held belief in the benefits of free trade.

This shift toward economic nationalism was one of the key drivers of Trump's appeal to working-class voters, many of whom had previously been Democrats but felt abandoned by their party's embrace of globalization. Trump's economic message, which focused on bringing back American jobs and revitalizing industries that had been hollowed out by globalization, helped him build a new coalition of voters who were less concerned with traditional Republican issues like tax cuts and deregulation and more focused on economic protectionism. This realignment of the GOP's economic priorities, from free markets to economic nationalism, became a defining feature of Trump's presidency and reshaped the party's platform.

Perhaps the most significant change Trump brought to the Republican Party was his approach to immigration. Prior to Trump, the GOP had been deeply divided on the issue, with establishment Republicans generally supporting a more moderate approach that included immigration reform and pathways to citizenship for undocumented immigrants. Trump's hardline stance on immigration—his promise to build a wall along the southern border, crack down on illegal immigration, and impose travel bans on certain countries—redefined the party's position on this issue. Trump framed immigration as not only an economic threat but also a cultural one, arguing that lax immigration policies were eroding American identity and security.

This message resonated deeply with Trump's base, particularly among white working-class voters who felt that their communities and livelihoods were under threat from both illegal and legal immigration. Trump's rhetoric about protecting American workers from foreign labor, combined with his focus on securing the border, became central to the Republican platform. Under Trump's leadership, the party embraced a more restrictive approach to immigration, positioning itself as the defender of American sovereignty and cultural values in the face of demographic changes. This hardline stance on immigration solidified Trump's hold on the GOP and alienated more moderate voices within the party who had advocated for immigration reform.

Trump's foreign policy also marked a significant departure from traditional Republican principles. For decades, the GOP had been the party of strong international alliances, military interventionism, and a commitment to promoting democracy abroad. Trump, however, adopted a more isolationist and transactional approach to foreign policy. His "America First" doctrine prioritized national sovereignty and economic interests over global partnerships and multilateral agreements. He questioned the value of long-standing alliances like NATO, criticized U.S. involvement in foreign wars, and pulled the country out of international agreements like the Paris Climate Accord and the Iran nuclear deal.

While this approach was deeply unpopular among establishment Republicans and foreign policy experts, it resonated with Trump's populist base, who were weary of costly foreign interventions and skeptical of international institutions. Trump's foreign policy emphasized a narrow definition of national interest, focusing on economic deals and military disengagement. His willingness to challenge the foreign policy consensus and prioritize American interests over global responsibilities reshaped the GOP's stance on international relations and cemented his hold on the party's direction.

Another key aspect of Trump's transformation of the Republican Party was his approach to social and cultural issues. While traditional Republican conservatism had long focused on issues like abortion, family values, and religious freedom, Trump tapped into a broader cultural backlash against political correctness, liberal elites, and progressive social movements. His rhetoric on these issues, often combative and provocative, energized a base of voters who felt that their values were under attack by a liberal cultural establishment. Trump's rejection of political correctness became a central part of his appeal, and he used it to frame himself as a champion of free speech and traditional American values.

This cultural battle extended to Trump's relationship with the media and other institutions of power, which he framed as corrupt and biased against his supporters. His constant attacks on the "fake news" media, the "deep state," and the political elite further solidified his image as an outsider fighting against entrenched forces in Washington. For Trump's base, this narrative of defiance and resistance became a rallying cry, and it reshaped the way many Republicans viewed institutions that had once been pillars of American democracy.

As a result of Trump's influence, the Republican Party underwent a dramatic transformation, becoming more populist, nationalist, and culturally conservative. The traditional pillars of Republicanism—free markets, international alliances, and conservative social values—were replaced or overshadowed by Trump's focus on economic nationalism, immigration control, and cultural warfare. This transformation created a new Republican coalition, one that was driven by working-class voters, rural Americans, and social conservatives who saw Trump as their champion. At the same time, it alienated many traditional Republicans, particularly in the suburbs and among the business elite, who were uncomfortable with Trump's rhetoric and policies.

The internal divisions within the Republican Party, between Trump loyalists and more traditional conservatives, became a defining feature of the GOP during and after Trump's presidency. These tensions were evident in the aftermath of the 2020 election, as some Republicans distanced themselves from Trump's claims of election fraud while others embraced them. The future of the party remains uncertain, as it grapples with how to navigate a post-Trump political landscape while still being heavily influenced by his legacy.

In conclusion, Donald Trump's transformation of the Republican Party has been one of the most significant political realignments in modern American history. His populist, nationalist agenda reshaped the party's platform, voter base, and internal dynamics, creating a new coalition that prioritized economic nationalism, immigration control, and cultural conservatism. While this transformation energized a new base of Republican voters, it also created deep divisions within the party, as traditional conservatives struggled to reconcile Trump's influence with the GOP's long-standing principles. As the Republican Party moves forward, it will continue to grapple with Trump's legacy and the lasting impact he has had on its identity and future direction.

The Cultural Legacy of Donald Trump—Division and Identity Politics

Donald Trump's presidency did more than alter the political landscape—it left an indelible mark on the culture of America, intensifying divisions and bringing identity politics to the forefront of national discourse. His candidacy and time in office reflected and deepened the cultural divides between urban and rural America, conservative and liberal values, and different racial and ethnic groups. More than any modern political figure, Trump stoked the fires of cultural conflict, rallying his supporters by championing their grievances against what he portrayed as a liberal elite, while simultaneously becoming a lightning rod for opposition. His rhetoric, policies, and public persona amplified the forces of division that had been simmering in American society, leaving a cultural legacy that continues to shape public life even after his presidency.

One of the most significant aspects of Trump's cultural legacy was his unapologetic embrace of identity politics, particularly with regard to race and immigration. From the very beginning of his presidential campaign, Trump used inflammatory language that played on fears and anxieties about demographic and cultural changes in America. His rhetoric about building a wall along the U.S.-Mexico border, characterizing Mexican immigrants as "rapists" and criminals, and instituting a travel ban targeting Muslim-majority countries tapped into a long-standing cultural divide over immigration and national identity. These issues, which had previously been discussed in more measured tones by both parties, became central to Trump's political identity and the cultural polarization of the country.

Trump's emphasis on immigration as a threat to American security and culture resonated deeply with many of his supporters, particularly white, working-class voters who felt that their way of life was being eroded by changing demographics. For these voters, Trump's rhetoric about protecting America from immigrants, refugees, and foreign influences wasn't just about policy—it was about preserving their vision of the country. His focus on nationalism and cultural protectionism framed immigration as a zero-sum game in which new arrivals threatened the jobs, safety, and cultural values of native-born Americans. This heightened rhetoric on immigration fed into broader debates about race and national identity, fueling cultural conflicts that had long been brewing in American society.

At the same time, Trump's presidency sparked a powerful counter-movement, particularly among racial minorities, immigrants, and progressive activists who saw his rhetoric and policies as an attack on their rights and identity. The Black Lives Matter movement, which had begun during the Obama years in response to police violence, gained new momentum under Trump as his administration was seen as indifferent or hostile to the concerns of Black Americans. Trump's response to incidents of racial injustice—most notably, his comments on the white supremacist rally in Charlottesville, Virginia, where he claimed there were "very fine people on both sides"—fueled widespread outrage and deepened the cultural divide over race in America.

Trump's handling of race-related issues, from his public comments to his administration's policies, laid bare the racial tensions that had been simmering for years. His opponents accused him of stoking white nationalist sentiments and emboldening far-right extremists, while his supporters argued that he was simply defending American values against attacks from the left. This conflict over race and identity became one of the defining cultural battles of Trump's presidency, with both sides using his actions to mobilize their bases and solidify their positions. Trump's presidency exposed the fault lines in American society over race, identity, and national belonging, intensifying debates that would continue to resonate long after he left office.

Trump's impact on identity politics wasn't limited to race and immigration. His presidency also amplified the cultural conflicts around gender, sexual orientation, and political correctness. Trump's brash, unapologetic style was seen by many of his supporters as a refreshing rejection of what they viewed as the stifling political correctness that had taken hold in American public life. His frequent attacks on "cancel culture" and his disdain for what he called the "woke" left resonated with a large segment of the population that felt alienated by progressive social movements. Trump positioned himself as a defender of free speech and traditional American values, arguing that the left's focus on social justice and identity politics was undermining the country's unity and freedom of expression.

For many of Trump's supporters, particularly in rural and conservative communities, his rejection of political correctness was a rallying cry against a cultural elite that they felt looked down on them and their values. Trump's disdain for the norms of polite political discourse and his willingness to challenge progressive orthodoxy on issues of race, gender, and sexuality made him a hero to those who felt that their voices were being silenced by liberal elites. In this way, Trump's presidency wasn't just about policy—it was about cultural resistance. His rhetoric gave voice to those who felt marginalized by the changing social norms around diversity, inclusivity, and political correctness.

However, Trump's cultural legacy was not limited to the divisions he stoked. His presidency also mobilized a new generation of activists and movements that sought to push back against his policies and rhetoric. The Women's March, held the day after Trump's inauguration, was one of the largest protests in U.S. history, signaling the rise of a powerful opposition movement centered around issues of gender equality, reproductive rights, and social justice. The #MeToo movement, which gained momentum during Trump's presidency, also reflected a cultural reckoning with issues of sexual harassment and assault, issues that had been highlighted by Trump's own controversies, including the *Access Hollywood* tape.

In many ways, Trump's presidency galvanized both sides of the cultural divide. His supporters rallied around his rejection of progressive social movements, while his opponents found new energy in resisting his agenda. This cultural polarization, with Trump at its center, became one of the most defining features of his presidency. It wasn't just about political battles—it was about a deeper cultural conflict over what kind of country America would become. The debates that raged during Trump's time in office—from immigration and race to gender and free speech—weren't just political issues; they were cultural flashpoints that reflected the deep divisions in American society.

As Trump left office, the cultural divisions he had amplified remained unresolved. His presidency had brought issues of identity politics to the forefront, forcing Americans to confront the underlying tensions around race, gender, immigration, and national identity that had been simmering for decades. Trump's cultural legacy, for better or worse, was that he had made these divisions impossible to ignore. He had forced the country to grapple with its identity, its values, and its future in a way that no president before him had done.

In conclusion, Donald Trump's cultural legacy is one of division and identity politics. His presidency brought to the surface deep cultural conflicts over race, immigration, gender, and political correctness, polarizing the country in ways that will continue to shape American society for years to come. Trump's ability to tap into the fears and frustrations of his supporters, while also mobilizing a powerful opposition, ensured that his cultural impact would extend far beyond his time in office. His legacy is one of both resistance and defiance, leaving the country more divided, but also more engaged, in the ongoing struggle over what it means to be American.

Epilogue: Reflections on Fame and Influence

As the story of Donald Trump's rise to fame and influence comes to a close, it is clear that his legacy will be studied, debated, and felt for generations to come. From his beginnings as a real estate mogul to his transformation into a celebrity and, eventually, the 45th president of the United States, Trump's journey has been anything but ordinary. His life has been a testament to the power of branding, media, and the sheer force of personality in shaping public perception, bending institutions to his will, and redefining the boundaries of politics, culture, and power.

Trump's ascent, first in the world of business and later in the realm of politics, was built on the foundation of fame. He understood, perhaps better than anyone else of his generation, that in a media-saturated world, visibility is power. His ability to command attention—whether through skyscrapers emblazoned with his name, a hit reality TV show, or bombastic political rallies—ensured that Donald Trump was always in the spotlight. Fame was not just a byproduct of Trump's ambition; it was the very currency that fueled his rise. His journey from real estate to reality television to the White House blurred the lines between entertainment and politics, and in doing so, Trump carved out a new path for how modern leaders could use celebrity to shape their destiny.

At the heart of Trump's enduring influence is his understanding of media and the public's appetite for spectacle. Long before his presidency, Trump was a master of self-promotion, using tabloid headlines and television appearances to keep his brand at the forefront of American culture. His larger-than-life persona—part billionaire, part showman—captured the imagination of a public increasingly drawn to personalities who broke the mold. Trump's brand was always about more than wealth; it was about an image of success that he crafted and sold to millions. Whether it was through the gleaming towers that bore his name or the boardroom scenes of *The Apprentice*, Trump knew how to sell a story, and he was always the star of it.

Trump's ability to leverage his celebrity status and turn it into political power was nothing short of remarkable. His 2016 presidential campaign was unconventional in almost every sense, defying the expectations of political experts and the norms of American electoral politics. But for Trump, this was simply an extension of his lifelong strategy—turning attention into influence. He understood that in a crowded field of political candidates, he could stand out not by following the rules, but by breaking them. His rallies became must-watch events, his tweets ignited media firestorms, and his provocative statements ensured that no matter what, the conversation was always about him. In a media-driven age, Trump's dominance of the narrative was a testament to the power of fame as a political tool.

However, Trump's legacy is also a cautionary tale about the limits of fame. While his ability to captivate the public and dominate the news cycle was key to his success, it also fueled intense polarization. His presidency was defined by division—between political parties, between regions, and between the many cultural identities that make up the United States. Trump's brand of politics was confrontational, his rhetoric often incendiary, and his style of leadership fundamentally different from what the country had seen before. In the end, Trump's reliance on fame as a tool for influence was a double-edged sword, bringing him unprecedented power while also deepening the cultural and political divides in America.

As Trump's post-presidency unfolds, his influence remains palpable. His presence still looms large over the Republican Party, his base remains fiercely loyal, and his potential return to the political stage in 2024 keeps the nation on edge. Whether he chooses to run for office again or continues to shape American politics from the outside, Trump's fame and influence are likely to persist for years to come. His ability to stay relevant, even after leaving office, speaks to the enduring power of his personal brand. Trump's legacy may not fit neatly into the traditional categories of political achievement, but it cannot be denied that his impact on the culture and politics of America is profound.

Looking back, it is clear that Donald Trump's journey was never just about building towers, hosting a television show, or running a country. It was about redefining what influence means in the modern world. Trump showed that fame—cultivated, maintained, and wielded strategically—can be a powerful tool for achieving success in business, politics, and beyond. His rise to the presidency marked a new era where celebrity and political power became deeply intertwined, and where the rules of engagement in public life were forever altered.

Ultimately, Trump's story is one of a man who understood how to make the world pay attention and how to turn that attention into influence. His legacy will be debated for decades, but one thing is certain: Donald Trump mastered the art of fame, and in doing so, he changed the game for everyone who follows. Whether admired or reviled, his ability to leverage his celebrity and reshape the political landscape stands as a testament to the evolving power dynamics of the 21st century. His rise, reign, and continued influence will serve as a lasting reflection on the intersection of fame and power in American life.

www.ingramcontent.com/pod-product-compliance
Ingram Content Group UK Ltd.
Pitfield, Milton Keynes, MK11 3LW, UK
UKHW030629180325
456389UK00011B/98